THE LEGEND OF ROWAN

THE LEGEND OF
ROWAN

JEFFREY L. RODENGEN

Edited by Alex Lieber and Jon VanZile

Also by Jeff Rodengen

The Legend of Chris-Craft

IRON FIST: The Lives of Carl Kiekhaefer

Evinrude-Johnson and The Legend of OMC

Serving The Silent Service: The Legend of Electric Boat

The Legend of Dr Pepper/Seven-Up

The Legend of Honeywell

The Legend of Briggs & Stratton

The Legend of Ingersoll-Rand

The Legend of Stanley: 150 Years of The Stanley Works

The MicroAge Way

The Legend of Halliburton

The Legend of York International

The Legend of Nucor Corporation

The Legend of Goodyear: The First 100 Years

The Legend of AMP

The Legend of Cessna

The Legend of VF Corporation

New Horizons: The Story of Ashland Inc.

The Spirit of AMD

The Legend of American Standard

The Legend of Federal-Mogul

The Legend of Pfizer

The Legend of Amdahl

The Legend of Echlin

Connected: The History of Inter-Tel

Applied Materials: Pioneering the Information Age

The Boston Scientific Story

Publisher's Cataloging in Publication

Rodengen, Jeffrey L.
   The legend of Rowan/Jeffrey L. Rodengen.
 1st ed.
 p. cm.
   Includes bibliographical references and index.
   ISBN 0-945903-45-6

   1. Rowan Companies. 2. Oil field equipment and supplies industry. 3. Petroleum industry and trade. 4. Oil well drilling rigs. I. Title

   HD9569.R69R69 1998   338.7'223'382
                                QBI97-41439

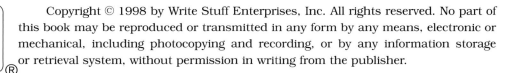

Write Stuff Enterprises, Inc.

1515 Southeast 4th Avenue • Fort Lauderdale, FL 33316
1-800-900-Book (1-800-900-2665) • (954) 462-6657

Library of Congress Catalog Card Number 97-062154

ISBN 0-945903-45-6

Completely produced in the United States of America
10 9 8 7 6 5 4 3 2 1

TABLE OF CONTENTS

INTRODUCTION

WHEN OIL PRODUCTION at the Wortham Field had fallen flat in 1925, Rowan Drilling struggled to meet its obligations. Rumors swirled that the company was going broke, and creditors questioned whether it would survive. But employees stuck by Arch and Charlie Rowan even if it meant going without pay until times improved.

As it turned out, the Rowan brothers were able to meet their obligations. But that expression of loyalty from the company's workers was something Arch and Charlie said they would never forget. It was an expression that today underscores the familial ties binding Rowan and its employees together. Rowan workers knew early that their personal well-being and the well-being of their individual families depended on maintaining the same sense of kinship throughout the company. Blood is thicker than water, but oil is thicker than both.

As in a family, such loyalty comes with high expectations and responsibilities. One of the earliest Rowanites, Bess Brants, recalled the day she was able to balance Rowan's books. (Brants had to learn bookkeeping on her own.) She expected a pat on the back, but instead Arch gruffly told her, "That's the way they're supposed to be, isn't it?"

As Rowan celebrates its 75th year, the traits passed down by the Rowan brothers still permeate this family of 5,000 employees. With $695 million in revenues in 1997, the company and its subsidiaries, Era Aviation and LeTourneau, maintain the kind of atmosphere that discourages impersonal memos and the tedious, slow-moving pace of a top-heavy bureaucracy.

In a speech delivered to business leaders attending the 1997-98 corporate partners breakfast series, Rowan Chairman and CEO Bob Palmer summed up the management philosophy: "We believe the best way to manage people is to let them know what is expected and then get out of the way so they can do it. ... The competence, well-being and loyalty of our employees is definitely a major priority."

Palmer recognizes that Rowan Companies only has three assets to manage: employees, money and machines. In the field, Rowan has earned a sterling reputation among roughnecks as a great place to work. Retired or active, Rowan workers are proud to recount that their company was one of the first independent contract oil companies to offer a comprehensive benefit program, devised by longtime Rowanite Mark Hart and adopted in 1949. The company today offers higher wages and benefits (including a recently expanded college scholarship program) than many other companies in its industry.

In managing money, Rowan's leaders have taken the calculated risks required in an industry as volatile as the oil business, but avoided the kind of debt that destroys corporations during downturns. Acquisitions over the years have been few, and they have always related in some way to Rowan's primary business of contract drilling, such as the 1967 ERA acquisition. The purchase of ERA (the name would change in 1988 to Era Aviation) brought a pioneering helicopter service and its pioneering founder, Carl Brady, into the Rowan family. ERA delivered crews, equipment and supplies to roughnecks drilling for oil on Alaska's brutally cold North Slope. It also moved into the passenger airline and freight business; today, Era Aviation's helicopters and fixed-wing aircraft are used in a variety of missions, including the cleanup efforts following the *Exxon-Valdez* disaster and the catastrophic forest fires that ravaged northern Florida in 1998.

One of Rowan's biggest risks came on the heels of a recession that resulted in losses exceeding $44 million. Instead of laying off its workers, as many oil business-related companies had done, Rowan kept its experienced workforce and the new Gorilla rigs ready for the upturn that Palmer knew would come.

The Gorilla rigs, together with its crews, represent the Rowan Difference. The four Gorilla-class rigs built by LeTourneau were the best in the business, capable of drilling in more than 300 feet of water. The upturn found Rowan with the right equipment and personnel at the right time. The risk of holding onto employees and building the Gorillas earned Palmer praise as a "visionary" from industry analysts and business magazines. Yet another recession threatened to shut down the builder of these magnificent machines, LeTourneau.

Bob Palmer's decision to buy LeTourneau shocked the industry, and analysts openly questioned what business Rowan had in purchasing a company that produces alloy steel and steel plate; manufacture heavy earth-moving machinery for the mining and timber industries; as well as build mobile offshore jack-up rigs. The move appeared especially puzzling because LeTourneau's marine division had not built a jack-up rig in years. But the company shared a can-do attitude similar to Rowan, and had supplied the drilling company with the most advanced equipment in the industry.

The gamble has paid off. The industry returned to profitability, and by the end of 1997 Rowan achieved the highest earnings in its history, $147 million, and ordered the next class of jack-up, the Super Gorillas. The first of this new class, the *Gorilla V*, started its journey down the Mississippi River in July 1998 for final outfitting at Sabine Pass, Texas, and then to the turbulent North Sea. The *Gorilla V* is the only jack-up rig capable of drilling in 400 feet of water, and is the only one that can operate as a fully operational production facility. Before its completion, the *Gorilla V* had won contracts, and work had begun on Gorillas *VI* and *VII*.

Palmer well understands the risk Rowan is taking by building the additional Super Gorillas, but with a "feel for the deal," he remains confident. "It is the way Rowan plays the game," he told his audience of executives in 1998. "The 'thrill of the chase' has overcome the fear of failure."

With the legacy of Arch and Charlie still strong within Rowan, Palmer knows an enterprise has two choices; to grow or die. The Rowan family has chosen to grow.

FOREWORD

by
The Honorable Walter J. Hickel
Former Governor of Alaska

I'VE LONG BEEN A BELIEVER in capital balanced with risk. Capital and production represent real wealth. Otherwise, why couldn't the government appropriate $5 trillion and live off the interest? You can hand out anything you want, but at some point, you'd have nothing left. Someone has to produce. Someone has to cut down a tree. Someone has to dig a hole or catch a fish.

Yet the effective use of capital and risk require both discipline and courage. This is what makes Rowan and Bob Palmer worthy of admiration. The company and the man possess vision. It is not a backward looking company, not a company willing to live off grandpa's wealth. Rowan remembers how its money was made and is not afraid to take the same kind of risks.

Fifteen years ago, there was an internal debate over whether to invest in the Gorilla rigs. I was on the board at the time and at that meeting, I said, "You'll see the day that customers will be willing to pay $100,000 a day for the Gorilla." That was when $20,000 a day was a lot of money, so it seemed amazing. But just recently, Palmer called me up and said, "Wally, we're getting $135,000 a day for the Gorilla."

The Gorilla wasn't the only thing that helped Rowan. It was a great move to buy LeTourneau

and keep the production plant operating. But that's how Rowan views capital. The company has never been afraid to gamble. And it always treats its people right. Rowan keeps its employees on during slow times because the company believes in its people.

I give a lot of credit to Bob Palmer for what Rowan is today. I've known a lot of executives in my private and public life. Bob is very unique. He feels responsible for Rowan as if he owned it totally, yet he remains aware of the long-term interests of investors. I've been to many board meetings and I've sat on the boards of other companies. The board meetings at Rowan are different. They don't take long. Bob addresses the board in simplicity and he tells the same story no matter where he goes, whether he's in New York or in Alaska.

Rowan has also done a great job of looking at the industry and seeing what it needs. The oil industry is dependent upon technology and investment. The industry needed a more efficient way to drill offshore and overcome disagreeable weather, like in the North Sea. Building the Gorillas, and most recently, the Super Gorillas, took confidence. But that's the difference between knowledge, confidence, and fear. You can have all the engineering, but if you have that internal doubt, you're going to fail. Or you can come from little or no schooling and see a picture, and believe you're going to make it work.

I've been around the oil business for a long time. I helped dig the first cellar on a Standard rig in 1936 when they were using cable rigs. As governor of Alaska, I saw the oil industry's interest in the whole northern world. I watched as Rowan's roughnecks battled freezing weather, snow, ice, darkness. Things are different in the north. You can change anything you want in the tropic, semitropic or temperate zones. In the Arctic, you can't do that. You take the land as God created it.

Later, as Secretary of the Interior under President Richard Nixon, I helped pass absolute liability legislation to require that if you had a lease on the ocean and there was pollution on it, you had to clean it up. Before that, if you had an oil slick in the ocean and it went across your lease, you didn't have to clean it up.

But the oil industry had to be a quick learner out of necessity. I have a story I like to tell about working in the Arctic. In 1994, a pipeline burst in the Russian Arctic. The company that owned the pipeline didn't want Moscow involved because people who live in the Arctic have an exploited mentality, whether they're dealing with Moscow or Washington D.C. They see others arrive, take their resources and go back.

So when that pipeline broke, they didn't want Moscow or Washington, D.C., insiders to handle it. I took a jet to Siberia, and that's an awfully big place, as big as two United States. Basically, it was a disaster. An oil company had hit oil and wanted to get the oil out through an existing pipeline that was about 20 inches in diameter. The Russians don't have standards like we do, so this pipeline was not built like our above-ground Alaskan pipeline. It was just laying on the surface. At one point, it went across a river bed and just hung down. It was already leaking, not too bad, but leaking.

The company wanted its oil out and Russia says, "Oh, sure. Yeah, yeah, go ahead." Rather than check anything, they just tapped into the existing pipeline and increased the pressure. It just exploded. You never saw such a mess. It was an unmitigated disaster. I wrote an opinion piece for *The New York Times* and laid out the problem, which was poor engineering in the pipeline. I also arranged for about $100 million from the World Bank to clean it up.

I use that story to illustrate a point. The disaster showed a lack of understanding for the Arctic. Oil companies have had to learn quick, had to adapt to changing technology and demands placed upon them. I don't mean outside demands, either. I mean moral demands. The oil industry needs to have a conscience, and this is one of the greatest reasons I admire Rowan.

The company is like a tough father. It has a conscience. Rowan takes care of its people with a lot of caring and a lot of discipline, but you can't have both without being a little tough. It is a company that is willing to take calculated risks without sacrificing its people or its integrity in the industry. These are the tools that gave Rowan the courage to invest when others stopped building and made the company what it is today.

Walter J. Hickel was twice elected Governor of Alaska. He first won, against heavy odds, in 1966. As Governor, Hickel put the state on sound financial footing by opening the North Slope for oil development. He initiated forceful environmental and anti-pollution action. In 1968, Hickel was named Secretary of the U.S. Department of the Interior, and became known for his strong actions on behalf of a national energy policy and the environment. Among his achievements, Hickel helped to upgrade offshore oil drilling regulations, and placed all eight species of great whales on the Endangered Species List. Hickel served as Governor of Alaska again in 1990, running under the Alaskan Independence Party banner. Hickel's second record as Governor includes the collection of about $4 billion in oil back taxes. He chose not to seek re-election in 1994. In private life, Hickel is the sole proprietor of the Hickel Investment Company, which builds and operates hotels, office buildings and shopping centers in Alaska.

ACKNOWLEDGEMENTS

A GREAT MANY PEOPLE assisted in the research, preparation and publication of *The Legend of Rowan*. The principal archival research, including the development of historical timelines, was accomplished by my determined and relentless researcher, Joan Thompson. Joan is a professional of the highest caliber, and has assisted me in the past. Once again, she helped to uncover fascinating facts, stories and high-quality images to bring Rowan's past to life.

However, this book would have been impossible to write without the generous cooperation and recollections of executives of Rowan Companies, past and present, as well as the Rowan family. I am thankful for the help provided by Bob Palmer, chairman, president and CEO of Rowan Companies, for his time, anecdotes, and his extraordinary memory; Mary Cocca, his assistant, who helped with many requests for information and materials, often on short notice; Era Aviation President Chuck Johnson; and LeTourneau President and CEO Dan Eckermann.

I am grateful to the following Rowan executives for their insights: C.W. "Scooter" Yeargain, a Rowan consultant and chairman of LeTourneau; R.G. Croyle, executive vice president; senior vice presidents Ed Thiele, Danny McNease and Paul L. Kelly; Mike Marcom, managing director of Rowan Drilling U.K. Ltd.; William C. Provine, vice president of investor relations; vice presidents Bill Person, Mark Keller, John L. Buvens and Walter Couch. (I am particularly grateful to Walter Couch for his generous contribution of photos of the sinking of the *Gorilla I*); Lynda A. Aycock, assistant treasurer and secretary; Mark Hay, secretary; Charles Wharton, editor of the *Grapevine*. Rowan's loyal retirees were very helpful as well. The recollections of John Jackson, retired vice president, and retired workers Charles Gardner and Mildred Rucker were most valuable; Ernie Walston and Rielley Euper contributed photographs as well as anecdotes.

A special word of thanks is due to the Rowan family. They have been very gracious in lending their time and personal photographs that have helped make the early chapters so complete. Among the family members I would like to thank: Jean Rowan McNab; Eloise Frame Rowan; Sue Rowan Pittman; Martha Rowan Hyder; Lorena Rowan Brock. Family members of a number of Rowan's leaders were also helpful: Heddie Rowe, Ina Yancey, Lucy Blanchard, Elizabeth Magner, Clayton Brants.

I would also like to extend my sincere appreciation for the time spent with Cecil Provine, retired vice chairman of Rowan's board. Mr. Provine passed away shortly following his interview in 1998, but he lives on in the memories of those who have known him.

The people at Era Aviation were most kind in providing their time and insights, which helped pull together the subsidiary's compelling history. I would like to thank ERA founder and former president Carl Brady, a pioneer whose stories illuminated the way of life for early Alaskan helicopter pilots; Al Meyer, senior vice president and manager of the Gulf Coast Division; Era pilots Gus Lapthorne, Danny Purvis and Larry Schmidt for sharing their experiences with me; pilot Mike Doebler for his thoughts and for a terrific ride aboard Era Classic Airlines; as well as Karin Griffith at Era Aviation.

I would also like to express thanks to the people at LeTourneau for their insights and memories: Don Cross, vice president of Vicksburg Marine; Rudy Harris, vice president of operations; Jack McElroy, vice president of financial services; Bart McCoy, director of operational improvement; George Cupstid, manager of project and engineering; Ronnie Neihaus, logistics coordinator at the Vicksburg Yard; and Robert Rimlinger, the *Gorilla V's* project manager; retirees Jim Golden, Edgar "Ish" Loflin and Price Stratton. Brenda Breitenberg was helpful in tracking down images and information.

At LeTourneau University, I would like to thank P.J. Sharp and Gerrie Forbis for their help in finding images as well.

I am also grateful to former Texas Governor Bill Clements for his views. I am especially grateful to former Alaska Governor Walter J. Hickel for his interesting and perceptive Foreword.

Among the many people and institutions who have helped in the gathering of images or information, I would like to thank: Betty Orbeck, director of archives at The Petroleum Museum; Bill Ennis at the Texas Oil & Gas Association; Houston Public Library; San Antonio Conservation Society Foundation; Joe White, director of the East Texas Oil Museum at Kilgore College.

And as always, a very special thanks to the dedicated staff at Write Stuff Enterprises, Inc., and key consultants, especially my executive assistants Colleen Azcona and Jill Thomas; Executive Editor Alex Lieber; Jon VanZile and Melody Alder, associate editors; Senior Art Director Sandy Cruz; Jill Apolinario and Kyle Newton, art directors; Fred Moll, production manager; Ivan Bial, sales and promotion manager; Karine Rodengen, project coordinator; Rafael Santiago, logistics coordinator; and Marianne Roberts, office manager.

The Goose Creek Oil Field, circa 1917, where Arch and Charlie Rowan worked as roughnecks. *(Photo courtesy of Houston Metropolitan Research Center, Houston Public Library.)*

CHAPTER ONE

HUMBLE BEGINNINGS

"There was a rumor on the street we were going to go broke, and some of our good employees came to me and told me that if we were hard up for money, why, they would stay on without pay until we got a payday and finish the well. That was certainly a great expression of loyalty that I never forgot."

— Arch Rowan, date unknown[1]

IN 1924, THE FORD MOTOR COMPANY sold its 10 millionth Model T. Affordable and popular, the Model T put America on wheels, and the nation's thirst for oil and petroleum products quickly became insatiable, prompting thousands of young men to stream to the alternately dusty and muddy Texas oilfields, dragging huge rigs across the prairie in the hunt for profitable wells.

Charlie Rowan, a 33-year-old drilling superintendent for Humble Oil, was among these early wildcatters. "Charlie Rowan had a dream born of the grease and sweat and hard work of the oilfields of the 1920s. That dream was to own a drilling rig like the tall wooden derricks he was working on in the Goose Creek Field in 1923," a magazine suggested many years later.[2]

When drillers discovered the Powell Field near Corsicana, Texas, in 1922, it was natural for the young man to jump at the chance. "I decided that the opening of this new major oilfield, which created the need for a larger number of drilling rigs, offered an opportunity to get into the contracting business," Charlie later remarked.[3]

The oil industry was a young, brawny business with plenty of room for another entrepreneur when the Rowan Drilling Company was founded in 1923. The world's first well drilled specifically to find oil was in 1859 in Titusville, Pennsylvania. By the turn of the century, crude oil production worldwide was almost 150 million barrels, half of

which was produced in Russia. Most of this crude was refined into kerosene for lamps, with a small amount used for fuel oil. By 1910, just as the automobile was beginning to make an impact as means for transportation, demand for gasoline began to outstrip demand for kerosene. Within a decade, worldwide oil production would surpass 1 billion barrels, driven mostly by the need for refined gasoline.

The Powell oilfield where Charlie Rowan made his gamble lay eight miles outside of Corsicana, a town southeast of Dallas. Corsicana witnessed the birth of the Texas oil industry when workers drilling for water in the 1890s struck oil instead, much to their surprise and initial disappointment. When news of the strike at Powell reached Rowan, he promptly resigned his job at Humble Oil, persuaded his brother Arch Rowan to join him, and the two invested in a rig with a wooden derrick. The Humble Oil and Refining Company was a substantial leaseholder in the field, Charlie Rowan later wrote.

"After talking the matter over with Mr. W.W. Fondren, who at that time was vice president of

A wooden derrick in the Goose Creek Oil Field, similar to the ones Charlie Rowan worked on in 1923.

The Boyd Oil Co's Simmons No. 1
11/27/24

TEXAS FIRST OIL FIELD - CORSICANA 1898   BY TAYLOR STUDIO Corsicana Texas

First Oil Field West of Mississippi River
Discovered in 1894. By 1898 over 1000 producing wells in
City of Corsicana, some of these wells still producing ---

Above: Corsicana, birthplace of the Texas oil industry and
headquarters to Rowan Drilling Company during the mid-1920s.
(Photo courtesy of the Navarro County Historical Society.)

Left: Simmons No. 1, the oil well that opened up the Wortham Oil Field
on November 27, 1924. *(Photo courtesy of Virginia Simmons.)*

1859 — The world's first oil well is drilled in
Titusville, Pennsylvania.

November 27, 1924 — Rowan Drilling brings
in the Simmons No. 1 and touches off an oil
boom in Wortham, Texas.

1923 — Charlie Rowan founds the Rowan
Drilling Company and begins drilling in the
Powell Field in Corsicana, Texas.

the Humble Oil and Refining Company, I resigned my position as drilling superintendent, and with my brother, A.H. Rowan, as a partner bought a drilling rig."[4]

This first Rowan oil rig was a steam unit that could drill 3,000 feet, a little more than a half-mile deep. It was powered by a single-cylinder engine and two 45-horsepower boilers. The brothers bought it from the Oil Well Supply Company. Arch Rowan recalls that they "paid a reasonable amount down and got a line of credit. My recollection is that first rig cost $16,000."[5] It would later be described as "small," but that was not its description in those days. "This was considered a large rig and quite adequate for the 3,000-foot wells in the Powell Field," wrote Charlie.[6]

For their first contract, the brothers turned to Charlie's former employer, W.W. Fondren, the same Humble executive who accepted Charlie's resignation. A Rowan company historian later noted that Fondren "recognized a free spirit when he saw one, gave him his blessing (plus a promise of some business) and sent him on his way."[7]

Their early survival was difficult, but the Powell Field was rich. Despite a close call when "a

Rowan Drilling Company purchased its second rig at auction for $5,500. The rig was sent to work in the Powell Field.

string of drill pipe was lost in the hole," Rowan soon had enough money to purchase a second, larger oil rig.[8] In 1924, the year it incorporated, the young company bought a used American Well and Prospecting Company rig at a sheriff's sale in Corsicana for about $5,500.[9] It had a 72-horsepower boiler and a 66-horsepower boiler.

September 1, 1927 — Bess Brants reports for her first day at work.

1927 — Rowan Oil Company is founded to manage the company's leases. Rowan Drilling sends its first rigs to West Texas.

1928 — Rowan rigs are active in New Mexico, East and West Texas.

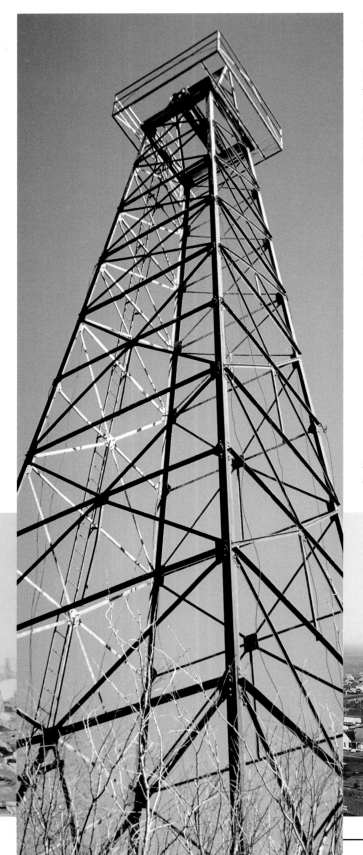

Employees reconditioned the rig, added some equipment and put it to work in the Powell Field.

With two rigs, the brothers incorporated their fledgling Rowan Drilling Company in May 1924, with total capital stock of $30,000. Charlie, Arch, and another brother, attorney Spencer Rowan, formed the first board of directors, with Charlie as president.[10] Charlie and Arch voted themselves annual salaries of $4,800.[11]

Turkey Day Gusher

Thus incorporated, the Rowan brothers began to look for new opportunities. On a fall day in a field 20 miles southeast of Corsicana, their efforts were rewarded, as Charlie later wrote.

"The company drilled the discovery well [on November 27], Simmons No. 1, for the Humphreys Oil Company on the outskirts of the town of Wortham. This well came in on Thanksgiving Day. It was a large producer and opened the Wortham Field. These were the days of lax spacing rules and town lot drilling and the bringing in of this prolific field created a large and fast drilling boom."[12]

Roughnecks erected derricks close together and inside town limits as companies hastily drilled competing wells to extract as much oil as possible from the field. Charlie had identified their customer as Humphreys Oil but they were really working for Humphreys subsidiary, Boyd Oil Company. Boyd had struck oil just days earlier a little more than a mile away, but that well flowed oil intermittently, yielding about 1,800 barrels a day. Five days later on Thanksgiving Day, Simmons No. 1 gushed forth 8,000 barrels its first day, according to one newspaper account.

"Shooting a stream of oil 200 feet into the air, the Boyd Oil Company's Simmons No. 1 roared into action about noon Thursday, ushering in the first oilfield of Freestone County and shattering the Thanksgiving quiet of the countryside for miles around. The well's initial production was estimated at 8,000 barrels, and it increased its

Opposite page: This rusted derrick stands as the lone reminder of the many that had been erected to tap into the Wortham Field. *(Photo by Joan Thompson.)*

Below: Pictured in 1925, Wortham, Texas, boomed after oil was struck on November 27, 1924.

Right: A historical marker acknowledging Wortham's contribution to the Texas oil industry. *(Photo by Joan Thompson.)*

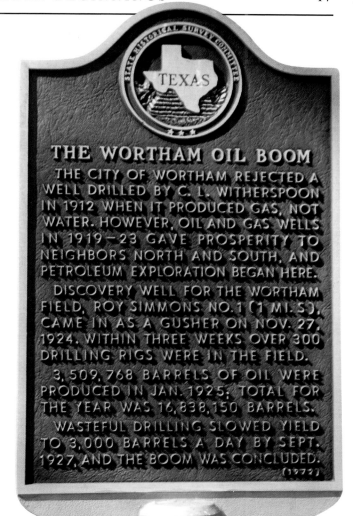

THE WORTHAM OIL BOOM

THE CITY OF WORTHAM REJECTED A WELL DRILLED BY C. L. WITHERSPOON IN 1912 WHEN IT PRODUCED GAS, NOT WATER. HOWEVER, OIL AND GAS WELLS IN 1919–23 GAVE PROSPERITY TO NEIGHBORS NORTH AND SOUTH, AND PETROLEUM EXPLORATION BEGAN HERE.

DISCOVERY WELL FOR THE WORTHAM FIELD, ROY SIMMONS NO. 1 (1 MI. S), CAME IN AS A GUSHER ON NOV. 27, 1924. WITHIN THREE WEEKS OVER 300 DRILLING RIGS WERE IN THE FIELD.

3,509,768 BARRELS OF OIL WERE PRODUCED IN JAN. 1925; TOTAL FOR THE YEAR WAS 16,838,150 BARRELS.

WASTEFUL DRILLING SLOWED YIELD TO 3,000 BARRELS A DAY BY SEPT. 1927, AND THE BOOM WAS CONCLUDED.

(1972)

Right: 2010 Crocker Street, Houston, Texas. This house is where three Rowan brothers convened their first meeting of Rowan Drilling Company board of directors. *(Photo courtesy of Jean Rowan McNab.)*

Below: An original $25 stock certificate for the newly formed Rowan Drilling Company, issued in May 1924.

"With the vast impetus known only to a full-fledged oil stampede, the little city of Wortham has been galvanized into hectic life. Fourteen new business houses have opened their doors this week; the streets are jammed with traffic and lined with pedestrians; city land values have doubled and trebled in the last few hours; and from every point of the compass, visitors are flocking in. ... Hospitable citizens have thrown open their houses to newcomers unable to secure hotel accommodations. The 'night life' typical of an oil town already is a reality — many people are on the streets at all hours."[15]

flow steadily during the afternoon. Early Thursday night, it was estimated to be throwing fluid from the hole at the rate of 15,000 barrels per day. ... That the well will have a big influence immediately upon the oil situation in Texas was indicated by oil men Thursday. 'Another Powell' was the way they described it. The well is so located that a town lot drilling campaign will be inevitable. Already more than 100 locations [or well sites] have been made."[13]

By bringing in another large oilfield, the Rowan brothers found themselves in the chaotic middle of a unique phenomena in American history: a Texas boom town. The well touched off so great a rush of business "that the oilfield supply houses and lumber yards at Mexia and Wortham have had to keep open all night to load out trucks and wagons for the active area."[14]

A local newspaper article depicted the excitement:

A later article described trainloads of workers and materials for drilling and pipeline work arriving in Mexia. It noted that "Mexia's population has jumped within one week from 12,000 to a number estimated at 18,000, with streets jammed ... as a result of the Thanksgiving discovery near Wortham."[16]

The discovery of the Wortham Field was notably different from previous discoveries, according to an article in the Houston *Post-Dispatch*.

"Before a barrel of oil was found, three big pipeline companies were tying into their main lines with pipelines to serve the field. It is said that for the first time in history a pipeline was laid by such companies to a wildcat field. The Simmons

was the first wildcat well ever to be offset before it came in. Within two hours after the Boyd wildcats came in, in each case, their production was flowing into markets.[17]

The Wortham Field meant increased business for Rowan Drilling and a third rig, one with twin-engines powered by 66-horsepower boilers. Charlie wrote that the rig "was considered about the newest and best type of drilling equipment then on the market."[18]

The brothers continued to work in the Wortham Field but the field's promise as "another Powell" was short-lived. By November 13, 1923, the Powell Field was delivering 354,893 barrels of oil daily. By 1924, the field had yielded a total of 40 million barrels. The Wortham Field, by comparison, peaked at an average daily production of 154,000 barrels in mid-January 1925.[19] By 1925, Wortham had pro-

duced just 16.8 million barrels of oil that flowed from 300 wells.[20]

Once the drilling boom at Wortham faded, it was time for the rigs to move on to other fields. The Rowan brothers shipped one rig to the town of Liberty, in southeast Texas, while another went outside Texas to Smackover, Arkansas, to take part in another Smackover boom. In 1926, the Rowans sent a rig to East Texas to drill wildcat wells for the Humphreys Oil Company around Jacksonville. Charlie wrote that "these wells showed some oil but were not commercial producers. They stimulated interest in this area, however, and no doubt hastened the discovery of the great East Texas Field."[21]

Mexia, Texas, at the height of the oil boom in the late 1920s. *(Photo courtesy of Texas Oil & Gas Association, Austin.)*

Production at Wortham Field declined in the years following 1925, and Rowan Drilling struggled amid rumors it was going broke. But employees stuck by the Rowan brothers. Arch recalled that "some of our good employees came to me and told me that if we were hard up for money, why, they would stay on without pay until we got a payday and finished the well. That was certainly a great expression of loyalty that I never forgot."[22]

Their banker, however, was more susceptible to the rumors and approached Arch on the street about the loan.[23]

"We had experienced some bad luck on two or three wells in a row, when I met the banker on the street one day. The banker said, 'Street talk has it that you boys are broke.' I asked, 'Do you do business by street talk?' 'Yes, I do,' answered the banker. 'All right, I'll have your money for you in the morning,' I said, and the next morning, when the bank opened, I was there with the full amount."[24]

Following Fortune

The Rowan rigs gradually migrated westward in the search for oil. Rowan first began drilling in West Texas in 1927, moving a rig into the Hendrick pool in Winkler County. Oil had been found on the ranch of T.G. Hendrick near Kermit, 40 miles west of Odessa, in mid-1926. Arch and Charlie added two more rigs to the field, where

Charlie noted "these rigs were kept busy for a year or two."[25]

The company also worked in the Salt Flat Field, north of Luling, and the Darst Creek Field, both in southwest Texas. Oil was discovered in Salt Flat in 1928, while Darst Creek began producing in July 1929. For Rowan, it was the beginning of a long era of drilling in West Texas and in New Mexico, the location of the vast Permian Basin where an inland sea had existed about 200 million years ago.

As it followed the wildcatters searching for a successful strike, Rowan established itself as an innovator. It was one of the first companies in semi-arid West Texas to use drilling mud, for example. Mud had been an important ingredient in rotary drilling since 1900 when a driller at Spindletop pumped mud down a drill stem to flush out cuttings from around the bit. Mud lubricated the whirling bit and counteracted pressures from gas, oil or water to prevent blowouts. Also, the mud plastered onto the sides of drilling holes, thereby reducing the possibility of cave-ins and keeping gas and water from seeping through the side walls. Oil historian Walter Rundell noted that "most wells struck the kinds of shales and clay needed to provide the basic ingredients of mud, and to these chemicals were added. If natural muds were not available, drillers could import dehydrated mud in paper bags and add water and chemicals."[26]

There were no mud companies, however, in 1927 when Rowan first went to Wink, Texas, to drill. Arch recalled making a proposal to a company near Fort Worth that manufactured paving bricks:

"I asked them if they would grind mud for me so that I could ship it out to West Texas. They told me frankly that they were not in the mud business, they were in the brick business and they refused to have anything to do with mud. I was forced to ship our mud in from Los Angeles. The brick

Left to right: Charlie Rowan, his wife Merle and a friend near Jacksonville in 1926. (*Photo courtesy of the Petroleum Museum, Midland, Texas.*)

company later went broke while the mud compa-nies that quickly appeared during the West Texas boom went on to make great fortunes."[27]

Rowan Oil Company

As Rowan Drilling ventured into West Texas in 1927, a second company was established called Rowan Oil Company. Rowan Oil focused on sell-ing the oil drilled from its sister company's wells. The new firm was created "when a little surplus had built up in the young drilling company."[28] Charlie and Arch, along with Arch's wife, Stella, founded Rowan Oil in May with $3,000 in capital stock. The company issued 120 shares of stock, valued at $25 a share. With cash payments, Charlie paid $1,500 for 60 shares of stock, while Arch put in $1,200 for 48 shares. Stella paid $300 for 12 shares. They became directors of a company formed "to establish and maintain an oil business with authority to contract for the lease and purchase of the right to prospect for, develop,

and use coal and other minerals, petroleum, and gas; and also the right to erect, build, and own all necessary oil tanks, cars, and pipes necessary for the operation of the business."[29] The company's main offices were in San Antonio.

In filing the charter with the state of Texas, Arch and Stella listed their residence and post office box in the San Antonio Frost National Bank Building. Charlie, who spent most of his time in the oilfields, also listed a post office box in the building. The documents went on to note that "his residence is only constructive, and he moves from place to place, and has no permanent residence."[30]

Rowan Oil hired a geologist named E.B. Stiles, and his assistant, A.C. Allen (who would one day become a vice president of Rowan) to find

Rowan Drilling had offices on the fifth floor of the Frost National Bank Building. Beside it is the historic San Fernando Cathedral, marking the exact geographic center of San Antonio. *(Photo courtesy of the San Antonio Conservation Society.)*

likely wildcatting sites. Money for this venture was tight; Rowan Oil's first balance sheet showed $269.77 cash in the bank and accounts payable of $54.96. By the end of 1927, its cash had dwindled to $2.73, with December's total revenues only $68.83. It wasn't until 1928 that "things picked up and the Rowan Oil Company was a going concern."[31] The company would exist for a half-dozen years before it was dissolved and later resurrected under the same name.

While it existed, Rowan Oil moved to where the action was. Beginning in San Antonio, Rowan Oil relocated to Fort Worth in 1927 following the discovery of oil on a farm 60 miles west of Fort Worth in 1917. The discovery turned the little cow-

During the heyday of Corsicana there were more than 1,000 oil producing wells in the town. *(Photo courtesy of the Navarro County Historical Society.)*

town into a boom town. Arch would remark that in 1927, "Fort Worth was in a little bit of boom then, and office space was hard to get."[32] He hired his wife's sister, Bess Seiders, who later became Bess Brants, as his secretary on September 1, 1927. She had studied accounting before going to work for the Rowans in their new offices in Fort Worth's Petroleum Building.

For seven years Bess Brants was the only office employee. An early example of the extraordinary loyalty demonstrated by Rowan's workers, she would remain close to the company for decades to come. She eventually became secretary/treasurer of both the Rowan Drilling and Rowan Oil companies, and also a member of each company's board of directors.

As the Rowan brothers complemented each other, Bess Brants complemented the both of them, particularly when they disagreed. "Bess had the ability to reason with them," recalled retired Rowan President Cecil Provine in October

1997. Interviewed shortly before he died on January 10, 1998, he said Brants was "one of the very few ladies in the business who had that much influence."[33]

In 1938, a boat used in Rowan's marine drilling operations in Louisiana was christened the *Bessie B*. A 1949 company magazine article about her lengthy service compared her to a tool pusher, or rig manager, and noted:

"There is a legend that Bess can run a drilling rig, and if office experience could qualify her, she would be the best tool pusher that the company has. ... A close friend remarked that in 22 years of association with her she never heard her say that she was tired. She is well-known for her quick thinking, sense of humor and a down-to-earth quality that makes her a natural in handling personnel problems and getting along with others. If anyone in the Rowan organization can approach the state of being indispensable, Bess can most nearly claim that distinction because of her many years of experience and the esteem in which she is held."[34]

The brothers were on their way to a successful future as the decade closed out. They had paid off the remaining balance on Rowan Drilling and also created an oil company. They had become not only drilling contractors but independent oilmen and part of the legendary breed of Texas wildcatters, which had surpassed Oklahoma as the leading state in oil production in 1928. The discovery of the East Texas supergiant oilfield in the woods of Rusk County two years later provided the Rowans and other contractors a seemingly limitless opportunity for growth.

The Rowan family shown gathered on the porch of their home in Alvin, Texas, circa late 1890s to early 1900s. *(Photo courtesy of Sue Rowan Pittman.)*

CHAPTER TWO

OIL AND WATER

1870–1929

"From the accounts of those who knew and worked with them, they were as different as, well, oil and water. 'Mr. Arch,' as he was known, was Marine-tough, an aggressive but highly respected businessman who defended his beliefs with a passion second to none. 'Mr. Charlie,' on the other hand is described as a sweet, soft-spoken individual who was loved by those who knew him."

—from *Oil Legends of Fort Worth*, 1993[1]

CHARLES LOUIS ROWAN WAS born in the southeast Texas town of Bryan on August 29, 1890. His brother Archibald was born four years later on October 9, 1894. They were two of four Rowan brothers, including Spencer and Robert, all children of William Albert Rowan and Maria Louise Ford. William's daughter from a previous marriage died in Alvin, Texas, in 1894, the year Arch was born.[2]

William and Maria, both remarkable, were an odd match considering the post-Civil War climate of the day. William had moved from New York to Texas in 1870 with his brother Louis. Both had served in the Union army during the Civil War; William was a captain in the 14th New York Volunteers, while Louis achieved the rank of colonel.

Maria Louise Ford, however, was a native of Texas, and proud of her southern heritage, and she was elected vice president of the Alvin Chapter of the United Daughters of the Confederacy.[3] Family members said Mrs. Rowan, who had been educated in private schools in Bryan, was an important, strong influence on her sons. Arch's youngest daughter, Sue Rowan Pittman, recalled in a 1998 interview that "she was the force in their lives."[4] Mrs. Pittman said that "she taught them Latin because my father understood Latin. ... They

all could recite the Bible backwards and forwards."[5]

William and Louis took a chance by moving to Texas, which still simmered with resentment following the war and the ensuing Reconstruction era. But the Rowans' war service did not appear to affect their standing in the community. They were described by local historical sources as "wide-awake, progressive men who are thoroughly in sympathy with all movements designed for the upbuilding of the country, and few gentlemen land-holders in southeastern Texas have a wider circle of friends."[6]

Around town, William became affectionately known as "Captain Rowan." Indeed, he was elected to the Liverpool school board in 1882, justice of the peace in 1885, and county commissioner from 1885 until 1887. He was also a member of the school board in nearby Alvin and sat as its board president in 1905.

"At that time most of the people living in the Liverpool area were Southern Confederates, and

The four Rowan boys, clockwise from top: Arch, Spencer Ford, Robert and Charlie. *(Photo courtesy of Sue Rowan Pittman.)*

there was still much hatred and resentment of Northerners. 'Damnedyankee' was still just one word. In spite of all this, 'Captain Rowan' was very popular and was liked by all members of the community."[7]

In 1877, William and his brothers joined with a land investor to buy a 30,900-acre tract of land south of Houston in Brazoria County. The ranch was on Chocolate Bayou, a deep natural inlet where, according to legend, pirates buried booty plundered from ships in the Gulf of Mexico. (As an interesting historical sidenote, the Rowan Ranch was on the site that had been defended by Stephen F. Austin, the "father of Texas," who led the successful rebellion against Mexico. Austin picked the site for his sister.)

In a book titled *The History of Liverpool, Texas and Its People*, a local historian recorded that the Rowans built "a substantial homestead where two of the brothers, William A. and Louis H., were to reside and manage the ranch."

"It was purely a family affair with strict regulations explicitly written, including one which forbade hard liquor of any kind on the premises. ... William A. and Louis H. Rowan were both lawyers by profession and practiced law in Angleton and Alvin from the 1880s to 1910 in addition to managing the ranch and other land development projects."[6]

An account written in the late 1890s described the Rowan Ranch, also known as Pleasant Bayou Ranch, as an idyllic area with a rich soil ideal for orchards and other fruit crops.

"It is bounded upon one side by Hall's Bayou and on the opposite side by Chocolate Bayou, navigable for twenty miles. Ten and one-half

Above and opposite right: William Albert Rowan and Maria Louise Ford Rowan. (Photos courtesy of Jean Rowan McNab.)

1877 — William Albert Rowan and Maria Louise Rowan move to Pleasant Bayou Ranch near Houston, Texas.

October 9, 1894 — Arch Rowan is born.

August 29, 1890 — Charlie Rowan is born.

1916 — Arch takes his first job in the oil industry working for the company that would later become Texaco. Charlie is roughnecking in the Goose Creek Oil Field.

miles of the best wire fence, running from Chocolate to Hall's Bayou, completes the enclosure, which embraces 31,540 acres of land, 3,000 of which are heavily timbered. A number of never-failing streams water the place. ... The line of the Mexican Central R.R. passes directly through the estate, and a depot is situated six miles distant from the dwelling house, which is a typical and beautiful old-time Southern home. ... Boats land within a short distance of the mansion house, and from the balcony of its second story can be viewed wide expanses of Galveston Bay, and the Gulf of Mexico beyond. ... The house is surrounded by a magnificent grove of fig trees that bear two crops a year. There are about 3,000 head of cattle on the place."[7]

The Formative Years

Raised in this setting, Charlie and Arch developed very different personalities.[8] Arch became an impassioned fighter, while Charlie had the "softest touch in the oilfield," according to the book, *Oil Legends of Fort Worth*:

> *"From the accounts of those who knew and worked with them, they were as different as, well, oil and water. 'Mr. Arch,' as he was known, was Marine-tough, an aggressive but highly respected businessman who defended his beliefs with a passion second to none. 'Mr. Charlie,' on the other hand is described as a sweet, soft-spoken individual who was loved by those who knew him."[9]*

In 1917, a youthful Charlie joined the army after America entered World War I, but never made it across the Atlantic. Years later, Charlie wrote an article for the Rowan company magazine, *Grapevine*, and said, "Since World War I, which I fought at Kelly Field, San Antonio, I have had a yen to see Europe."[10] When the war ended, he went to work for Humble Oil and was quickly pro-

1917 — The brothers join the military to fight in World War I. Arch sees action in Europe, while Charlie is stationed in San Antonio.

1921 — Arch Rowan quits the oil industry to work in the automobile industry.

1919 — Charlie Rowan begins working for Humble Oil and is quickly promoted to a drilling superintendent.

Above: Arch Rowan, left, and his older brother Spencer Ford Rowan both served in Europe during World War I. *(Photo courtesy of Lorena Rowan Brock.)*

Below: Shown in 1916, the Goose Creek Oil Field is where both Charlie and Arch Rowan began as roughnecks. *(Photo courtesy of Sterling Municipal Library, Baytown, Texas.)*

moted to drilling superintendent, which would be his last job working for somebody else.

Arch's first job in the oil business was as an employee of the Texas Company (now Texaco) in 1916 in Houston. Only a year later, he, too, enlisted in the armed forces and served for two years, including a tour of duty in Europe, where he became a regimental sergeant major. Arch returned from France to a job offer from the Texas Company.

"They wanted me to go to Tulsa, and I didn't want to go to Tulsa, and my brother, Charlie, suggested that I go to Goose Creek and take a job as a roughneck on a drilling rig and learn something about field operations in the oil business. Well, I was a young man and fresh out of the Marine Corps, in good health and good physical condition, and so I went down and worked as a roughneck. In those days, roughnecking was more manual labor than it is now [in 1973]. They've got a lot of mechanical devices that do a lot of the things that we did manually back in those days. Well, I thought I was in great physical condition. I found out that work is pretty hard and pretty rough and pretty dirty. I stayed with it for quite a while until I had a health problem with my kidneys, and then I had to leave it and stay out of the oil business for a period of two to three years."[11]

After quitting the oil industry, Arch tried his hand at the automobile industry because of his experience in operating and maintaining machinery. He worked for Southern Motors in

Health problems drove Arch from the oilfields in 1921, when he left the Texas Company (later Texaco) to work for Southern Motors. *(Photo courtesy of Sue Rowan Pittman.)*

1921 as assistant chief engineer and later as works manager.[12] He might have never returned to the oil industry had not his brother drawn him back in.

"Mr. Charlie"

Although they possessed different personalities, Arch and Charlie were both problem solvers who believed in hard work and learning. Arch described his brother as one who sought the challenge of starting up new producing wells. In a 1973 interview, Arch recounted that Charlie "loved drilling tools, and he loved to drill wells. ... I suppose one of the interesting things about the drilling industry is that every field is a different drilling problem. It was these problems that Charlie Rowan loved to solve."[13]

Charlie's son-in-law Elton Hyder Jr., a Fort Worth attorney, described how the brothers divided the company workload: "Arch did the business and the contacts. Charlie handled the drilling and the engineering. He was a practical, self-trained engineer."[14] Hamilton Rogers, a future president of Rowan Oil Company, remembered that "Charlie had a mental inventory of every damned rig. But he stuttered, so Arch was always the front guy."[15]

Charlie's daughter, Martha Rowan Hyder, recalled in 1998 how the slight stammer didn't stop him from doing what he wanted; he preferred

the field whereas Arch handled the administrative side of the business. And the impediment didn't impede his ability to tell a good story: "Once he got going he told the best stories," she said.[16]

They shared integrity, foresight and perseverance as traits; their differences tempered each other's essential nature. Charlie Rowan's gentle manner, for example, offset Arch's stern personality. A memorial article appeared in the company magazine, the *Grapevine*, in 1961 recalling "Mr. Charlie's" compassion.

"Derelicts from the oilfield frequently put in an appearance at the office and claimed to have worked for 'Mr. Charlie.' Although they could not name their tool pusher and were vague about where or when they worked, they never went away empty-handed. He always justified his gullibility by saying 'I would rather be taken in by 10 bums than to pass up one deserving man.'"[17]

Arch Rowan said in an interview years later that his brother deserved to be held in high esteem: "Everybody ... just loved Charlie Rowan. ... I don't believe he had an enemy in the world. If he did, there was something wrong with the other person."[18]

In one account, Arch described how a boilerman blew a boiler on a drilling rig in South Texas. "First thing, I asked (Charlie) when I talked to him on the phone was, 'Did he fire the boilerman?' The boilerman, incidentally, got blown about 50 feet from the boiler but was uninjured except for a few bruises. Charlie said, 'No, he'll be the best boilerman we ever have from now on out.' And he kept him on the payroll."[19]

Retired Rowan worker Charles Gardner, at the time working as a mechanic, recalled how Charlie came up to him one day with his hand outstretched to greet him. "I told him I couldn't. My hand was all greasy. He said, 'If your hand wasn't greasy, you wouldn't be working for me.' I loved the man because he was a working man's friend."[20]

With the right people working for Rowan, Charlie believed the future of oil drilling had no bounds. More importantly, he believed in himself and his workers, noted the *Grapevine*:

"The Rowan Drilling Company was not built from a one-rig beginning to its present size by men

A TOWN CALLED ROWAN

IN 1905, FIVE YEARS AFTER A HURRICANE devastated their hometown of Alvin, William and Louis Rowan platted a new town in a dusty prairie on the other side of the Chocolate Bayou from Liverpool. The men had helped rebuild Alvin and the surrounding area, and for reasons not officially recorded, decided to establish the Rowan legacy by creating a municipality under the family name.

The brothers established the town on a new railroad line, which brought new families and the promise of bustling commerce. A land boom for fruit and garden farms was at its peak, and citrus, fig orchards and strawberry farms were under development in the Texas Gulf Coast area.

Louis became the town's first mayor. The town of Rowan (or Rowanville, as it was sometimes called) "started off with great expectations," wrote historian J.W. Moore.

"Roads were graded and shelled, a post office and a depot were built, as were stock pens for shipping cattle. Office buildings, packing sheds, hay barns and a hotel were also built. The town was laid out on both sides of the rail-

After the Rowan homestead on Pleasant Bayou Ranch (above) and the town of Alvin (below) were destroyed in the storm of 1900, the Rowans founded a town named Rowan. *(Photo courtesy of Sue Rowan Pittman.)*

Opposite page: Plat records, filed in 1908, for the town of Rowan in Brazoria County. *(Photo by Joan Thompson.)*

road, with the greater portion of the town on the southeastern side. Many of the town-site lots were sold, and several residences were built.

Rowan continued to grow in spite of a terrible fire in September 1907 which destroyed more than half of the town's buildings."[1]

In 1908, a road was built from Alvin to Rowan Station. Two years later, the first street-light was installed. An article that appeared in the weekly newspaper in 1910, the *Alvin Sun,* noted that "there was a great deal of excitement in town Thursday. The streets were crowded with admiring citizens to see the erection of our first street lamp. The police had a great deal of trouble in keeping back the crowds so called upon the Liverpool Department."[2]

Sadly, Louis Rowan didn't live to see his town bustling with activity. In 1909, he sustained a serious injury from a buggy accident, and died at his home, according to the March 5 edition of the *Alvin Sun:*

"Col. Rowan was in Alvin Tuesday afternoon mingling with his many friends, and in his jolly humor, and late in the afternoon started for his home in company with a gentleman from his neighborhood. A few miles out the neck yoke of his buggy snapped and the pole dropped to the ground, which

caused his team to run, jerking him over the dash board and breaking his neck. He was carried to his residence where he lingered until death relieved him."[3]

A year later, just two months after the streetlight was installed, the town was disbanded, after it and a large portion of the Rowan Ranch were sold to an orchard development company. Moore described the scene in 1996:

"Today the old town of Rowan is not even a ghost town. There is no visible evidence of old buildings or ruins to serve as a tombstone for the once-thriving and bustling town. The depot, the hotel, the store buildings, the packing sheds and the stock pens are all gone, leaving nothing but their silent memories in a cow pasture now overgrown with tallow trees."[4]

Capt. William Rowan, Charlie and Arch's father, died in 1917 at his home in Houston, where the family had moved after leaving Alvin. Their mother, Louise F. Rowan, died in 1937, at the age of 76.

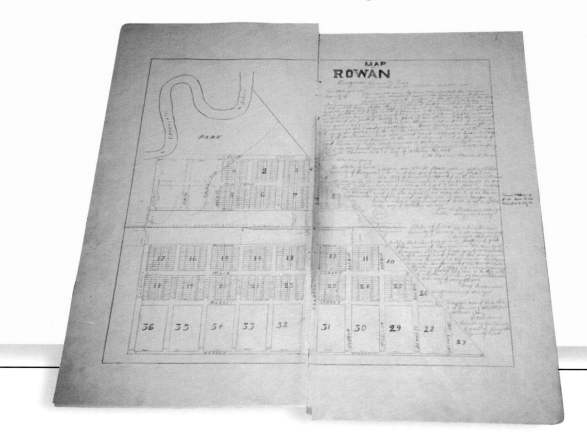

of faint heart and short vision. This was sharply brought to your editor's attention a few years ago when he wrote in an article, 'drilling equipment has been greatly improved, but has gone about as far as it can go ... .' He sent it in to Mr. Charlie Rowan for approval and got it back with a firm line drawn through the words 'but has gone about as far as it can go.' Mr. Charlie never lost his vision or faith in the future of the drilling industry under the Free Enterprise system."[21]

"Mr. Arch"

Where Charlie was affable and kind, Arch was determined and uncompromising in his expectations of himself and his workers. Self-educated in business and law, Arch was a consummate businessman. Percy Gresham, a minister and long-time family friend, recounted his work ethic:

"He not only believed in hard work, but practiced it. Many times when I was his guest at the Wade plantation in Georgia, I arose for breakfast at what I felt to be a reasonable hour only to find that Mr. Arch had already been in the fields. His wife, Stella, and I would welcome him home for breakfast at about 7:30 or 8:00. He always had a project — whether it was drilling wells, selling a company, building a house, perfecting an agri-

cultural practice or electing a candidate — he was always on the job."[22]

A future Rowan president, C.R. "Bob" Palmer, recalled that "Mr. Arch was constantly looking for problems to solve. Arch would often work around the clock. Work was his life and midnight was as good a time as 8 a.m."[23]

Arch left school at age 12 but would eventually receive an honorary college degree, according to an account by the company:

"Mr. Arch pursued law with such thoroughness that in June 1962 he received an honorary doctor of law degree from Bethany College, Bethany, West Virginia. Yet even before the honor was bestowed, his associates jokingly stated: 'Arch has been practicing law without a license for more than 30 years.' In fact, while being represented by counsel, Mr. Arch's remarks once forced a judge to advise the lawyer, 'Counselor, I believe your client has won the case for you.'"[24]

Hamilton Rogers, a lawyer who went to work for the Rowans in 1941 and later headed Rowan Oil Company, said Arch was "a better lawyer than I was, and probably more aggressive."[25]

Rogers recalled a lawsuit in which Arch was being represented by prominent Texas attorney Gillis Johnson. "The opposing lawyer approached Gillis about a settlement. Replied Gillis: 'Arch isn't going to settle this. Peace troubles his soul.'"[26] A Rowan vice president, Mark Hart, once recalled that "while my good friend, Mr. Arch Rowan was a self-educated man, his great organizational ability and his thorough knowledge in engineering, accounting, law and politics made him the best businessman I have ever known."[27]

Why he left school has been lost to history, but a 1973 maga-

Charlie and Arch with their mother, Maria Louise, circa 1920s. *(Photo courtesy of Sue Rowan Pittman.)*

zine article noted it may have been due to family circumstances. He attended primary schools in Alvin and later in Houston where the family had moved but "vicissitudes of fortune on the part of his family meant leaving school at the age of 12 to make his own living. He had reached the seventh grade."[28]

Houston's city directory of 1908 listed Arch as working as a delivery clerk for a clothing store and Charlie as a student, while their father worked in real estate. Other jobs that later city directories list for Arch include collector, a clerk for Houston Land & Trust Company and a stenographer. Charlie worked in clerical jobs for a railroad and a clothing store between 1910 and 1912.[29]

Arch always believed his workers were the company's greatest assets, but he didn't pamper them with praise for a job well done. Bess Brants, the company's first office worker and later its secretary-treasurer, recalled the day she learned that Arch didn't give points for merely doing one's job:

> *"Once, after working especially hard learning bookkeeping I managed to balance the books for the first time. I told Arch about it and he replied with only a grunt. I felt sure he hadn't understood me, so later I repeated that the books were in balance, fully expecting a pat on the back. His reply was, 'That's the way they are supposed to be, isn't it?' I never fished for a compliment again, but I always knew I was appreciated."*[30]

Arch's daughter, Sue Rowan Pittman, said she once showed off a straight-A report card. Arch responded that that was the least he expected of her. She said both her father and Charlie had a great love of learning, and passed that trait along to their children. But as the offspring of men who fought the land and the elements, the children sometimes learned a few things they shouldn't have, she said.

> *"The language on the drilling platforms was not the best in the world. When I was around the men tried to keep me from hearing all those words but I picked up quite a bit anyways. One day I came in while the minister of the University Christian Church and his wife were visiting for Sunday lunch. I walked into the living room and opened a little leather purse I had, and said, 'Goddamn! Here's a nickel!' It was the only time I had my mouth washed out with soap."*[31]

Charlie and Arch were dedicated to the oil business, a booming industry throughout the 1920s. By 1929, however, the Rowan brothers' fortunes were about to change. The stock market crash of October 1929 signaled the beginning of the Great Depression, when demand for oil would slacken. At the same time, the oil industry received a remarkable piece of news. One of the world's largest oilfields had been discovered — and it was in Texas.

Columbus "Dad" Joiner, left, shakes hands with his geologist. A.D. "Doc" Lloyd in front of the Daisy Bradford No. 3, the well that first struck oil in the East Texas Oil Field. H.L. Hunt, cigar in mouth, is second from the right. *(Photo courtesy of Texas Oil & Gas Association, Austin.)*

CHAPTER THREE

THE TRAVELING ROWAN RIGS

1930–1940

"Mr. Charlie could not understand why it took only one day to tear down, skid, set up and spud a West Texas rig, while at the same time, it would take four to five days to do the same in the Gulf Coast. Mr. Charlie found that Cecil [Provine] and Ira [French] had unitized certain equipment, making it easier to rig down and rig up, but more astonishing was the fact Cecil could disconnect and move the boiler with a full head of steam and be ready to spud in as soon as they set down."

— Grapevine, 1973[1]

COLUMBUS "DAD" JOINER brought in the East Texas gusher, the only known supergiant oilfield in the United States. An Alabama-born wildcatter who had made and lost two fortunes in Oklahoma, Joiner had been drilling in the hilly land of Rusk County since 1927. Work was slow, his equipment secondhand. Joiner spent much of his time peddling percentages of his project to raise cash. After two dry holes, Joiner asked an oil scout for a major company to look over the third site. The scout dismissed its potential, suspecting that a suspiciously promising core sample from it had been "salted," or deliberately spiked with oil, to dupe investors.[2] Undeterred, Joiner sought out more trusting partners, including Arch Rowan. But Arch was among the dubious. In an interview years later, he recounted what might have been:

"We were at Jacksonville when Dad Joiner discovered his East Texas oil field. Joiner was broke and did not have enough money to set pipe, and he came to me and offered to give me an interest in his block (of leases) if I would furnish him a string of pipe. I told him I would furnish the pipe if he would let me take a core and look at the sand and that I would be responsible for the rig

and the well while I was coring. This he refused to do. So I didn't make a deal with him. I thought the core that he had might have been salted. Most of the geologists thought so, too. Afterward, he made the now-famous deal with H.L. Hunt."[3]

At the time, Joiner was just another small-time player in the oilfields. Oil historian Daniel Yergin described him as the "caricature of the classic down-on-his-luck, woebegone but always optimistic, silver-tongued and ever-persuasive wildcat promoter."[4] He bought into the belief that oil existed in East Texas by an even more persuasive man by the name of Doc Lloyd, a self-trained "geologist." Trained geologists (meaning those actually holding degrees) laughed at the idea of oil in East Texas, recounted Yergin in his book, *The Prize*:

"Doc Lloyd had provided Dad Joiner with a description of the geology of the East Texas region. To say it was misleading would be an understatement; it was totally incorrect, fabricated. ... But Doc

A 1936 marker honors the site of "Dad" Joiner's well. *(Photo by Joan Thompson.)*

Lloyd did one memorable thing; he told Joiner exactly where to drill, when almost everybody thought the idea was completely ridiculous."[5]

Joiner struck black gold on his third try. On October 3, 1930, the Daisy Bradford Test No. 3 shot out a stream of oil. He had tapped into the southern end of an underground oil pool that stretched 43 miles and was about five miles wide. Joiner had discovered the only known supergiant oilfield in the continental United States, and one of only about 40 worldwide. (A supergiant is a field that contains at least 5 billion barrels of recoverable oil).

Hundreds flocked to see the Joiner well on Daisy Bradford's farm, the first in East Texas. *(Photo courtesy of Texas Oil & Gas Association, Austin.)*

1930 — Columbus "Dad" Joiner brings in the East Texas Oil Field. Rowan moves all available rigs to the booming field for drilling work. Cecil Provine joins Rowan as a water pumper.

1935 — The company buys its first diesel electric rig.

December 12, 1933 — The brothers dissolve Rowan Oil Company and set up Rowan Drilling as a Delaware corporation.

Joiner, 70 years old and suffering from the effects of rheumatic fever, suddenly found himself at the center of one of America's greatest oil booms. Investors and drilling companies, Rowan included, descended on East Texas. Charlie recalled that with the field's discovery, Rowan "moved all of its suitable rigs into this field and drilled several hundred wells during the next two or three years."[6] By the end of 1931, oil companies had taken 109 million barrels from 3,612 producing wells.[7] Oil deluged markets. In Texas, the average price of crude oil plummeted from $1.10 a barrel at the time of the Joiner discovery to less than 10 cents in 1931.[8] For a time in 1931, Texas Governor Ross S. Sterling ordered the East Texas wells shut down and sent in National Guard to enforce the order. The Texas Railroad Commission, which administered oil and gas resources, issued various proration orders aimed at regulating oil flow. But for small operators even a nickel a barrel was better than no money coming in. It was a time of protest, martial law, turmoil and "hot," or illegal, oil.

While most of the nation was mired in the Great Depression, East Texas was booming with production and drilling jobs. When work in the field even-

tually subsided, Rowan rigs had again gone on the move to new fields in a pattern that was becoming familiar to the company. Workers drilled in Conroe, Amelia, Cayuga, Tomball, Fairbanks, Pearsall, Taft, Bunkie and Winnsboro and other sites across West Texas, as well as in southeastern New Mexico. Sites in New Mexico included Monument, Seminole, Wasson, Slaughter, Eunice and Barnhart.

In September 1930, the brothers created Rowan and Nichols Oil Company with lease broker Roy Nichols, who handled most of the leasing for Rowan Oil Company. The capital stock of the new company was $20,000, divided into 800 shares worth $25 each. Arch and Charlie each paid cash for $7,500 in company stock, while Nichols paid $5,000.[9] They based their new company in Fort Worth.

Rowan and Nichols soon began racking up a list of its own leases, many in the East Texas fields. According to a *Grapevine* article, "Lease No. 106, B.C. Todd, was routinely entered in the lease records of June 1931. But this was destined to be no ordinary lease, for it marked the first big production for the company. When the East Texas field was drilled up, this lease turned out to be in the very heart of it."[10] The magazine article boasted that the leased field was still flowing strong in 1957.

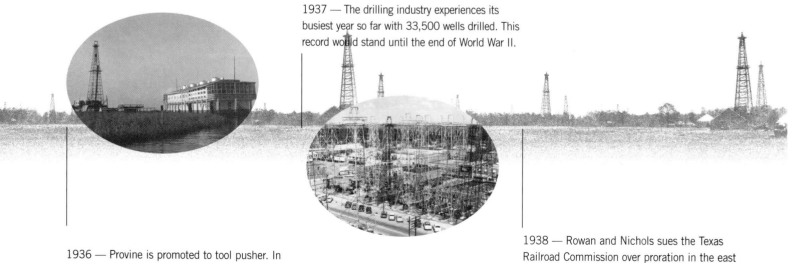

1937 — The drilling industry experiences its busiest year so far with 33,500 wells drilled. This record would stand until the end of World War II.

1936 — Provine is promoted to tool pusher. In the coastal flats of Louisiana, Rowan pioneers the self-contained drilling barge.

1938 — Rowan and Nichols sues the Texas Railroad Commission over proration in the east Texas field. The case goes all the way to U.S. Supreme Court.

Cecil Provine

The same year Joiner made his discovery, Cecil Provine joined Rowan as a water pumper for the summer before his senior year in college. When his summer vacation was over, he returned to school and graduated from Texas Christian University in 1931 with a bachelor's degree in business administration. He considered going to work in a bank for $90 a month. "This was the Depression," he said in a 1997 interview. "Ninety bucks a month was the best you could do."

However, Bess Brants happened to be friends with Provine's older sister, and he met Arch. "He said, 'Why don't you come work for me,'" Provine recalled.

Left: Cecil Provine's graduation notice from Texas Christian University. By the time he received his degree in business administration, he had already worked for Rowan for a summer.

Below: The flood of cheap oil from East Texas caused a sharp drop in prices, prompting Texas Governor Ross Sterling to issue a shut-down order. He sent the National Guard to enforce the order. *(Photo courtesy of Texas Oil & Gas Association, Austin.)*

With the discovery of Joiner's oilfield, nearby Kilgore and other towns underwent boom times. *(Photo courtesy of Texas Oil & Gas Association, Austin.)*

"I asked him what he did and he said he was a drilling contractor. Of course, I didn't know what a drilling contractor was, so I asked how much he paid. He said $6 a day for a 12-hour day. And don't ask for overtime. 'Come to work for me and I'll show you the ropes,' he told me. That was the beginning of our friendship. They were the only people I ever worked for."[11]

Brants recalled visiting Provine at the Todd lease in East Texas. She said she found Provine "lolling in the wet sand under the pipe racks reading comic books. He had engineered a float so that he could do his job from a reclining position."[12]

Arch Rowan had more in mind for Provine than reading comic books and sitting under shade trees. He instructed the young man on the duties of a water pumper, saying "the pump would not need attention constantly and he could fill it up with gas, oil it and, instead of sitting in the shade of a tree, he could go up on the derrick floor and learn how to be a roughneck. He took this advice and it wasn't long until he started up the ladder from roughneck to president of the company."[13] Provine worked two months as a water pumper. He roughnecked for a year and a half before becoming a driller.

Provine, like other drillers, picked his own crew to journey with him on assignments. His first drilling job was on a steam rig for Humble at Pistol Hill in East Texas. Crewmembers who stayed with him to work on rigs in New Mexico, Louisiana, and East Texas included Dick Luse, Cajon LeJaun, Hunk Novack, Jack Rogers and Lacy Boyd.

Boyd, a wheat farmer, had gone to work for Rowan in the spring of 1931. He worked on two wells in Kilgore, and on sites near Longview and in New London. While working in New London, Boyd's family contacted him to help with their wheat crop.

"I told Charlie Rowan I wanted to go home by the fifth of June. ... He asked if I would stay long enough to stab a string of pipe. We ran pipe on May 25. He told the driller to make my time out to the first of June. The driller told him, 'I'll have to hire someone to take his place.' Charlie Rowan said, 'Don't hire anyone to take his place. Just get you an extra pair of (work gloves) and get after it. If you get behind, get me a pair and I'll help you.'"[14]

Boyd, who retired in 1965, described Charlie as "one of the best men who ever owned a drilling rig. He was my idol of a man to work for. If you just did a good job, he'd stand by you."[15]

In 1934, Provine and another man, Ira French, were transferred to West Texas to set up the company's West Texas-New Mexico Division. Arch and Charlie, realizing the magnitude of the newly found Permian Basin, purchased additional rigs to work this rich area. An office also was opened in Houston to take care of Gulf Coast operations. Earl Hessor and E.O. Buck were in charge.

Two years later, Provine was promoted to a tool pusher, or rig superintendent. At the time, one pusher was responsible for five or six rotary rigs, as well as two or three cable-tool rigs. A company magazine article relates this story about the inventiveness of Provine and French:

"Mr. Charlie could not understand why it took only one day to tear down, skid, set up and spud a West Texas rig, while at the same time, it would take four to five days to do the same in the Gulf Coast. Mr. Charlie found that Cecil and Ira had unitized certain equipment, making it easier to rig down and rig up, but more astonishing was the fact Cecil could disconnect and move the boiler with a full head of steam and be ready to spud in as soon as they set down."[16]

Provine proved tough enough to handle the strenuous and dangerous work. Rowan executive Mark Hart recalled going to work for Cecil in 1936 in the Monument Pool in New Mexico, where Cecil was the day driller on a steam rig:

"The tool pusher, Ira French, introduced him to me by pointing to me and saying, 'This is the guy they sent out from Fort Worth.' Having the best crew in the oilfield, Cecil was not happy to have a 'weevil' [a novice] replace his pipe racker. ... Another day while I was still roughneck-ing for Cecil, the crew was picking up drill pipe from the racks when the derrickman, who was 'tailing it in,' let it slip. The pipe hit the backup man, Dick Luse, in the head and dropped him bleeding across the rotary table. Cecil lit into the derrickman with both barrels and two vocabularies — one of which he did not learn at Texas Christian University. It was years later that I realized

A view of the East Texas Oil Field where Cecil Provine and his early crew worked. *(Photo courtesy of Texas Oil & Gas Association, Austin.)*

that this must have been the first Rowan safety meeting I attended."[17]

Hart, a fellow Texas Christian University graduate, later assumed responsibility for safety issues.

Paper Changes

Back at the office, Rowan was undergoing paper changes. The brothers dissolved Rowan Oil Company on December 12, 1933. Signing the dissolution papers were the four stockholders: Arch, president and treasurer; Charlie, vice president; A.A. Klein, a Humble employee living in Houston; and Bess Brants, secretary.[18] Taxes for the company's last month of operation were $10.02.[19] Within the next few months, the Rowan brothers took steps to set up Rowan Drilling as a Delaware corporation with capital stock of $90,000.

The stock of Rowan Drilling was issued in 3,600 shares, valued at $25 each. Charlie had the most stock with 2,304 shares. He was followed by Arch with 1,110 shares, A.A. Klein with 180 shares, and Bess Brants with six shares. The Delaware incorporation papers detailed that the company could not only "establish and maintain a drilling business" but also buy and sell mineral rights, as well as "establish and maintain an oil business" to contract for prospecting rights and own oil storage and transportation facilities.[20] Its offices in Texas were in the Trinity Life Building in Fort Worth.

The brothers then dissolved Rowan Drilling as a Texas corporation. The stockholders gathered in the Trinity Life Building on April 14, 1934, and voted to approve the company's dissolution as a Texas corporation. The voting stockholders were Charlie, Arch, Bess Brants and A.A. Klein, voting by proxy.[21] After signing the appropriate documents, the transfer of Rowan Drilling assets to that of the Delaware corporation was complete.

The Rowan brothers established a geological department in 1935 for exploration, and A.C. "Charlie" Allen was the geologist charged with the task of gathering well data. Allen graduated in 1925 from Southern Methodist University with a degree in geology and physics. He was originally hired to work as a geologist with Rowan Drilling Company in its earliest years, "then in its infancy and in lean circumstances. After two years on special work, and leaner ones for the Rowans, he was reluctantly released."[22] He worked for a couple of other oil companies before returning to Rowan.

Rowan and Nichols already had producing leases with B.C. Todd "A" and "B" leases. Its third was the Will Cary lease in Lea County in southeast New Mexico. It was drilled as a joint enterprise with N.G. Penrose in 1936. The following year, Allen did surface work in North Texas that resulted in production on several leases. Then, under orders from Arch, Allen started gathering geological information in the Gulf Coast area of Texas.

Rowan Drilling also was on the move with new technology. In 1935, the company bought its first diesel electric rig, one of the first companies to do so. Most rigs at the time were still drilling with steam power, and the new contraption raised a few eyebrows. Arch later recalled that "we had a superintendent on that rig who was really scared by that electricity. But he finally got used to it and began to like it very much."[23]

Pioneering in Marsh Country

The Louisiana marshes held the promise of oil but drilling was extremely difficult. One company that tried the usual derrick-method lost both the derrick and the drilling equipment when the well cratered. Soon the Tidewater Oil Company (now Getty) took over the troubled leases and brought in Rowan to solve the problem. The company pioneered the concept of the self-contained drilling barge in 1936 when the company was contracted to drill a well at the mouth of the Mississippi River. The concept involved mounting the derrick, hoist and hoist motor on pilings in the marsh, while the engines, generators and mud pumps were placed on a converted cargo barge. Rowan's diesel electric Rig No. 1 was moved to Houston for shipment by barges through the Intracoastal Canal to New Orleans and then 75 miles south to the Venice Field. The drilling site was eight miles by water to Venice, the nearest small town.

Louis Hartmangruber journeyed in August 1936 from the dry prairies of West Texas to become Rowan's first superintendent in the Louisiana area. He described the exhausting work after the arrival of equipment at the drilling site on August 14, 1936:

"The unloading and setting up of machinery started and we finished about three the next morning. Everyone was worn out working and fighting mosquitoes. I often think how lucky 22 men were that night getting back to Venice in a boat made to carry eight men. We did not know this until the next day. Rigging up was slow since most of the men left us after the first night. Arch Rowan took over the job of getting supplies, and I took over the job of rigging up."[24]

This page and next: The *Delta Queen*, a 110-foot quarterboat, housed drilling crews working at West Bay, which was several hours by boat from Venice, Louisiana. Rowan was one of the first companies to drill in Louisiana's bayous.

The Pennsylvania Shipyard at Beaumont, Texas, built the barges which Rowan leased and then eventually bought — the forerunners of Rowan's future fleet.

Workers dreaded the mosquito-infested job site, and even Hartmangruber admitted his urge to leave. The nearest telephone was 22 miles away in Buras, Louisiana, and the supply houses were 135 miles away by land in Houma. Road conditions were poor. Some of the Rowan workers found small apartments along a levee but Hartmangruber had to settle on a place for his family in New Orleans. Seventeen years later, the wives of Rowan workers still complained about the living conditions. Ina Yancey, wife of Clifford Yancey, a drilling superintendent at the time, said Venice was "the end of the road in those days. There was a ballroom and a post office. But they were in what someone called a hotel. That was all of it."[25]

Clifford Yancey eventually rose to become president of the domestic drilling division of Rowan Drilling. Ina recalled that her husband would never have worked anywhere else. "People offered him jobs but he stayed. Like a lot of the others, he started out at the bottom and went to the top."[26]

But the grueling work in the Venice area put loyalty to the test because families suffered under the same conditions. Conditions would improve years later but were still bad enough to prompt a 1953 letter to Charlie Rowan signed by "A Group of Displaced Wives Existing Under Venice Conditions." Charlie reminded them when Rowan first came to Venice, the area had no paved or graveled roads, there was one store but no boarding houses, and "the nearest place to get a meal was Buras, and it was nothing to write home about."[27] On its 50th anniversary, Rowan noted that its work in the Venice Field for Tidewater was "one of the longest well-to-well drilling contracts on record."[28] Of the initial five holes that Rowan drilled, three were dry with the third and fourth turning out to be producers. Rowan would eventually drill more than 150 wells in the area.[29]

Besides the remoteness and mosquitoes, the conditions beneath the marshes called for cautious work. Millions of years ago, the area had been the site of a huge salt dome. Drilling hazards included marsh gas, hot water flows, heaving shale — and the worst — abnormal pressures. Charlie described it as a "dangerous and treacherous area. High pressure gas is prevalent and on account of soft sand and unconsolidated formations, a blowout can mean loss of well or rig."[30] Twelve years after going to work in the Venice Field or Venice Dome, Charlie Rowan noted no serious fires or blowouts had occurred and congratulated Hartmangruber and his workers for their careful work. Hartmangruber continued to supervise the fleet of mobile barges until his retirement in 1956.

In 1937, in Brazoria County where Arch and Charlie spent their boyhoods, Rowan drilled a discovery well in Danbury. Rowan Drilling had taken the Thomas Jamison lease on a farm-out from Shell. Oil had been found in Danbury seven years earlier at 1,560 feet but commercial production did not begin until September 1937.[31] It was a busy year for the drilling industry and one that would not be outpaced for 11 years. That year the industry drilled a total of 33,500 wells.[32] By the end of 1938, Rowan had more than survived the Great Depression. The brothers were able to increase the company's capital stock from $90,000 to $450,000, divided into 18,000 shares at $25 a share.[33]

But the decade was not to end without issues still remaining from the discovery of the prolific East Texas Oil Field.

Like other East Texas towns, Kilgore, Texas, was overcrowded with oil wells. Rowan initiated a legal battle over proration, which dictated how much oil could be removed from the ground. The case went to the Supreme Court. *(Photo courtesy of Texas Oil & Gas Association, Austin.)*

Battle Over East Texas

In 1938, Rowan and Nichols sued the Texas Railroad Commission over a production allowance order the state agency had issued in August for the East Texas Oil Field. The commission's order allowed each well in the field to produce 2.32 percent of its hourly capacity under unrestricted flow. However, "marginal wells," with low productive capacity, were given a "special status" since such wells would be prematurely abandoned if they had to adhere to the same percentage as the better-producing wells.[34]

Under the 1938 order, these low-producing wells — of which there were many in the East Texas field — could produce up to 20 barrels a day. Wells like those of Rowan and Nichols were capped at about 22 barrels a day apiece. Rowan and Nichols obtained a lower court injunction blocking the proration order. The company complained that the order unfairly allowed small neighboring wells to drain away the oil under its leases.

Lower courts, in backing Rowan and Nichols, said the commission should have considered other factors besides production capacity in devising its order. Those included the estimated amount of oil under the land. But the U.S. Supreme Court, in a 6-3 decision in June 1940, upheld the validity of the commission's proration formula and threw out the injunction. The justices' majority opinion stated that it was not up to the federal courts to supplant the judgment of state regulatory agencies on the fairness of production quotas.

Rowan and Nichols' action against the commission was considered a test case for proration. In a front-page story, *The Wall Street Journal* reported that the nation's highest court, by its decision, "avoided what otherwise might have developed into a serious situation not alone in Texas but possibly in other states which are operating under legislative conservation measures.

"By the ruling the Railroad Commission is given wider latitude in setting allowances, and hence, will be in a position to enforce stricter proration than in the past. Had the decision of the Supreme Court been in the other direction, it is conceivable that the state temporarily at least, would have experienced a period of unsettlement which would have reacted on crude prices generally throughout the oil producing area in the Southwest."[35]

Rowan finished the court fight in time to prepare for what would become the most destructive conflict in human history; a conflict that was started, in large part, over the viscous black fluid that was about to become the lifeblood of civilization.

Charlie Rowan (above) would become president of Rowan Drilling and chairman of Rowan Oil.

CHAPTER FOUR

RISING TO THE TOP

1941–1949

> *"The success which this company has attained could not have been obtained without the intelligent and wholehearted cooperation of our many employees. The management of this company appreciates their loyalty and efforts and will endeavor to be fair, generous and appreciative of those employed by it."*
>
> — Charlie Rowan, 1948[1]

I N JULY 1941, PRESIDENT FRANKLIN Roosevelt froze Japanese assets in the United States to protest Japan's takeover of French Indochina. Without these funds, Japan could not purchase the oil it needed for civilian or military use, since only about six percent was produced in the island nation.

Relations between the United States and Japan had grown progressively worse following Japan's attack on China in 1937. With its attention on the war in Europe, the United States tried to use oil as a diplomatic weapon and not as a military provocation, but oil was Japan's Achilles heel. Without fuel Japan would not be able to bring its half of the world under the "Greater East Asia Co-Prosperity Sphere," a euphemistic policy to ensure that Japan had the oil and other raw materials it needed. Its strategists drew up plans to take over oil-producing Dutch and British colonies. In 1940, with the prospect of war looming, the United States instituted the first peacetime draft in American history.

That year Rowan improved its drilling technology. In June 1940, Arch and H.E. Dralle, who was with Westinghouse Electric & Manufacturing Company, wrote an article, "Barge Mounted Diesel Electric Rigs," for *World Petroleum* magazine. The technical piece discussed generators and motor designs, noting that Rowan Drilling had two diesel electric rigs operating on barges in the Louisiana Gulf Coast, and that such rigs were more economical than steam ones because of the savings in fuel and fresh water costs. The rigs had an engine generator capacity of 800 kilowatts, or 1,075 horsepower, and could drill to depths of 12,000 feet.

"All fresh water must be transported to the location over long distances by barge. It remains only to contrast the amount of fresh water required in the engine water jackets for cooling with that required for boilers when steam equipment is used to realize the tremendous advantages in favor of the Diesel electrics."[2]

The War Effort

On December 7, 1941, 360 Japanese aircraft attacked the U.S. Pacific Fleet at Pearl Harbor. After more than two hours, eight battleships were sunk or damaged and more than 170 aircraft destroyed. With the United States' entry

---

Humble Oil and Rowan Drilling Company boasted one of the longest-running contractor relationships in the industry, bringing in many wells together.

into World War II, supplies and workers became scarce. Cecil Provine entered the Army as a private, and emerged as a captain, spending half of his four-year service in the Transportation Corps in India. For him, there was no doubt he would return to Rowan, which continued to pay him during the war. "I was in the Army four years but they compensated me while I was in the Army," he said in a 1997 interview. "I never thought about going to work for anybody else."[3]

Throughout the conflict, America's ability to produce and move oil was severely tested. As a "war of motion," World War II signaled the era of oil as the most important strategic resource in a nation's arsenal. All the elements of modern warfare — tanks, jeeps, planes, ships — ran on petroleum-based fuels. The importance of oil was underscored by the fact that tankers ranked high as targets for German submarines operating off the United States' coastlines.

Oil drilling and production in the United States increased dramatically. Arch, who at age 47 tried to enlist in the Marines, was instead invited to work on various national boards to boost productivity. He became a member of the Petroleum Industry War Council, heading up the council's manpower section. "We codified and classified all of the jobs in the petroleum industry — production, pipelines and refining. This was a big job and required a great deal of work. Much of my time was devoted to this vital effort," he later recalled.[4]

Never sedentary for long, Rowan's Rig No. 8 spent 1941 working in Mississippi.

1941 — The United States enters World War II when the Japanese bomb Pearl Harbor. Drilling activity drops off as production levels from existing wells are dramatically increased.

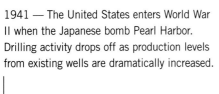

1948 — Rowan purchases its first airplane.

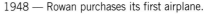

1944 — Gilbert Rowe joins the company to reengineer its equipment in the expectation that the war will soon end in an Allied victory.

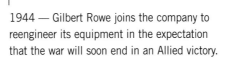

The National Petroleum Council grew out of this organization, and Arch was reappointed each year. By 1973, he would be one of only two original members still serving on the council.

By 1945, the United States was producing seven times more oil than projected, leading one general to remark that the industry "squeezed it out of a hat."[5] The draft and rationing of both raw materials resulted in a scarcity of men and rigs, even as companies clamored for new wells. Rowan, busy throughout the war, chose patriotism over profits. "We could have gotten higher prices by going to new customers," recalled Arch, "but we stayed with our old customers all during the war."[6] Rowan Drilling reported that for 1943, it had $1.2 million in gross receipts, with $1 million earned in Texas.[7]

In 1944, Marcus Gilbert Rowe joined Rowan and succeeded Arch in oversight of the engineering of all company equipment. Materials were scarce, and Arch recalled that the Rowan rigs "were not maintained in their best condition. I hired Gilbert Rowe and made him chief engineer with the charge that he would modernize and bring up to date all our equipment so that it would be the best equipment." Rowe would later become the first non-family member to be named president of Rowan.[8]

Rowe had been a shop superintendent and chief engineer for the Hunt Tool Company before coming to Rowan. He fell in love with oilfields at the young age of 14.[9] During his high school summers, he had worked for Yount-Lee Oil Company and later studied mechanical engineering at Texas A&M University. Like Arch and Charlie, he also had been employed by Humble Oil and Refining Company. Later, he spent six years in Venezuela working as a master mechanic and assistant drilling superintendent for Standard Oil.

Rowe advanced rather quickly through the Rowan management ranks. He worked three years as chief mechanical engineer before his promotion to assistant vice president. Seven months later, in January 1948, he became vice president while continuing to direct Rowan's engineering activities. Among his responsibilities was design and construction of Rowan's barge fleet, which was stationed in Louisiana.

Reorganization

American industry emerged from the war primed to move. Between 1945 and 1950, the number of automobiles burgeoned from 26 mil-

1948 — The *Grapevine* is founded with Mark Hart as its first editor. The first issue is published as the October-November edition.

1949 — Rowan celebrates its 25th anniversary after enjoying its busiest year since the late 1930s. Rowan's 22 rigs generate more than $6.5 million in revenue.

October 1, 1948 — Rowan Drilling is again split into two companies as Rowan Oil is resurrected as an oil lease company. It is incorporated in Delaware.

lion to 40 million. Gasoline sales increased 42 percent during the same period as oil replaced coal as America's primary energy source. During the war, the industry had kept pace with demand, but rising demand coupled with the shift from production of high-octane aircraft fuels to low-octane gasoline and home heating fuel proved too difficult.

"Right after the war was a tough time in the drilling business," remembered William Clements, Jr. When Clements wanted to set up his own drilling business in 1947, he turned to the Rowan brothers for advice. "They were highly respected," Clements said. "One of the brothers was what I could call Mr. Inside, and the other brother was Mr. Outside and that was Arch."[10] Clements later was elected governor of Texas.

In 1948, America imported more oil than it exported for the first time in its history. The rise in power of the Middle Eastern oil producers had begun.[11]

That same year, the Rowan brothers again split Rowan Drilling Company into two separate companies — one that drilled on contract and another that sought and produced oil and gas. Rowan and Nichols had been dissolved in 1941 and the assets divided by agreement. Roy Nichols went on to become an independent oil operator in San Antonio.

Oil production was a growing part of Rowan operations, but recent Texas law held that a drilling contractor could be liable to an oil company for causing damage to underground reservoirs. Rowan's oil and gas properties had been a small part of the business but had become sizable in

Gilbert Rowe, left, was a shop superintendent for Hunt Tool Company before joining Rowan as the company's chief engineer.

As demand rose, Rowan rigs were expected to drill deeper in more demanding conditions. The company constantly upgraded its rigs, including installing this huge, 42,650-pound drawworks on Rig 1, which spent 1948 in Venice, Louisiana.

recent years. To protect their oil and gas investments from potential liabilities incurred by the drilling company, the brothers resurrected Rowan Oil in December 1947 under a new charter as a Delaware corporation. Rowan Drilling transferred all of its leases and oil interests to Rowan Oil, in exchange for all of Rowan Oil's capital stock.[12]

The reorganization went into effect October 1, 1948. Each company had $225,000 in capital stock, divided into 18,000 shares, and both Rowan Oil and Rowan Drilling had offices in the Commercial Standard Building in Fort Worth. The brothers switched off roles in each company: Arch was chairman of the board of Rowan Drilling and president of Rowan Oil, while Charlie was president of Rowan Drilling and chairman of the board of Rowan Oil.

Other officers of Rowan Drilling were F.W. Brigance, who was vice president; Gilbert Rowe, assistant vice president; Bess Brants, secretary-treasurer; and Mark L. Hart, assistant secretary-treasurer. For Rowan Oil, there was A.C. "Charlie" Allen, vice president; Bess Brants, secretary-treasurer; and Hamilton Rogers, assistant secretary.

Before the reorganization, and as of August 31, 1948, Rowan Oil listed $1.7 million in assets, with $264,000 in lands, leases and royalties, and $181,250 in debt.[13] Rowan had wells in New Mexico, in addition to the wells in the Rowan, Danbury and West Midfield Fields of South Texas. The Rowan Field got its name from the town of Rowan, which had been founded by the brothers' father and uncle. In fact, good production was found in Rowan Oil's No. 1 Hubbard, the discovery well of the Rowan Field in Brazoria County.[14] The company also had wells in the TXL Field in West Texas, and the Eunice area in southeastern New Mexico.

Rowan Drilling's balance sheet showed general revenue to be about $610,000.[15] The compa-

Old time Rowanites fondly remember the company's parties. Pictured here at the 1948 Christmas party are (left to right): Gilbert Rowe and wife Heddie; Elizabeth Brigance and her husband F. Weldon Brigance.

ny owned 20 rigs, with 16 of them working in West Texas and New Mexico (as well as two on barges in South Louisiana and two in South Texas) and maintained division offices in Midland and Houston.

The *Grapevine*

In 1948, Rowan officials decided to create a company magazine that would be called *The Rowan Grapevine*, later shortened to the *Grapevine*. The publication grew out of a tour of Rowan rigs in West Texas by company officials Mark Hart, Gilbert Rowe and F. Weldon Brigance.

An article that appeared in the *Grapevine* years later noted that on the tour, Hart asked workers, "'What do you think should be done to make this a better company to work for?' Up speaks an unknown hero and says, 'Start a company paper.' On the drive back, Mark agrees to edit such a publication. Weldon Brigance is quite skeptical, and says so."[16]

Arch Rowan shared Brigance's skepticism. He admitted he did not expect the magazine to publish beyond two or three issues. But Arch was mistaken. Following publication of the seventh issue, the paper's first anniversary, Arch congratulated the magazine staff and recalled that "when the proposition was made to publish this paper, I consented with some misgivings."[17] Indeed, it was first put together by a staff untrained in journalism who could only manage writing and layout assignments during any spare time from their regular, heavy workload. Yet, the young newsletter became a labor of love and a source of considerable enjoyment for readers.

To Mark Hart fell the job of ensuring the magazine's first publication. Fortunately, he was a man of firsts, as would be noted at his retirement from Rowan in 1969. It was recorded that he was Rowan's "first trainee, the first purchasing agent, the first editor of the *Grapevine*, and developer of the first group insurance and safety programs for Rowan."[18] The Texas-born Hart, supporting himself on a scholarship and part-time jobs cleaning office buildings and cutting hair, earned a bachelor's degree in business administration from Texas Christian University in 1935. He began working for Rowan as a roughneck a year later in Hobbs, New Mexico.

Following eight months in the field, he joined the Fort Worth office staff, becoming the company's personnel director in 1946. Six years later, he was appointed Rowan Drilling's vice president in charge of personnel, payroll, safety and insurance. By then, he had shed his *Grapevine* duties, resigning as editor in late 1950. But he remained in close contact with the field, spending two months each spring and fall at crew meetings to talk about operations and to explain insurance and safety programs.

Rowan employee John Jackson recalled, "Crew meetings were his greatest joy. ... The men in the field really liked Mark and they always felt free to discuss any grievances with him."[19] When Hart's promotion to vice president was announced in 1952, Arch proclaimed it well-deserved, describing Hart as a "valuable, loyal and tireless employee."[20] Hart remained at Rowan for 33 years.

In 1948, Hart used his spare time to publish the inaugural issue of the *Grapevine*. Helping him as art editor was Tommy Nichols, an assistant geologist and draftsman for Rowan, who illustrated the magazine with cartoons and other drawings. Nichols, like Hart, became editor of the magazine. Nichols joined Rowan in 1935 and retired in 1967. However, after his retirement, he spent two more years assembling the *Grapevine* from the attic of his Fort Worth home. Regarding Nichols' 1969 retirement from the *Grapevine* editorship after 14 years, then-President Gilbert Rowe wrote that "from a 'temporary draftsman that can type' to editor-in-chief may seem like a long, hard climb, but for Tommy it was a natural progression. In addition to his duties as geologist, he always found time to lend a creative hand on the *Grapevine* and was instrumental in molding it from a pioneer publication to the award-winning magazine we have today."[21] In 1963, Nichols received the Benjamin Franklin award from the Texas Manufacturers Association "in recognition of outstanding achievement in the field of employee communications through a company magazine."[22]

For the first issue, published for October-November 1948, Nichols sketched a drawing to illustrate that the magazine needed a name. He depicted workers puzzling over some equipment labeled Rowan Drilling Company. Beneath the cartoon was the caption: "It's your baby, you name it!" Employees were told they should have a hand

Also pictured at the 1948 Christmas party are (left to right): Arch Rowan, Merle Rowan and Stella Rowan, all standing, and Charlie Rowan, seated.

The *Grapevine* created a family atmosphere across the company and kept the far-flung crews informed. Charlie Rowan here enjoys the second issue of the magazine. *(Photo courtesy of the Petroleum Museum, Midland, Texas.)*

in naming the magazine "because it is for you, and we hope it will be filled with news from you and about you and your family."[23] They were encouraged to mail entries in a company-wide contest. Company executives would judge the submissions and a winner and two runner-ups would receive cash prizes totaling $100.

Eighty-five employees sent in 257 submissions. In announcing the winner, company officials had decided the name "should be one that could be used for both the oil drilling and producing business; it should be used in or suggest the oilfield; it should be one that could fit into our industrial relations; and, the name should be one that could be used as an appropriate masthead on the cover page of the publication. The committee thought that the *Grapevine* had all of these qualifications."[24] The second issue bore that name in a masthead surrounded by a vine, bearing leaves and clusters of grapes, that wound from the office headquarters to a der-

rick, to an equipment building and finally to a worker wearing a hard hat.

The winner was office worker Dorice Swanson, a native of New York, and a four-year Rowan employee. She received a $50 cash prize. Two runners-up each received $25 for the names of "Circulating with Rowan" sent in by Clyde McHam, the chief clerk in the West Texas Division office in Midland, and "The Dope Bucket," submitted independently by both Robert J. Kuitu and L.B. Mize. The deadline rule decided who got the runner-up prize for "The Dope Bucket," oil-field lingo for the grease bucket. Kuitu received the $25 prize because his entry was postmarked at 1 p.m. on October 28, while Mize's entry had a 2 p.m. Oct. 31 postmark. Other submissions included "The Rowan Inkwell," "Rowan Shale Shaker," "Rowan Rotary Review" and "Rowanotes."

Dorice Swanson was surprised that others had not submitted the name *The Rowan Grapevine*, for it was a phrase she had heard at the office from Mark Hart. She recalled him telling her, in a conversation about material control, that "'Dorice, you are going to have to get a lot of your information through the grapevine.'"[25] She also discovered the peculiar vocabulary of the oilfield from her Fort Worth desk. While a dope bucket referred to a container holding lubricants for equipment, other terms born to the oil industry included everything from tool-pushing to roughnecks and weevils to tour (pronounced like "tower" and meaning "shift"). She wrote about her introduction to this new language:

"I shall never forget one of the first drilling reports I took over the phone from one of our tool-pushers ... when he told me they would 'break tour in the morning,' I assumed that 'tour' was spelled 'tower' indicating some sort of a small mound or something and that it meant breaking the ground preparatory to drilling the well. I really got a laugh on that one. How green I was."[26]

But she did learn the lexicon, as one man once remarked:

"A gentleman awaiting attention in the office while I was busy on the telephone, remarked after I had completed my conversations, 'I came

in to ask to see Mr. Rowan but I think I shall talk to you — you sound just like a toolpusher and seem to know the answers.' Needless to say, I felt very much complimented."[27]

The first issue of the magazine announced its intent. It was "to be of the people, by the people and for the people of Rowan Drilling Company, Inc., and Rowan Oil Company. The aim of the paper is to improve the spirit of our organization, to create good will within and toward the company, to improve morale, and finally, but not least, to keep our people well-informed on company news."[28]

Articles in the first publication included Charlie Rowan's history of the company's 25 years in the contracting business. In the final lines of the history, Charlie wrote, "The success which this company has attained could not have been obtained without the intelligent and whole-hearted cooperation of our many employees. The management of this company appreciates their loyalty and efforts and will endeavor to be fair, generous and appreciative of those employed by it."[29] Other news items in the inaugural issue included a listing of the company's 20 rigs and

field workers, promotions, wedding announcements and information on crew meetings.

Items in later *Grapevine* issues would include births, business trips, jokes, new and retired employees, and information on safety, taxes and the oil industry. The magazine published photos and news of employee events from newborn babies to children's graduations to vacations. Employees were paid a dollar for each published photo to encourage them to send in family snapshots. Clifford Yancey was drafted as the *Grapevine*'s first staff photographer. At the time, Yancey was the safety director, and the only employee who regularly visited all the rigs. He was given a camera, and his photos of rigs, workers and crew meetings kept readers updated.

Yancey had gone to work for Rowan in the late 1930s after graduating from Oklahoma A&M. "He was a chemical engineer but you could make more money roughnecking than you could being a chemical engineer," his wife, Ina, said in a 1998 interview.[30] He would rise to president and chief operating officer of Rowan's domestic drilling division in 1971. "Mr. Charlie Rowan decided that Clifford would be a good one to get the thing organized and get it going," Mrs. Yancey said. "So he just carried a camera around with him while he was getting the rigs organized and getting the safety program started."[31]

Rowan prided itself on its early and consistent emphasis on safety. Bess Brants' son, Clayton Brants, went to work in his family's insurance business after college, and handled Rowan's insurance needs for two decades. In a 1998 interview, he described Rowan as an "industry leader in safety awareness and safety procedures."[32] He said the company began one of the first safety programs to promote awareness on how to avoid worker accidents, and "they've managed to excel in that category. So as an insurance risk, they were highly desirable and usually led the parade in setting rates for their unblemished safety record."[33]

More than a newsletter, the *Grapevine* was a forum for Rowan workers and their families, like this picture of Drilling Superintendent J.C. Beard and his son, James.

Ending their shift in the summer of 1949, workers on a Rowan rig west of Fort Worth pose for a *Grapevine* photograph.

Charley Wharton, who became the *Grapevine* editor in the early 1980s, said the magazine emphasized safety awareness through statistics and articles. He said in a 1998 interview that "every issue has at least one page in it that's nothing but a statistical report on who the safest people are in our business or in our company and who has the safest rigs."[34]

"Quite a few of our rigs and quite a few of our equipment yards, count in months and some count in years, how long it's been since they've had a lost time accident, and that's pretty incredible in our business."[35]

It was a busy time for Rowan and the industry in general, which recorded its best year in 1948 with a total of 38,500 drilled wells. Rowan drilled 78 wells for a total of 610,821 feet, or nearly 116 miles, with 55 wells in Texas alone. Workers drilled another 12 in New Mexico and 11 in Louisiana.[36] Arch became chairman of Rowan

Drilling in October, relinquishing his duties as vice president and general manager. F.W. Brigance took over that position, while Gilbert Rowe also became a vice president. Rowe was in charge of engineering and rig operations.

In 1949, Rowan celebrated its 25th anniversary. In the May-June 1949 issue of the *Grapevine*, the event was noted with a drawing of an anniversary cake topped with derricks as candles with glowing flames and an article called "The Fruits of Free Enterprise." The article praised the free-enterprise system and those who believed in it.

"In a sense, the story of the success of any small business is, in varying degrees, the story of the success of our whole enterprise system. The success of our company is indirectly a reward earned by all American citizens for their faith. ... It is a memorable day — for the owners who have provided the capital, taken the risk and furnished the initiative and know-how — and for each of us, for we have a common share."[37]

In another article of the same issue, the *Grapevine* spotlighted the history of employee

Dick S. Luse to illustrate the importance that Rowan placed on individual workers for its success. Luse, then acting division drilling superintendent of Rowan's West Texas and New Mexico division, had more than 20 years of employment with the company in 1949 to make him the field employee with the greatest length of service. The Mississippi native and former carpenter roughnecked for several contractors in South Texas before joining Rowan in 1929 because "after inquiry, he found that, and quoting Dick, 'the Rowan organization was the best.'"[38]

Luse's work history with Rowan resembles a road map of rig travels. He began in 1929 on Rowan's original Rig No. 1, then moving to the Salt Flat field north of Luling, Texas. It was a time when Charlie Rowan was still in the field, working as a toolpusher and rig supervisor to build the company. Luse later helped move the Rowan rigs to East Texas after the momentous oil discovery there, and then followed the rigs to various places in West Texas and Oklahoma. The article noted that "on the 25th anniversary of the Rowan organization, it is fitting and proper that Dick Luse, Rowan's only field employee with over 20 years service, should by virtue of his enviable reputation as a fine man personally and as a 'well-man' professionally, be the recipient of the expressed appreciation and affection of the Rowan companies."[39]

Rowan had also become airborne in 1948, buying a twin-engine Beechcraft. In 1950, the Beechcraft would be sold and replaced with a roomier Lockheed Lodestar that was based in Fort Worth. A Grumman Widgeon was added and flown out of New Orleans to barge rigs in Louisiana's marshlands.

As the decade drew to a close, Rowan bought another rig to bring its total to 22. The latest rig was put to work in Hamilton County in Central Texas.[40] By the end of 1949, Rowan's rigs generated more than $6.5 million in revenues with pretax income of more than $1 million.[41]

As Rowan rigs moved to more remote locations, the company soon found it was easier to transport men and equipment with airplanes than by truck. For work in Louisiana, Rowan purchased the Grumman-made Widgeon. Standing next to the plane is Louis Hartmangruber.

Rowan went to Alaska in the 1950s. These workers are setting the surface casing on a rig to begin drilling for General Petroleum Service , a subsidiary of Mobil Oil.

CHAPTER FIVE

STRIKING ITS FUTURE

1950–1959

"I have found that whether on a mountain trail in Wyoming, in a rough sea off the coast, under a derrick floor with blow-out preventers smoking from high pressure, or fighting for a principle he believes in, regardless of how it affected him personally or financially, when the chips were down, [Arch] was always there."

— *Grapevine*, 1957[1]

BY 1950 A STEADY STREAM of American goods circulated the globe as the nation entered a period of unparalleled prosperity. Sales of new homes, domestic appliances and automobiles all skyrocketed as the population made up for two decades of denial. The nation's gross national product almost doubled between 1945 and 1960 and the automobile became a focal point of daily life.

For companies like Rowan, the 1950s represented both a tremendous growth opportunity and considerable challenge. Competition in the oil industry was as fierce as ever, with oil drilling companies competing hard for contracts. Staying ahead was often defined by who could drill the deepest and who was the fastest.

The majority of the company's rigs at this time were diesel-electric land-based rigs. In 1950, the company bought its 23rd rig, followed by its 24th a year later. Both went to West Texas, where, along with New Mexico and Louisiana, most of Rowan's drilling was located. Since only one Rowan rig remained at work near Houston, the company closed its South Texas-Louisiana Division office in that city, moving it in the fall of 1950 into the National Bank of Commerce Building in New Orleans. By the time the Houston office was closed, however, Rowan was developing a new and formidable expertise — one that held great promise for the decades to come.

Rowan Afloat

At the end of 1949, Rowan had two barge-mounted rigs working in Louisiana. That year, the company reinforced its flotilla by adding two more rigs, while building an office, maintenance and repair shop for the Gulf Coast Division in Harvey, Louisiana.

The first of the new rigs, Rig No. 13, weighed more than 1 million pounds and had worked in Texas, Mississippi and Louisiana before its conversion to marine drilling. The rig was installed on a two-barge outfit consisting of a drill unit connected to a 100-foot power barge. The three-deck power barge ran on four 675-horsepower diesel engines. The lowermost deck was reserved for mud pits and the pump room, while the center deck was used to store mud and pipe racks. The top deck housed the drawworks, motors, crew lockers, offices, quarters and the kitchen. The

Arch Rowan received several honors in the 1950s, including being honored by the Texas Independent Producers and Royalty Owners as chief Roughneck of 1957.

In 1950, Rowan doubled the size of its fleet of floating rigs from two to four. Rig No. 13 was mounted on two barges for marine drilling.

1950 — The company buys its 23rd rig and opens an office in downtown New Orleans to service its growing fleet of four barge-mounted rigs.

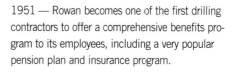

1951 — Rowan Oil and Rowan Drilling establish joint headquarters in Fort Worth, Texas. In December, the company sends its first rig north to drill in North Dakota.

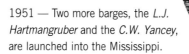

1951 — Two more barges, the *L.J. Hartmangruber* and the *C.W. Yancey*, are launched into the Mississippi.

1951 — Rowan becomes one of the first drilling contractors to offer a comprehensive benefits program to its employees, including a very popular pension plan and insurance program.

derrick on the drilling barge measured 154 feet by 30 feet, but could be converted to 187 feet by 38 feet by adding sections to the base.[2]

On the crew barge, a visitors room featured such comforts as Pullman-type bunks, a kitchen with electric refrigerator and showers.[3] The huge rig was built in Harvey, Louisiana, and according to the *Grapevine*, "looks like a city block floating more than it does a barge. The rear of the power barge slightly resembles a broadside of a battleship. The four exhaust pipes, 44 feet and 9 inches long and 10 inches diameter, look somewhat like four cannons."[4] The converted rig was one of the most powerful, diesel-electric drilling barges in the industry.

The conversion of Rig 13 to drilling by Avondale Marine Ways Inc. prompted visits from oil company representatives and Fort Worth employees to see the behemoth. Office workers were flown in and taken to the rig "for a look at what in the world caused all that extra paper work recently."[5] Rowan liked to ensure that even those in the office learned about the bread and butter of its existence — the rigs. In a 1997 interview, Gilbert Rowe's wife, Heddie, said the trips were a learning experience for office workers who

had never seen a rig: "They didn't know how it worked or anything. They'd take them out and let them see how it worked."[6]

Rig 13 went to work in Timbalier Bay in Louisiana for the Gulf Oil Corporation. Slightly more than a year after its conversion, the rig was drilling its sixth well in that vicinity for Gulf Oil.

The *M.G. Rowe*, the company's fourth barge, was launched into the muddy waters of the Mississippi River on August 22, 1950. At 200 feet long and 54 feet wide, it was the largest drilling rig barge designed for tideland waters. It was named after Gilbert Rowe, its design engineer. Unlike Rig 13, it was a self-contained unit, with the drilling equipment and power supply on the same barge. It was designed for a standard 30-foot base derrick 150 feet high but could accommodate a 33-foot base unit. The barge could carry a load of 1.5 million pounds. The *Grapevine* described its latest barge as "another example of experienced oil men working with experienced marine men to produce better equipment for oil production."[7]

Rowan began adding barges in quick succession, launching two more in 1951, including the *L.J. Hartmangruber* on May 8, and the *C.W. Yancey* three months later. The *L.J. Hartmangruber* was

1954 — The company attempts its first platform-mounted drilling job in deep water. Although successful, the job is tormented by bad weather.

1955 — Arch receives the Golden Deed award from the Exchange Club of Fort Worth. Construction begins on the Rowan Building in Fort Worth.

1955 — Arch and Charlie retire at the same time. Hamilton Rogers is appointed president of Rowan Oil; Gilbert Rowe is appointed president of Rowan Drilling.

1957 — Barge-mounted rigs outnumber the company's land rigs for the first time. Working for Humble, the first Rowan crews are sent to drill in Alaska.

named after Louis Hartmangruber who had worked for Rowan more than 16 years, much of it in the marshes of south Louisiana.[8] The launching of the barge, the third built for Rowan by Avondale Marine Ways over the previous year, was sponsored by Hartmangruber's wife, Cecilia. The ceremony, held at Avondale's Harvey plant in Louisiana, included champagne, red roses and colorful bunting. This barge, like the *M.G. Rowe*, was a single, integrated unit that was fully equipped. In fact, Rig No. 1 had been taken off its former drilling barge and placed on the *L.J. Hartmangruber*. The new barge went to work for Gulf Oil in Timbalier Bay.

The *C.W. Yancey* was launched on August 3, 1951, with Yancey's wife, Ina, breaking a bottle of champagne on the 200-foot-long hull.

Left to right: Charlie Rowan, Ina Yancey and John H. Bull, president of Avondale Marine Ways, celebrate the launching of the drilling barge *C.W. Yancey* (below) in 1951.

Rowan Drilling had purchased the drilling barge, which once held Rig 1, and had it re-configured and enlarged by Avondale Marine Ways. The *M.G. Rowe*, *L.J. Hartmangruber* and *C.W. Yancey* were of similar design, each 200 feet long, 54 feet wide and 12 feet deep.[9] The *C.W. Yancey* headed down the Mississippi River to Hunt Tool Company to be fitted with a diesel-electric drilling rig. Its first contract was with Sun Oil Company in the Lake Verret area, and it became the sixth barge rig operating for Rowan in Louisiana.

By mid-1957, the number of Rowan rigs operating in Louisiana marshes outnumbered their land-locked counterparts in West Texas and New Mexico, with 13 land-based rigs, compared to 14 marine rigs.[10]

As marine drilling gradually overtook land-based operations, the company's administrative effort was run from increasingly crowded land-based offices. In 1951, Rowan Oil and Rowan Drilling moved to new headquarters on the top floor of the Fair Building in Fort Worth, bringing

Drilling barges were added in quick succession in the early 1950s. Rig No. 21 was mounted on a barge and sent to work at the mouth of the Mississippi River in 1954.

Rowan back together under one roof.[11] Rowan delayed its annual Christmas party by a week until the new offices were ready. That translated into a celebration of Christmas, the New Year and open house all on December 30, 1951. The *Grapevine* duly noted that the feast included two huge turkeys, two equally large hams and Stella Rowan's famous hogshead cheese.

Employees moved in before painters, carpenters and electricians had finished preparing the new facility. The *Grapevine* reported that "the pride of the employees is a coffee bar, centrally located for all hands."

"The walls are gray green, and the floor is salmon pink rubber tile with an ivory coffee cup

design and border. It has indirect lighting and acoustical ceiling. The tables are chrome and beige, with chartreuse chairs. The functional equipment is a sink and refrigerator unit of stainless steel and white enamel — a 48-cup coffee urn, and a two-burner hot plate. Each person has his coffee cup numbered in red on the bottom. Coffee and Cokes are furnished by the company."[12]

Elsewhere, the conference room "is the apple of Mr. Arch's eye. The floor is coffee and cream color, and the 16-foot walnut table with a desk at the end is an impressive sight indeed. This had been Mr. Arch's dream since he started trying to gather all supervisory personnel into one small office in the Commercial Standard Building."[13]

Left: Phillis Perryman of the Statistical Department in the new building's employee lounge, which was the "pride of the employees."

Below: This conference room in Rowan's new headquarters was described as "the apple of Mr. Arch's eye." As of 1998, the table and chairs were still in use, located in Rowan's conference room on the 55th floor.

The Frozen North

In December 1951, Rig No. 23 was prepared for a 1,500-mile journey to North Dakota, destined to drill for Amerada Petroleum Corporation in the Williston Basin. Seeking hardy volunteers for the field, Gilbert Rowe sent a letter to West Texas crews outlining the severe weather conditions and warned that winter temperatures far below zero were common. Operators had to winterize rigs by boxing in the derrick floor up to 25 feet, enclosing the structure to the ground and heating the rigs by steam. The company developed contingency plans to provide emergency food supplies at the rig in case the crew was snowed in. Rig 23's first location was in the Tioga-Beaver Lodge Field about six miles from Tioga, a town of approximately 650 people.

Fifteen years earlier in Louisiana, Rowan workers fought humidity, mosquitoes and snakes. In North Dakota, the challenge was different. Employees described their work experiences in early 1952:

"On January 7 at midnight we broke tour. The rigging up didn't break any speed records due to weather conditions, and we were held up by part of the equipment being snowbound enroute. After the substructure arrived, we got after it in typical

Rowan's introduction to cold-weather climes came in North Dakota, where Rig 23 was dispatched in 1951. This picture was taken four years later.

Rowan fashion — I mean fast. The entire substructure is enclosed and a house is built around the pumps and pits. The cold isn't bad until the wind blows. It is really better than you might think. When there is a gale, it's rough, but one day it was 36 degrees below and nice."[14]

Although new to the harsh environment, Rowan helped to pioneer rig winterization. Since the discovery of oil in the Williston Basin, contractors had labored over the problem of winter drilling:

"Rowan's contribution to the fund of know-how is a winter shed so constructed that it can be skidded intact, just as the derrick and substructure are skidded from one location to another. This saves the time and expense of building a wooden frame, covering it with sheet metal, then tearing it down and rebuilding it with each move."[15]

Rowan next moved crews to Alaska in 1957 under a contract with Humble that included drilling a wildcat well. Two seven-member crews lived in

Rowan Rig 23 being skidded to a new location in North Dakota.

barracks nestled on a hillside. The Bear Creek location was an hour by helicopter from King Salmon, an Army Air Base 270 miles southwest of Anchorage, where the wind often reached 80 knots. Temperatures literally fell off the scale because the mercury stopped moving in thermometers rated to minus 50 degrees Fahrenheit. Rowan workers discovered that knowledge gained from working in the northern and southern sections of the United States was not enough in the Alaskan badlands, noted Rielley Euper, who worked as a maintenance man with tough assignments that included Alaska and the North Sea.

"There were a lot of things that we didn't know about working in extreme cold. We learned to apply additives to diesel fuel because in cold weather it turns to jelly, and you have to heat it to bring it back to a fluid state. If you park a truck outside at night you're running on what feels like flat tires until they warm up. If you don't have heaters on the engines, they just won't start."[16]

The crews stayed in portable buildings (furnished by Humble Oil) at the camp for 30 days, and were flown to Anchorage for five days off. Two helicopters and crews were based at the camp, along with Humble engineers and geologists.

Deep Water Drilling

Until the advent of true offshore drilling, all of Rowan's barges operated in the swirling chocolate waters of the Louisiana bayou. But the knowledge that much more oil was located beneath the ocean floor drove Rowan from the protective lee of land to the open sea.

The first offshore oil well was brought in on a Sunday morning in October 1947 by a small company called Kerr-McGee. Unlike its counterparts on land, there was no rush to build platforms because the cost was simply too prohibitive. An offshore oil platform could cost five times as much as a land-based rig to build. Once in place, the rig was subjected to the planet's most inclement weather: hurricanes, raging winds and tides, waves, and the corrosive effect of salt water.

But the potential commercial rewards were tremendous. For the United States, offshore drilling would add about 5 percent of total reserves for oil.

In 1954, Rowan launched its first deep-water drilling job on a reconditioned rig, a 20-year veteran of the oilfields of West Texas, New Mexico and Mississippi. The rig had undergone improvements and modifications over the years, increasing its drilling depth capacity from 4,000-foot wells to depths below 12,000 feet. It had bogged down in mud and high pressures during its last drilling job, so another rig was mounted on a platform perched on pilings in the Gulf of Mexico.[17]

This first deep-water job was a baptism of foul weather, as the crew had just begun drilling when a storm struck. The drilling tender carrying supplies and crew members for the platform moved away from the drilling platform and swung around to face into the wind. The drilling tender's galley was stocked with more than a week's worth of food, which had not yet been unloaded. The supply vessel was too distant to secure a line, but the boat carrying the relief crew was near. However, it could not go alongside the supply tender because heavy seas threatened to smash them together. The boat's skipper "maneuvered between the tender and platform, took a line from the former and passed one to the latter. Thus, for 18 hours the drilling crew was fed. It is rumored that there were many landlubber stomachs on both [vessels]."[18]

With these hardships behind, Rowan counted the experience a success. In 1955, the

---

By the 1950s, Rowan's floating rigs actually outnumbered their land bound counterparts. The company's expertise in barge-mounted drilling helped it move into deeper waters.

company added a second rig to platform work. Within a year, crew members were ferried out to the platforms by helicopter instead of boats, saving hours of transport time. When bad weather grounded the helicopters, the slower-moving boats were called in again.

Taking Care of Their Own

With business strong and growing, Charlie and Arch instituted one of the first comprehensive benefits programs offered by an independent contract oil company. Rowan Oil and Rowan Drilling had a combined payroll of 553 workers. In addition to Rowan Oil, Rowan Drilling had contracts with the major oil companies of the day: Gulf, Houston Oil, Humble, Shell, Texas Pacific Coal and Oil, Texas Gulf Producing, Union Oil of California, Amerada, Pure, Seaboard, Stanolind and Tidewater.[19] The company passed the 1 million-foot mark in combined drilling footage in 1951.[20]

Rowan first offered group insurance to employees in the late 1930s, but later realized "the plan was expensive and did not meet the particular needs of the Rowan companies' employees, so it did not catch on very fast or go very far. In fact, only 25 percent of the eligible employees took up this insurance."[21] After World War II, the company began devising an improved plan. Mark Hart directed a new policy, which became effective in March 1949, and was immediately popular — 95 percent of eligible employees signed up.[22] Shortly after, the *Grapevine* published pictures of the first babies born under the plan. Paid vacations for drilling crews arrived a year later,

HADACOL CORNER AND THE SPRABERRY TREND

IN THE DUSTY FIELDS OF WEST TEXAS, about 45 miles from Midland, a settlement known as Hadacol Corner was thriving. A gusher had created a boom in Spraberry Trend by the summer of 1951, and Rowan developed several farm-outs in the area and put four rigs to work. Hadacol Corner was named after "Hadacol" Darkins, a Midland man who parked his trailer at a dusty crossroads and set up a business:

"He sold soda pop, sandwiches and candy to oilfield workers. It soon became a mecca for truckers who obtained directions to the locations to deposit their cargoes. His success was almost overnight. Others followed suit, hence the colorful, thriving community. ... A literal forest of oil wells extend out from Hadacol Corner."[1]

The Hadacol Corner site originally consisted of only a fence post showing directions to Rowan leases, as well as other oil company holdings. But six months after Hadacol began his trailer business, the site grew to at least 30 trailer houses, a cafe, filling station garage, grocery store and a welding shop.

The vast Spraberry Trend, a half-million acre area running through some half-dozen counties, prompted a legal battle over gas flaring, or burning away of the casinghead gas produced from the oil wells. Operators had to allow gas flow to produce oil. But what to do with the gas from so many wells not connected to gas gathering lines? The illegal flaring of gas was widespread in the Spraberry Trend. In their book, *Wildcatters: Texas Independent Oilmen*, Roger M. and Diana Davids Olien wrote that the scale of the trend was a formidable barrier to gas conservation. The cost of building pipelines to every well "would be staggering," considering that the price of gas was low and the cost of pipe for such gathering systems high.[2]

But the amount of gas wasted was also enormous. The Railroad Commission in April 1953 issued an order that shut down all the wells in the Trend, even those connected to gathering systems, until facilities were completed to market all of the gas.

"The decision to shut in all wells marked a departure from previous regulation of gas production, but it was designed to meet three important peculiarities of the situation: the amount of gas flared was great — an estimated 220 million cubic feet daily; a huge processing system was necessary, and it could not be completed quickly; and the Trend's geological characteristics permitted oil to migrate irregularly over great distances. The last was why all wells were shut down; if some remained in production, they would drain oil from those properties that were closed. Thus, the 468 wells that wasted no gas were shut down along with the more than 1,800 wells whose gas was flared."[3]

Needless to say, operators large and small were unhappy. Rowan Oil and other companies sued the commission. According to an article on Rowan Oil's court battle, "Arch's suit alleged the commission's order invalid on the basis it discriminated against some producers in the area. His contention was that he was not flaring any gas from his Spraberry wells."[4]

Elton Hyder, who had married Charlie's daughter, Martha, served as Rowan's attorney. He argued that the court should not "penalize the lawful operator because of the unlawful operator."[5]

Arch took the stand to say he would suffer irreparable damage if his wells were shut down. He feared that some wells, once shut down, could not be restored to production and he could lose some $2.5 million.[6] But Railroad commission chairman Ernest O. Thompson countered on the stand that the field wide shutdowns to prevent gas flaring was "a new assault on waste."[7]

The Texas courts ruled against the commission. The commission was told it could not shut down wells connected to gas gathering systems. Furthermore, the court said the order should be modified to exempt nonflaring producers from the production ban. The commission appealed the district court decision to the Texas Supreme Court. The Texas attorney general, who spoke for the commission, asked that the shutdown order be either upheld in its entirety or stricken. The state's high court in June 1953 noted the "commission has made a courageous effort to prevent the waste of gas," but it ruled that the portion of the order shutting down nonwasteful wells to prevent the loss of oil of shut-in well owners was void.[8] Since some of the order was invalid, the justices said, the entire order must be thrown out. With that, the commission "decided to minimize gas waste by cutting back oil production and set a limit of ten producing days a month for the Spraberry."[9]

providing for two weeks a year for employees with at least one year of service, three weeks for those with 15 years of employment, and four weeks for 25-year employees. In making the announcement, Charlie said, "The nature of the oil well contracting business, with its lack of continuous operations and its large labor turnover, has, in the past, rendered paid vacations for drilling crew employees impractical. Our drilling personnel, however, is of such quality and has stayed with the company so well that the management feels we can work out a satisfactory paid vacation plan for our field employees."[23] In the uncertain world of contracting, no other independent contractor offered such a benefit.

The company also began awarding service pins. The announcement was made in early 1951 after a written survey of employees who had worked for Rowan for five or more years. The appreciative gift was described as a "small gold, dignified looking pin with a large 'R' in the center with a stone which will indicate whether it is a five-, 10-, 15-, or 25-year pin."[24] The stones ranged from a ruby for the five-year pin, to a half-carat diamond for the 25-year pin. For 10 years of service, Rowan employees received a sapphire pin, followed by an emerald for 15 years and a one-quarter carat diamond for 20

Above: J.T. "Pappy" May in 1953 became the first employee to retire under the Rowan pension plan, which proved immensely popular.

Left: In 1951, Rowan instituted the practice of awarding service pins. That year, Mr. Arch presented a pin to A.C. Allen, vice president of Rowan Oil.

years of service. Rowan already had 71 employees who warranted pins, and expected 22 more to become eligible during 1951.[25]

Charlie Rowan announced the establishment of a voluntary pension plan in November 1952. The pension was established because Charlie and Arch were "firm in their belief that the average American does not want a dole or handout but, rather, an opportunity to provide for his own welfare."

"That is why the insurance plans have been of the voluntary, employee participation type, and the pension plan is the same. Those who consider it good and want it are invited to join with the companies in insuring their well-being and that of their families."[26]

The plan also included death and permanent disability benefits. Any employee with at least one year of service was eligible. Contributions to the plan from the company and the employees were placed in a trust fund.

The pension plan, described as "the brain child of Mr. Arch more than anyone else," did not leave the Rowan old-timers with lost, unpaid years. Instead, according to a company document, "the Rowan companies dig into their tills and pay every person in the company up to date. Thus, all of our pension credits start from the time we were employed rather than from the date of the Plan's inception. This cost the companies many thousands of dollars."[27] One hundred percent employee participation was achieved by 1954.

John Jackson, who retired in 1978 as vice president in charge of personnel, recalled helping enact the pension, and Rowans' reasons behind it: "They had the employees on their minds all the time. They were first class people who honored their employees in every way."[28]

The New Generation

The Rowan brothers had been at the helm of their companies for 30 years; they decided it was time for a new generation of leaders to move into place. The Rowans were well-known for their ability to identify potential in an employee, and few were so universally entrusted as Cecil Provine. In 1953, he was elected to the board of directors and named vice president of Rowan Drilling. Mildred Rucker, one of the early receptionists for Rowan Drilling, remembered the atmosphere at the Fort Worth headquarters throughout this period. The Rowan brothers and Bess Brants worked seven days a week, with Brants "sitting on the beach and working." On weekends, Brants would find time to throw parties at her house, at which Rowanites gathered in a large congenial crowd. At the office, meanwhile, Provine made a distinct impression on the young receptionist.

"He was really a character. He was a marvelous oil man with a heart of gold, but he always came on like gangbusters. He was a strong person and his language was always a little bit earthy, but you never resented it. He was always the kind of fellow that when I was the reception-

Left to right: Cecil Provine, Bess Brants, and Fort Worth National Bank employees Jack Kelly and W.B. Duke at the 1956 Christmas party.

Mr. Arch, left, with Hamilton Rogers, who succeeded Arch as president of Rowan Oil Company when Rowan stepped down in 1955.

ist, no matter who was at my desk and wanted to see him, he would see them even if they weren't important people."[29]

Also in 1953, Hamilton Rogers was named vice president of Rowan Oil. A Texas native who graduated from the University of Texas Law School, Rogers joined Rowan in 1941, and was elected to the board of directors of Rowan Oil in 1947.

That summer, Charles Robert "Bob" Palmer began working for the company as part of a work program through Southern Methodist University's placement service. The 18-year-old student was described in a *Grapevine* article as a "man with a purpose" who went to college to prepare himself for a career in the drilling industry.[30] In the co-op program, he alternated going to school for two months with working for Rowan for two months. By the end of that first year, he knew that working for Rowan was his goal. Marriage and a family caused him to work in another company's geological lab closer to home for a short time, but he soon returned to roughneck for Rowan. In June

1957, he graduated with a bachelor's degree in mechanical engineering, but he worked for Rowan as an engineman on a drilling crew because, among other reasons, the job paid 50 percent more than as an engineer. In 1960, he worked in Fort Worth, supervising engineering and purchasing. He returned to Southern Methodist in 1965 to earn his master's degree in engineering administration, and gradually rose through the ranks to eventually become chairman and CEO in 1972.

In 1954, Rowan management suffered a terrible loss with the death of F. Weldon Brigance. He had worked for Rowan Drilling for 20 years, and had made a significant contribution to its growth and success. Brigance, who rose to be the company's executive vice president, died from cancer at the age of 56.

Arch and Charlie planned to retire at the same time in 1955. Charlie would be 65 that summer, while Arch would be 61. Although Arch had a few years remaining before retirement age, they agreed to step down together. For successors, Arch appointed Hamilton Rogers president of Rowan Oil Company, while Gilbert Rowe became president of Rowan Drilling. Others had been at Rowan Drilling longer than Rowe but his wife, Heddie, said the Rowan brothers "saw the possibilities, I think, of what he could do."[31] Rogers and Rowe had gradually assumed greater responsibilities over the years, and were "known qualities and not a blind gamble."[32]

When the Rowan brothers gave up these positions, it marked the first time since the founding of Rowan Drilling 32 years previously, and the inception of Rowan Oil, that the brothers were not heading their companies. The *Grapevine* described it as a "delicate and crucial shift."

"It is not easy for the founders of a successful business to hand the reins over to someone else. They suffer the same misgivings and apprehensions inherent in a father giving his daughter in marriage to another man, after the father has nurtured and cared for her from birth. We are fortunate that the heads of our companies have had the wisdom and forethought to train two such able young executives as Gilbert Rowe and Hamilton Rogers, thus assuring that the business will be carried on in the same traditions that have made the name Rowan respected and honored in oil circles."[33]

Arch and Charlie would still be available for counsel and guidance and would continue to serve as chairmen of their respective boards. Arch's son, Arch, Jr., was elected to both boards of directors.

In only seven years, Rowan Oil had doubled the number of producing oil and gas wells in which it had an interest, from 60 in 1948 to 120 wells in 1955. As for Rowan Drilling, it had doubled the number of wells drilled, as well as more than doubled its drilling footage during the same seven-year period. In 1948, Rowan drilled 77 wells for a total of 603,209 feet, compared to 145 wells for 1.4 million feet in 1954. The company continued to drill deeper in the search for oil. Its average depth in 1948 had been 7,800 feet, but by 1954 it was drilling to 9,700 feet.[34]

Honors

Arch had become a respected member of the Texas oil elite, and received a number of accolades for his leadership within the industry. The first came in October 1951, when he received the Texas Mid-Continent Oil and Gas Association's 1951 Distinguished Service Award for his work on behalf of the industry. Along with a Humble executive similarly honored, Arch received the award at the asso-

ciation's annual meeting in Beaumont. F.J. Adams, the Gulf Oil executive who presented the award, told of Arch's childhood, his initial foray into roughnecking, and his co-founding of Rowan Drilling. Adams said Arch's "business acumen and fair dealing with operators, and his understanding of requirements to keep abreast of all new developments, now rank Rowan as one of the most outstanding well-drilling organizations in the industry."[35] Adams went on to talk about Arch's involvement in various organizations, including the National Petroleum Council, the American Association of Oilwell Drilling Contractors, and the Independent Petroleum Association of America.

"Businessman Arch as a citizen and family man is also an outstanding person. When time will permit, he lives as a country gentleman at Rowanoak Farm on Mary's Creek, just west of Fort Worth, where he conducts a farm and ranch business as well as a place where he is a hospitable host on many occasions. In all of these surroundings, he has the excellent help of his lovely wife, Stella, and three children, Jean, Sonny (Arch Jr.), and Sue."[36]

Arch H. Rowan, left, received the Golden Deeds award for 1955 from the Exchange Club of Fort Worth. *(Photo courtesy of The Petroleum Museum, Midland, Texas.)*

In 1956, the company moved into the Rowan Building, 6000 Camp Bowie Blvd., in Fort Worth. The rose brick building was more than 37,000 square feet.

Arch received the Golden Deeds Award for 1955 from the Exchange Club of Fort Worth. Nearly 500 people, including businessmen and Texas Governor Allan Shivers, attended the banquet in Arch's honor. The *Grapevine* reported that "affectionately known by his friends for the courage to exemplify by acts and deeds the convictions of his mind, his name was subscribed to the Book of Golden Deeds, and he was presented with an achievement award bearing the personal signatures of all in attendance."[37] In his acceptance speech, Arch paid tribute to his family, and

"the most wonderful character and the finest friend I ever had — my mother — long since this life departed. She was possessed of a magnificent mind and a beautiful philosophy of life. She was a Christian lady."[38] He also spoke of his brother, "whom I have been associated with for 32 years without a harsh word or discordant note."[39]

Arch's business and civic leadership included serving as a director of the Chamber of Commerce, the United Fund and the Cancer Society, as well as being a former president of the Exchange Club, vice chairman of the Texas Turnpike Authority, and a deacon of the University Christian Church. The Texas Turnpike Authority was a state agency, overseeing the construction of the Fort Worth-Dallas Toll Road. As part of his work for the agency, Arch traveled throughout the United States to inspect toll roads and even to Europe to ride on a superhighway. Laughingly, he would describe it as "one of the most time-consuming jobs I've ever had."[40]

Shortly after Arch was honored with the Exchange Club award, the Rowan companies announced its new headquarters — the Rowan Building in Fort Worth. Construction of the three-story building on Camp Bowie Boulevard had begun in 1955, after the Rowan Pension Fund purchased the land. The air-conditioned structure, built of light rose brick trimmed with gray stone and aluminum, contained more than 37,000 square feet. Rowan, which began in Fort Worth by renting one office and a reception room, now spread out over 11,000 square feet. The balance of the facility was leased to tenants. The building was within 15 minutes of downtown via the freeway.

Presidents Gilbert Rowe and Hamilton Rogers announced in 1956 that the Rowan companies would provide seven $500 college scholarships, one of which was reserved for an employee's child. Eva Sharon Abbott, daughter of driller George Abbott Jr., became the first to be awarded the scholarship. She attended Louisiana State University and earned a bachelor of arts degree, majoring in English. She would later characterize her college education "a truly precious thing. I owe [Rowan] a great deal, and though words are so inadequate, Thank You!"[41] Over the years, Rowan would increase the number of scholarships for the children of employees to two in 1969 and then four in 1973. By 1999, Rowan will have established 20 scholarships, each awarding $2,500 a year for up to five years.

Arch's third honor struck close to the hearts of oil men — he was named chief roughneck of 1957. The award from the Texas Independent Producers and Royalty Owners honored outstanding oilmen who moved up through the ranks. It was given to Arch at the group's annual meeting in Galveston. The *Grapevine*, in its coverage of the event, quoted an un-named friend of Arch who spoke during the presentation.

"I have hunted and fished with Arch from Wyoming to the Gulf, have worked with him in most of the oil patches in Texas and Louisiana. I have found that whether on a mountain trail in Wyoming, in a rough sea off the coast, under a

derrick floor with blow-out preventers smoking from high pressure, or fighting for a principle he believes in, regardless of how it affected him personally or financially, when the chips were down, he was always there."[42]

Rowan Oil Is Sold

When the Rowan brothers founded their companies, they decided to split their drilling efforts between two separate entities because of Texas law. The decision, though, had become outdated, and it was becoming clear that the Rowan companies weren't benefiting from two separate organizations. In 1958, plans were announced to sell Rowan Oil Company to the Texas Pacific Coal & Oil Company in a $9.6 million stock deal. Texas Pacific swapped 275,408 shares of its stock for the Rowan Oil assets. Those assets included interests in 142 producing oil wells and 21 gas wells; an estimated 7 million barrels of oil reserves in Louisiana, Texas and New Mexico; and interests in 15,000 acres of productive leases and 41,000 undeveloped acres. Texas Pacific also received $2.5 million in liquid assets, including equipment, cash, accounts

The law prohibiting a drilling company from owning oil leases had changed by 1958, prompting the sale of Rowan Oil Company to Texas Pacific Coal and Oil Company.

receivable and inventories. H.B. Fuqua, Texas Pacific board chairman and president, said in a *Wall Street Journal* article that the purchase would "substantially increase our oil and gas reserves in areas where we wanted new production."[43]

Rowan had its own reasons. Historically, Texas law did not permit a drilling company to engage in the oil production business. The law had changed in recent years, permitting a drilling contractor to secure leases and produce oil. The *Grapevine* spelled out the thinking behind the deal:

"Since there was no reason for having two corporate charters and two companies engaged in competition with each other in the same office, it seemed advisable to make a sale of the assets of the Rowan Oil Company. One of the considerations in making this transaction was the willingness and the desire on the part of Texas Pacific Coal & Oil Company to invite the employees of the Rowan Oil Company to continue their jobs with the T.P. organization. Those who could not be absorbed by the young producing division of Rowan Drilling Company, Inc., will be afforded an opportunity to use their fine talents in the T.P. organization."[44]

Indeed, Rowan proclaimed that the expertise of Rowan Oil Company President Hamilton Rogers and Vice President A.C. "Charlie" Allen were "about as valuable an asset to T.P.C.&O. as the producing oil and gas properties. Every lease and agreement in the Rowan files is as familiar to Hamilton as the palm of his hand, and Charlie is personally acquainted with every whim and caprice of such temperamental areas as the Danbury Dome field."[45]

Texas Pacific had not been the only company interested in acquiring Rowan Oil. "When word got out that Rowan was considering trading or selling their oil holdings, several large companies presented attractive deals. Texas Pacific Coal and Oil Company was selected because of its fine management and financial soundness."[46] It also was a good deal for Rowan Oil employees. Texas Pacific, established in 1888 as a coal company, maintained headquarters in Fort Worth, meaning that Rowan Oil employees who went to Texas Pacific would not have to be uprooted. Arch was satisfied with the stock deal and said, "we don't feel that we are selling to Texas Pacific. We feel we are buying in with them."[47]

In the summer of 1958, Rowan began drilling operations in Mississippi. The company drilled a well with gas instead of mud as a lubricating medium, a technique it had used before in West Texas. Rowan first employed the technique while spudding a well for Humble on March 31, 1954, in northwest Texas. In the Texas Panhandle, drillers watched as their drilling fluid drained away into cavernous formations. They filled the cavities with hay, peanut hulls and other bulk materials that could be washed down the drilling pipe, but the effort was costly, time consuming, and not always successful. They next found they could force natural gas, or even compressed air, down the drill pipe to clear drill cuttings and cool the bit.[48] Great care had to be taken when working with natural gas. Safety mea-

The drilling operation was busy throughout the decade. These Rowan workers are welding, lifting and moving the flowline into position as they set up a rig.

The company experimented with gas drilling on Rig 24, which is pictured in Colorado. Gas drilling proved to be faster and more economical than mud drilling.

sures included pressure gauges and fencing-off the area to keep away smokers.

Rowan had joined with Humble to navigate their first joint effort with gas drilling back in 1954. Without safety guidelines for this demanding technique, the two companies' safety departments gathered all available information on gas drilling and met in a cafe to establish a set of rules before proceeding with the well. The *Grapevine* reported later that "how well they labored is attested by the fact that these basic rules were adopted by the AAODC (American Association of Oilwell Drilling Contractors), and have survived to this day [1964] with no appreciable changes."[49]

In 1958, four years after its first successful gas-drilled well, Rowan prepared to drill with gas in the Silome Area of Clay County, Mississippi. Several men experienced in gas drilling came from West Texas to share their knowledge with Rowan workers on the Gulf Coast. Two years later, the company finished drilling Shell's Federal Land Bank Unit No. 1 well with gas. Another local well had been

drilled using the mud method, and it was interesting to compare the cost of the two projects. It took 106 bits and 91 days for the well drilled with mud, while the gas-drilled well used only nine bits during the 23-day work.[50]

On November 16, 1959, Rowan brought in the Price No. 1 in a new field in Borden County in West Texas. It was the first oil well promoted and drilled by Rowan since Rowan Oil had been sold to Texas Pacific the year before. The field was dubbed the Romac Field after Rowan and McElroy Ranch, a partner in the venture. While bringing in the well, the crew killed more than 30 rattlesnakes.[51]

The new decade would bring a far greater change, however. Five years after his retirement, Charlie Rowan would die.

The drilling tender *Rowan I* would soon be joined by a sister ship. As Rowan increased its presence offshore, more tenders were needed.

CHAPTER SIX

DEEPENING WATERS

1960–1967

"[Arch] would not let the company go into debt to build drilling rigs that he probably would never see, and he would not place his family's fortune in jeopardy to guarantee those loans. It was really that issue that had precipitated the decision to go public, and let the Rowan family move out of the picture so we could go forward."

— C.R. Palmer, 1998[1]

CHARLIE ROWAN HAD SUFFERED a stroke in the late 1950s, but the tough roughneck recovered to lead an active life. Following his retirement, Charlie and his wife Merle traveled the world together and spent time with his family. Always seeking to acquire and dispense knowledge, Charlie would explain historical landmarks to his family to impress upon them the importance of understanding the past as a way to understand the present.

In 1961, Charlie fell while coming down the steps of an aircraft. "I think he didn't recover from that," recalled his daughter, Martha Rowan Hyder. "His strength failed. But after his first stroke, he had four or five good years with mother."[2]

Another tragedy struck the Rowan family a year later. Arch's only son, Arch, Jr., died from burns he suffered as he prepared to barbecue steaks in the back yard of his home near Fort Worth. A kerosene can exploded in his hands as he poured the liquid onto the glowing coals of a charcoal burner. Flames flashed back into his face and set his clothes afire.[3] His wife, Eloise, burned her hands as she desperately rolled him in a blanket to smother the flames. She was treated at the hospital for burns and released. Her husband, only 32 years old, died the next day on August 7, 1962.

Ironically, it was Arch, Jr., called "Sonny" by his family, who had worked to improve firefighting methods to save crews on burning aircraft. Horace Craig, aviation writer for the *Fort Worth Star-Telegram*, wrote that "people who fly lost a real friend." Craig noted that the younger Arch was president of Fire Control Engineering Company, which had developed a new method for "'cutting a path' through a raging fire quickly with sodium bicarbonate. The dry powder ... long had been known as a superior fire fighting agent, but it had been difficult to apply. Rowan's company, however, had learned to pump the dry powder through hoses, just like water."[4] (The powder was driven by compressed nitrogen, stored in conventional bottles.)

Craig had noted that the fire-smothering powder acted as a curtain against heat. Arch, Jr. became interested in sodium bicarbonate from his experience with oil well fires. Like aircraft fires, burning fuel is the cause of oil well fires. As a pilot, Arch, Jr. had noted that the heavier foam

Rowan found new quarters on the 30th floor of the Humble Building in downtown Houston. *(Photo courtesy of Houston Metropolitan Research Center, Houston Public Library.)*

trucks at airports could not get to a fire as quickly as one loaded with the lighter dry powder. Shortly before his death, he had written that "our object is to get to the scene in a hurry, drill a hole through the fire and rescue the crew of an airplane."[5] His company had sold some 150 dry-powder units.

At the time of his death, Arch, Jr. was in his seventh year as a director of the board of Rowan Drilling. He was an independent oil operator active in politics and civic affairs like his father. He had worked for Rowan in the oilfields during his college years and earned a bachelor's degree in geology and a master's degree in business administration from the University of Texas, and had served two years in the Air Force. Arch, Jr.'s daughter, Sydney, was three years old and his son, Arch III, just seven months old at the time of their father's death.

Arch, Jr.'s sister, Jean Rowan McNab, said if her brother had lived, he would have become more involved with Rowan Drilling. In a 1998 interview, she said "I think Sonny's plan was to go to Midland and spend a few years, just in the oil business but on his own, and then come back to the company after he … had a few independent years. But he died before he was able to do that."[6]

The accident occurred just two months after Arch, Sr. had received an honorary juris doctorate from Bethany College in Bethany, West Virginia. The citation acknowledged Arch's roles "in both the dramatic epic of oil and the glorious and dynamic state of mind called Texas."[7]

"Periodically, we do reaffirm our faith in fundamental and traditional values by paying our respects to self-determination, personal and social responsibility, initiative and sustained creative effort."[8]

Moving to Houston

The death of Charlie Rowan in 1961 coincided with dramatic changes for the company. At the beginning of the sixties, Rowan operated 32 rigs in eight states: Louisiana, Mississippi, Montana, Wyoming, North Dakota, New Mexico, Alaska and, of course, Texas. These rigs moved from field to field and state to state. A lone rig in Mississippi later joined Rowan's other land rigs in Louisiana. A rig working in West Texas

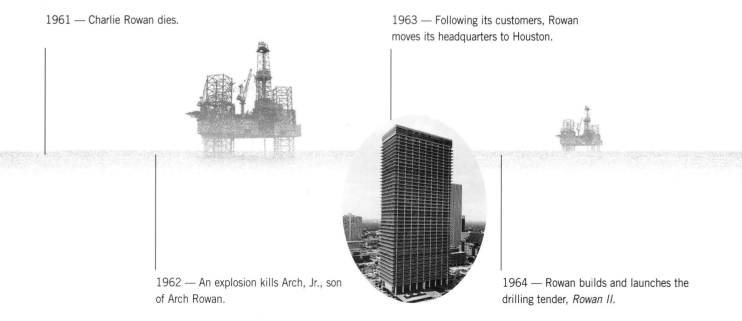

1961 — Charlie Rowan dies.

1962 — An explosion kills Arch, Jr., son of Arch Rowan.

1963 — Following its customers, Rowan moves its headquarters to Houston.

1964 — Rowan builds and launches the drilling tender, *Rowan II.*

Workers set up equipment for gas drilling in the Oklahoma towns of Poteau and Wilburton in 1962.

1965 — Rig No. 7, one of two split-level rigs, drills more than 21,000 feet in just 197 days.

1967 — Rowan announces a 5 percent pay raise for all its rig crews.

1967 — Rowan goes public with an initial offering of 323,000 shares.

Above: A high-pressure manifold, through which gas flows to the well, on a gas-drilling rig in Oklahoma.

Right: While Rowan's headquarters moved to Houston, engineer Bob Palmer cleaned out his files for his move to Midland.

went to southeastern Oklahoma in October 1961, and a rig from Montana soon followed. A third rig traveled from Wyoming to work in Oklahoma.

New to Oklahoma, the crews of two of the rigs settled into the small town of Wilburton, while other crew members took up residence in Poteau, an old mining town. A summer 1962 *Grapevine* article recounted that without a trailer park in Poteau equipped for big house trailers, "our men pitched in to 'rig up' the camp. They dug ditches and laid water pipe. An electric line was hastily strung and by now, no doubt, sewer connections have been made and normal living has been resumed."[9]

An even bigger move for Rowan was to come, however. More and more large oil companies were moving their headquarters to Houston, and Rowan officers soon felt the company should follow its customers. In 1963, Rowan located new

quarters on the 30th floor of the Humble Building in downtown Houston. By then, Rowan had performed contract work for Humble every year since its founding in 1923. (In the 1990s, the special relationship between Rowan and Humble would become known as an "alliance.")

From its new home, Rowan would administer operations, engineering, bids and purchasing. "This move is being made to permit closer relationship and contact with the ever-increasing concentration of our customer companies' management in Houston," according to President Gilbert Rowe.[10] Rowe and Cecil Provine, who had become executive vice president a year earlier, were among the top Rowan executives who made the move.

The company's general offices remained in Fort Worth, however. There, Vice President Mark Hart continued to supervise accounting and statistical operations, as well as his other duties in personnel and insurance management. J.C. Magner, vice president in charge of legal, land and

Left to right: Gilbert Rowe, Bess Brants, Lou Provine (Cecil Provine's wife), Heddie Rowe and Ina Yancey, (Clifford Yancey's wife), at the christening of the *Rowan II* drilling tender in 1964.

production departments, also remained in Fort Worth. Arch, chairman of the board, and secretary-treasurer Bess Brants also kept offices in Fort Worth. Engineer (and future chairman, president and CEO) Bob Palmer moved to Midland as a drilling engineer.

All Ahead Offshore

In the sixties Rowan went increasingly offshore as its competitors began recognizing the enormous potential in open-water drilling. The platforms of the day were mounted on pilings sunk deep into the ocean floor, with a conventional drilling rig operating through a hole in the platform. But Rowan, determined to stay on the cutting-edge of offshore technology, diverted more resources to offshore drilling designs and methods. In the spring of 1963, the company bought the *Carle Sharp*, a drilling tender that had serviced Rowan rigs, including the

existing offshore platforms, for eight years. It was partnered with the reconditioned Rig No. 18, which had been "enthroned on a brand-new three tier steel drilling structure and substructure" and placed on a Gulf Oil Corporation platform in the Gulf of Mexico.[11] The drilling structure and substructure had been designed by Rowan.

Rowan's continued expansion offshore coincided with a drop in its land-based oil drilling business. The year 1963 was described as a "hold-on year for the contracting industry" by company executives because drilling dropped 6 percent, or about 2,871 wells, to a total of 43,550 completions nationwide. This was the lowest level in a decade.[12] Rowan continued to upgrade its barge rigs because, according to the *Grapevine*, "offshore drilling is the one field where there is not more rigs than jobs. Rowan has always 'gone where the work is,' and will continue to do so."[13]

Following the purchase of the *Carle Sharp*, Rowan broke ground for a repair yard on the 20 acres it owned six miles east of Morgan City, Louisiana. The new facility, which replaced the Harvey Yard, had a 700-foot frontage on the Intracoastal Waterway and a slip 90 feet wide by 750 feet long and 12 feet deep.[14] Rowan built a

THE WIRE LINE GUIDE APPARATUS

ROWAN RECEIVED ITS FIRST PATENT IN 1961 for its wireline guide apparatus. The company had set up a generous policy for inventions in 1949 by agreeing to pay all costs for a patent and permitting the employee to receive a percentage of any royalties from outside licensing.

This new device was developed to reduce wear and tear on drilling equipment. Its most successful application use was in directional drilling on offshore rigs where multiple slope tests are necessary to determine the correct angle. To accomplish the tests, an instrument had to be run through the drill pipe on a wireline. But the friction between the wireline, the pipe and other parts wore out both line and equipment at a costly rate, noted an article in the *Grapevine*:

> *"Something had to be done. Jack Liem, our directional drilling expert, was assigned the task of starting the project. Before it was finished Clifford Yancey, Gilbert Rowe and Willard Wysick had all contributed their knowledge and skill."*[1]

They devised a guide that screws onto the top of the pipe but with an arm to hold the wireline to the side so it will clear the traveling block. The entire string of pipe could be raised, lowered or rotated, while the instrument on the wireline could be added or withdrawn without removing the guide. The device was tested extensively on Rowan rigs.

The company reached an agreement with the Hunt Tool Company to manufacture and market it.[2]

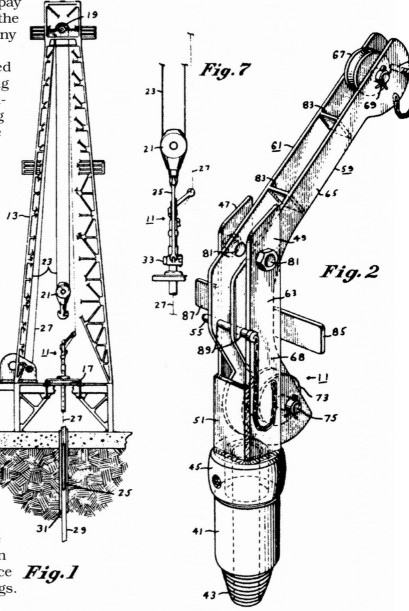

Fig. 7

Fig. 2

Fig. 1

A Rowan rig is installed on a Pan American platform in Cook Inlet, Alaska, in 1966.

new shop and office, craneway, and covered storage and cleaning area. The new yard, with its 440-foot radio tower, was to be the dispatching center for rig supplies and workers.

Even before the service yard was open, Rowan had launched its second drilling tender, a company-built vessel called the *Rowan II*, christened November 28, 1964, in Orange, Texas. Gilbert Rowe's wife, Heddie, broke a champagne bottle on the 260-foot-long and 54-foot wide tender, which had been built in just six and a half months. Its air-conditioned quarters could accommodate 50 workers and included a walk-in refrigerator, large recreation-television room and a laundry. Rowan engineer Bob Palmer had moved to Orange to serve as project manager of the expedited building program.

Rowan quickly added two more rigs for platform work, a drilling rig capable of drilling below

18,000 feet, and a completion rig. The former dug the hole and set casing, while the lighter completion rig followed to finish up the wells. Both went to work on a single platform and under a single derrick.[15]

The company also revived an old experiment with floating living quarters for crews working on the Gulf of Mexico. It bought three war surplus submarine net tenders that could be converted to living quarters. The conversion included air-conditioned living quarters, a recreation room and a galley to make Quarterboat No. 1 "a roughneck's dream of home away from home."[16] The revamped quarterboat was sent to work with a rig southwest of Venice, Louisiana. It later accompanied a Rowan rig to Florida to work for Mobil Oil near Crystal River.

In 1965, Hurricane Betsy slammed into the Gulf Coast. One rig was torn from its platform and another had to be towed to a shipyard for repairs after it shifted 26 feet during the storm. Yet another was idled for two weeks because of damage, and the Morgan City Yard suffered slight damage.[17]

The experience was not nearly as devastating as initially feared, however, and the rigs were

Above: Scattered ice floes float around a Pan American platform in Cook Inlet, Alaska. The legs could withstand ice floes moving at 7 miles an hour.

Below: Rowan Rig No. 7 before its conversion to a split-level rig.

In 1966, a division devoted to Alaska was formed to handle the increased activity prompted by discoveries in Cook Inlet. Prior to the contracts Alaska had been "sort of a stepchild," noted the *Grapevine*, because "our activity there waxed and waned, coming at times to a complete standstill without a single Rowan representative to be found in the entire 586,400 square miles of the state."[19] Ralph Coffman became the division's first superintendent.

Although the focus was gradually moving offshore, Rowan continued to set records on land. Rowan's Rig 7 was one of only two split-level land-based rigs in existence. Instead of a large rig floor to hold all of the drilling equipment, the substructure holding the drawworks and engines was five feet above the ground; another drill floor was nearly 29 feet above the ground. The gap between the two substructures could accommodate the blowout preventer equipment needed for extra-deep drilling, especially in the Delaware Basin, an area that covers portions of West Texas and southeast New Mexico.[20]

Rig 7 lived up to its novel design. Spudding in on August 26, 1965, the rig drilled a 21,472-foot

soon back in operation. By early 1966, Rowan was ready to make further initiatives offshore. The company announced it had been awarded two platform contracts that would test Rowan's expertise in two areas. These platforms were located in the near-freezing waters of Cook Inlet in southern Alaska. Pan American (now Amoco), which had hired Rowan, was the operator in a group that included Sinclair Oil & Gas, Skelly Oil and Phillips Petroleum. The group planned to build the platforms using four legs that were 14 feet in diameter. As many as eight wells could be drilled through each leg. The legs, fabricated with special steel, were designed to withstand the shock of a tidal ice floe of nearly seven miles an hour. Rowan's job was to furnish two rigs and crews for the platforms. To accomplish the job, Rowan traded in two older rigs and bought two new semi-electric rigs.[18]

hole in the record time of 197 days for the Delaware Basin. In comparison, another well that Rowan drilled in the same area took 487 days from spud to total depth. Of course, the credit for the drilling record also went to the Texaco officials who planned out the work, and the drilling crew members who "were no strangers to deep well drilling, having previously completed two wells in the 20,000 foot range in South Texas and in the process, setting a new depth record for our company as well as running the longest string of 9⅝-inch casing ever run at that time."[21] Rowan later added a second split-level rig. Rig 30 also had the Hi-Floor cantilever mast design, and was put to work in far West Texas. (As of 1998, both rigs continue to work in the United States, and have worked in Venezuela and Argentina. Although these rigs have been rebuilt over the years, the basic design remains the same.)

Going Public

Traditionally, Rowan employees and outside observers had known the company for its family-like atmosphere. It was run by a close-knit cadre of executives whose expertise and careers had been nurtured inside the company. It was always a company of hard work and integrity rather than one of secret processes and jealously guarded information, a private company with the imprint of the Rowan brothers' generosity and personalities indelibly stamped on it.

But Rowan's movement into offshore drilling posed a problem with this structure. Arch, who had come out of retirement at Rowe's request after Charlie's death to return as chairman of the board, remembered that "it appeared that the only way the company could have substantial growth was to go offshore or foreign. This would require and entail considerable capital, more than I wanted to invest in the drilling business after my retirement, and I proposed that the company go public ... and seek additional investors."[22]

On September 6, 1967, Rowan launched an initial public offering (IPO) of 323,000 shares of common stock, ending its 44-year history as a private company. In a Rowan prospectus released in late 1967, the company noted that "the expansion of offshore work, the increase in well depth

and the rapid obsolescence of equipment requires ever more operating capital."[23]

Rowan raised $6.2 million from the public offering. Net proceeds from the stock offering, along with $3 million in borrowed money, were to be used by the company to buy 18,630 shares of preferred stock, retire about $3.2 million in debt from the purchase in 1965 and 1966 of offshore rigs, and raise working capital for its offshore future.[24] The company applied for a listing on the American Stock Exchange for the 789,330 common shares to be outstanding after the offering.[25]

Thirty years later, Rowan President Bob Palmer noted that the IPO was a watershed event. In a 1992 speech, he outlined how public ownership, the next step in Rowan's evolution, came about. Rowan had moved its executive offices to Houston and was looking for deals but "the company did not own a mobile offshore drilling rig, and we did not have enough money to buy one and for good reason."

"First, most of the cash flow from the time Rowan was founded had gone toward expansion of the family businesses or as dividends to the owners. Second, the owners avoided debt like the plague, and they were particularly disinclined to personally guarantee debt; and third, in those days, banks did not loan money on smoke and mirrors. Lenders wanted good, solid collateral, like (certificates of deposit) or long-term contracts with access to receivables. Thus, without a drilling contract to use as collateral, Rowan could not borrow the money to build an offshore rig; and without a rig, we could not get a drilling contract."[26]

Interviewed years later, Palmer said that Arch had told him he "would not let the company go into debt to build drilling rigs that he probably would never see, and he would not place his family's fortune in jeopardy to guarantee those loans. It was really that issue that had precipitated the decision to go public, and let the Rowan family move out of the picture so we could go forward."[27]

At the time of the IPO, Rowan President Gilbert Rowe stressed that the end of private ownership meant no major changes in management or objectives. "Our job is to operate the company successfully and profitably. This applies

Rig No. 27, located about 80 miles west of Bethel, Alaska. Inset: Rielley Euper stands outside the tents at Rig No. 27's location in Alaska. *(Photos courtesy of Rielley Euper.)*

whether we are a private or a public company," he said.[28] Two outside directors were added to the board for a total of 10. However, control of the company remained basically the same. In a 1967 interview with Rowe, *The Oil and Gas Journal* reported that "two-thirds of Rowan Drilling's outstanding common stock is still in the hands of veteran executives and key employees. No single stockholder owns more than 10 percent of the outstanding shares."[29]

Naturally, the biggest adjustment to leaving the private sphere was opening the company's financial records to public scrutiny. But Rowan could confidently report it was in a strong financial position. The company had assets, as of September 30, 1967, of $8.7 million. It owned six rigs on fixed platforms in the Gulf of Mexico, four in the icy waters of Cook Inlet in Alaska, and 23 onshore drilling rigs, which included the six inland barges.[30] By 1966, offshore work had become so important that it accounted for 42 percent of the company's contract-drilling revenues and 65 percent of its income from contract operations.[31]

Although offshore drilling clearly represented the future, Rowe did not expect to pull out of land drilling, even though activity in that area was depressed compared to the number of available land rigs. Rowe proclaimed that "the brightest area of land drilling is now in the 20,000-foot and deeper class."[32] Of the company's 23 inland rigs, 12 could drill below 18,000 feet. The remainder were in the medium-depth range, and Rowe expected they eventually would be sold or traded in for newer, larger equipment.

In early December 1967, Rowan announced an across-the-board 5 percent wage increase for all of its rig crews. Cecil Provine, by this time executive vice president of Rowan, said the hike "is something the boys in the field need," and would also serve as a means to attract better workers.[33] Rowe said the pay increase "will give dividends for our customers. It helps provide a stable labor force of experienced men who can do the work more efficiently."[34]

The pay hike stuck out in the oil industry. *The Oil and Gas Journal* reported that "some industry sources hailed Rowan's action as an encouraging step toward stabilizing the drilling labor force which is diminishing as workers leave for better-paying jobs." Indeed, Rowe said wages were boosted "to keep our crews' pay in line with comparable work."[35] The journal described the move as "doubly significant because Rowan Drilling is one of the few contractors who had adopted the shorter workweek."

"Rowan land and barge crews on the Gulf Coast work an average 42-hour week. Crewmen in West Texas, New Mexico, Oklahoma, Wyoming and Arkansas work 48-hour weeks. These shorter hours were introduced nearly two years ago. Offshore crewmen for Rowan are continuing on a 56-hour week, working 10 days with five days off. Before the latest hike, Rowan's wages were near the industry's top. Now portions of its scale lead the industry."[36]

With Rowan expanding into freezing, ever-more harsh environments, however, more workers were collecting their paychecks with numbed hands, knowing they had earned every penny.

Some of the supervisors responsible for Rig No. 34, the first air mobile rig, from left to right, Bob Keller, Leroy Rambin, Bob Palmer and Dick Watson.

CHAPTER SEVEN

A COLD DAY IN HELL

1967–1969

"I'd have on five or six pairs of pants and seven or eight shirts at one time."

— "Scooter" Yeargain, recalling life on the North Slope, 1997[1]

ALASKA'S OIL POTENTIAL HAD been identified as early as 1923, when President Warren Harding created a naval petroleum reserve on the Arctic coast. Over the next several decades, wildcatters poked around the state and occasionally ran across a respectable oil reserve, but nothing major. From about 1957 to 1967 oil workers had drilled in the frigid North Slope, attracted by the promising geology but disappointed by the results.

By the winter of 1966, a company called Arco (the result of a merger between Richfield and Atlantic Refining) was ready to call it quits. As partners with Humble, Arco had just one more exploratory well to drill before it shut down operations on Alaska's north coast.

The hole was spudded in the spring of 1967, dubbed the Prudhoe Bay State No. 1. Company officials half expected the hole to be dry, and wouldn't have drilled at all if not for the fact that the necessary equipment was already on site.

Then, on December 26, 1967, a loud humming began issuing from the well. It quickly turned into a rumble, then a roar. As onlookers huddled in the minus 30 degree Alaskan winter, a spout of natural gas shot from the hole. Geologists rushed to the scene and estimated that the field held 10 billion recoverable barrels of oil, making the Alaskan field one-and-a-half times larger than the East Texas field discovered decades earlier.

But the North Slope was perhaps the most hostile environment in which Rowan had ever been asked to drill. Roads did not exist. Cloaked in darkness for much of the year, the first few feet of tundra were frozen as solid as cement for months on end, and under that, the arctic permafrost extended for a thousand feet. Winter temperatures plummeted to 65 degrees below zero. In the summer, the prairie thawed into a sodden mush. Delivering crews and supplies posed a huge challenge.

Rowan, which purchased ERA Helicopters just three days later, was in the perfect position to benefit from this unique environment.

A Brief History of ERA Helicopters

The need for reliable transportation resulted in the company's first venture outside of the oil drilling and producing business. On December 29, 1967, Rowan paid $2.5 million in cash and stock to buy ERA Helicopters, Alaska's largest helicopter operation.[2]

Rowanite Ernest Walston, geared up for the cold. In an interview, Walston said workers kept an eye on each other for signs of frostbite.

The companies were well matched. Both had demonstrated a determined and pioneering spirit. ERA had consistently introduced new and larger helicopters, and was the first to introduce external load concepts and turbine equipment.[3] ERA had conducted year-round operations in the state since 1956 from its base at Merrill Field in Anchorage, where Rowan had a base office and 22,500-square-foot hangar. ERA had worked for oil, mining and construction companies, along with state agencies. It owned and operated two Bell 204Bs, a Sikorsky S-62A, three Sikorsky S-55s and 13 Bell helicopters. ERA also had two fixed-wing aircraft, a Cessna 402 and 185.[4] In 1967, the company showed a profit of $261,000.[5]

ERA's three founders continued as the company's officers: Carl Brady as president, and vice presidents Roy Falconer and Joe Seward. The three men had founded ERA in 1958 when they merged two separate companies: Economy Helicopters and Rotor Aids, Inc., a California firm. The name of ERA resulted from taking the first letter of Economy, Rotor and Aids. Both companies had existed nearly a dozen years before the merger.

Brady, a state senator at the time of the acquisition by Rowan, had grown up in Arkansas, and learned to fly in Yakima, Washington, in late 1941. "I was jerking sodas at an ice cream parlor and making $25 bucks a week," Brady recalls. "I'd spend $20 of it on flying lessons."[6] Immediately after getting his instructor's rating, he moved to Florida and served as a flight instructor for aviation cadets. He next joined the Army Air Corps in Detroit and went into the Air Transport Command, Ferry Division, where he spent World War II.

Following the war, Brady and several partners launched a wheat crop dusting service called Economy Pest Control. At about the same time, Bell Helicopters Corporation began experimenting with pest control using helicopters, and Brady learned to fly Bell's first demonstrator. He would later recall that "we hocked everything we had to scrape together enough money to buy our first helicopter. It cost $29,500. Actually, we lease-purchased it; we couldn't afford to buy anything."[7]

In 1948, the fledgling company won a contract from the U.S. Geological Survey for helicopter mapping in Alaska. That first summer, two-man crews flown by Brady mapped the northern half of Chichagof Island, which is west of Juneau, Alaska. "They had spent seven years

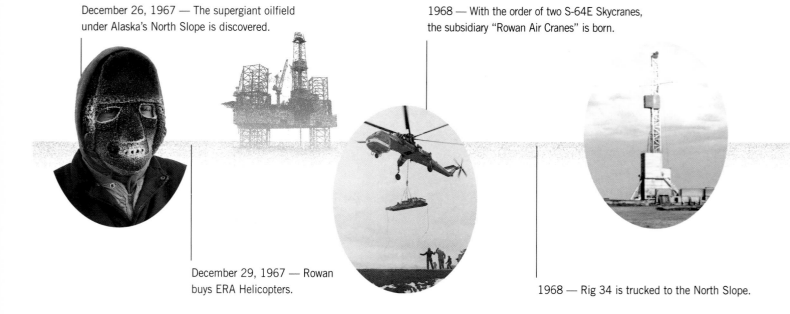

December 26, 1967 — The supergiant oilfield under Alaska's North Slope is discovered.

December 29, 1967 — Rowan buys ERA Helicopters.

1968 — With the order of two S-64E Skycranes, the subsidiary "Rowan Air Cranes" is born.

1968 — Rig 34 is trucked to the North Slope.

mapping the southern half," Brady said. "We mapped the northern half in 33 days."[8] That contract led to the first commercial helicopter operation in Alaska. With this new operation, the company's name was changed to Economy Helicopters Inc. But not only did the company have the first commercial helicopter operating in Alaska, "they had the only helicopter, Brady remembers, 'It was scary, because if we got stranded, there would be no other helicopter to come lift us out.'"[9]

Brady later adapted the early helicopters to use a skid-type landing gear. According to an article in *Alaska Business Monthly*, "Manufacturers then went to that as a general pattern." Other innovations soon followed.

"Brady had discovered, in the process of taking on more and more remote assignments, that the wheeled choppers had a disconcerting tendency to roll down mountain slopes. The skids put a stop to that. Other lessons from Brady's experience found their way into design modifications and pilot manuals. In those early years, Brady pioneered the use of helicopters in herding wild horses and driving wild elk from orchards,
where they overbrowsed valuable trees one bad winter. ... Brady hired his ships out to blow snow off telephone lines, re-seed forest lands, fly search and rescue, haul supplies to firefighters and conduct game counts. So commonplace now, such missions constantly made headlines then."[10]

A newspaper reporter, writing in the 1950s, quipped that Brady was the "early bird with the whirly-bird."[11] Brady and his crew returned to Alaska each summer to work. In the beginning, the contracts were mainly for geological surveys, and later, supported the work of oil companies on the North Slope. During the summers in Alaska, Brady got to know Joe Seward and Roy Falconer, also helicopter pilots. The three men frequently stayed in the same tent camps.

Rotor Aids, Inc.

Seward and Falconer had met in 1947 aboard an aircraft carrier where they both flew Corsair fighters. Seward had worked a night job as a tool designer for an aircraft company to pay for his college education. He graduated in 1943 from

1968 — Bess Brants retires as secretary-treasurer.

1969 — A helicopter crash that killed three workers underscores the hazardous environment of the North Slope.

October 1969 — Arch Rowan retires as chairman but remains a director; Gilbert Rowe becomes chairman and Cecil Provine is appointed president.

Above: Roy K. Falconer, one of the founders of ERA.

Below: ERA Helicopters working on powerlines in the 1950s.

the University of California at Los Angeles and entered the Navy afterward, serving aboard destroyers in the North Atlantic for several years before learning to fly. Falconer had enlisted in the Navy after his 1937 high school graduation. He briefly served on a light carrier before entering the Naval Academy. Following graduation in 1941, he spent several years on destroyers in the South Pacific before flight training and carrier duty brought him into contact with Seward.

The two became friends. The *Grapevine* gave this account of what happened next.

"They spent many nights discussing the slow rate of advancement and the lack of excitement following the stimulating years of wartime combat. This discussion expanded into the opportunities in commercial aviation, with Joe advancing the idea that helicopters might be a ripe field, since the helicopter had just recently been commercially certified and by its nature should be a valuable aid to industry, agriculture,

photography, etc. Hence, the name 'Rotor-Aids' was born."[12]

They learned to fly helicopters, resigned their commissions and set up Rotor-Aids. Seward and Falconer each chipped in $5,000 from their savings and borrowed the rest to buy a Bell 47D. They began earning money in agricultural flying, forest fire fighting and patrol, and movie photography.

By 1958, expanding oil industry operations had created the need for larger helicopters. Rotor-Aids and Economy formed a joint venture and bought two S-55s from Sikorsky. The joint venture was successful enough to prompt a merger between the two companies, and ERA was born in 1960. Economy was dissolved, with Brady's two partners remaining in Washington. Brady moved to Anchorage to take over daily management of ERA.

By the time Rowan purchased ERA, each man had more than 5,000 flight hours in helicopters, as well as thousands of hours in fixed-wing aircraft. "They understand all flight problems, and speak the same language as their pilots."[13] Like their Rowan counterparts who came up through the oilfields, ERA executives had gained their experience in the field.

Also like Rowan, improved technology, along with first-hand experience, had eased the hardships and special problems in their work. Helicopters in the early days "were extremely underpowered, and before the invention of the turbo engine, powerplant failures occurred with regularity. Radio communications were virtually nonexistent, as well as any form of navigational aid."[14] ERA in 1964 was the first to use turbine-powered helicopters in Alaska by flying a Bell 204-B. Other firsts by ERA included the first commercial use of a Sikorsky S-55 helicopter on a year-round basis in Alaska (in 1956), and in 1957, the first use of the Sikorsky S-55 and S-58 for external loads in Alaska.

Carl Brady, Sr., inset, piloted the first commercial helicopter in Alaska.

Brady recalled how the company, as it worked to map out uncharted territory, would drop off people in remote areas.

"We would fly out, always paying careful attention to visual references when we dropped men off, 'Let's see, the third ridge with the funny out-cropping, then the second valley beyond that.' Sometimes we would drop off five or six men a day under these circumstances. We were greatly dedicated to remembering where each man was, because all they had to rely on to get back was our memories."[15]

Several other helicopter companies entered the picture, and a friendly rivalry developed. All would pitch in to help in an emergency. Brady recalled one such incident that occurred during a Fourth of July celebration in the small town of Pelican, Alaska, where food and beer were plentiful in the best Independence Day tradition. Children, meanwhile, competed for a helicopter ride by decorating their wagons with tinsel to win a float contest.

Brady personally gave the winner a ride, but a snapped fan belt forced him to land. He had no tools or replacement fan belt, but Brady "and his company mechanics, with an ingenuity born out of no radio communications, had devised a list of ten things that might possibly go wrong with a helicopter," according to an article in *Alaska Flying*:

"A broken fan belt was a Number 5 on the list, so Brady tramped out a shaky numeral [in the

snow], and reinforced its shape with spruce boughs. The next morning the well-known aviator, Shel Simmons, dropped the necessary equipment off by small parachute. 'I'd never met Shel before,' Brady said, 'but after that, I looked on him as a lifelong friend!' Others apparently considered themselves Brady's friends as well, because after he had fixed the fan belt and returned home, he had to spend the next three or four hours picking up all the would-be rescuers, well-oiled with July 4th refreshments, who were scattered over the area in search for him."[16]

Rowan Skycranes

With the promise of work in the North Slope secure, Rowan in early 1968 ordered two S-64E "Skycrane" helicopters. Cecil Provine had been in Alaska when a Sikorsky Aircraft official told him how the huge helicopters were used to place bridges over streams and rivers in Korea. Provine said he discussed the possibility with Rowan officials and "[Atlantic Richfield] said if you'll only buy the cranes, we'll give you the work."[17] The purchase marked the first civilian procurement of the S-64E, which was a commercial version of the Army's CH-54A Flying Crane.

The Skycranes could lift loads up to 10 tons. They would be operated by Rowan under a newly formed subsidiary called Rowan Air Cranes, Inc.

Sikorsky Skycrane helicopters were originally used in Korea by the military. Rowan's purchase marked the helicopter's first civilian acquisition.

Rowan President Gilbert Rowe deemed the purchase in line with Rowan's policy of seeking new, improved techniques and equipment. He noted that, "as oil exploration moves farther and farther to remote inland and offshore areas, surface transportation becomes increasingly difficult, costly and time-consuming. Transporting rigs by air and subsequent logistics support of drilling sites by air is the logical alternative."[18]

Previous to the Skycranes, helicopters did not have the lift capacity for the heavier drilling rig pieces. Rowe said that the company planned to design, build and package rigs to the Skycrane's capacity, adding that "we also will use the Skycranes for heavy construction work, in forestry and powerline operations or wherever the job requires a heavy-lift machine."[19] Lee S. Johnson, president of the Sikorsky Aircraft division of United Aircraft Corporation described Rowan's plan to be the first commercial user of the Skycrane as a "major breakthrough for civilian helicopter operations."[20]

Rowan understood firsthand the Skycrane's abilities and promise. In late 1967, the company, along with other drilling contractors and an oil company, had tested the Skycrane to move equipment to offshore platforms. The Skycrane had unloaded 52 tons of drawworks, pumps, drill lines, winches, mast, bunk house, tool house and other equipment from five flatbed trailers in 23 minutes instead of the usual two hours. Then, in 11 trips, the Skycrane delivered the equipment to an offshore platform in the Gulf of Mexico. The job took a fraction of the 20 hours it normally took to ship by barge.

In another test, the helicopter moved a 360-ton rig a distance of 1.4 miles in 58 transfers. The trips included carrying loads that ranged from a half-ton compressor to a mud tank that weighed 9.5 tons. The helicopter's accuracy of placement was astonishing; for example, "a bunkhouse, 10 feet wide and 40 feet long, was lowered into an area which was only 10 feet 4 inches wide."[21]

The North Slope

With the purchase of ERA and the impending delivery of the Skycranes, Rowan quickly landed contracts to drill into the frozen tundra. Cecil

Rowan Air Cranes moving equipment to a new drilling location in Alaska. The Skycrane could lift up to 10 tons. *(Photo courtesy of Rielley Euper.)*

Provine, who spent much time in Alaska during this period, recalled flying over the North Slope and seeing the black smoke from what turned out to be the discovery well. "They wouldn't let us land because they didn't want anybody to know," he recalled in a 1997 interview. "If I had known and had any sense, I would have gone back in town and bought Atlantic Richfield stock because a tremendous amount of oil showed. Their stock went sky-high right after."[22]

Since there were no roads or airports, Rowan worked with manufacturers for months to develop portable drilling rigs that could be lifted by the Skycranes. Arco contracted for two of these "air mobile" rigs. One of the package rigs was to be ready by late December 1968 and the other to follow in early 1969. The rigs, each with a depth rating of 17,000 feet, would be taken by rail and truck to Fairbanks, Alaska. Both then would be airlifted to the Prudhoe area on the North Slope by a Lockheed L-382 Hercules fixed-wing aircraft, the civilian version of the U.S. Air Force's Lockheed C-130.[23] A rig already in Alaska, but at Standard Oil Company's Beluga River Camp near the Cook Inlet, was sent to work on the North Slope. It was to do exploratory drilling for Standard Oil of California.

Rig 34, the first of the "air mobile" rigs to go to the North Slope, made the trip by truck to Fairbanks. From there, L-382 Hercules aircraft made 55 flights, three a day, to the air strip at Prudhoe Bay 400 miles distant. Helicopters then carried the rig to the drilling location on the Arco-Humble lease. On January 29, 1969, an open house was held at the Odessa Yard to show off Rig 35, the second "air mobile" drilling rig, and then it, too, was taken north. Rowan's investment in the two new rigs and camp equipment was estimated at $3.5 million.[24] The men who supervised the creation of Rigs 34 and 35 were R.A. "Bob" Keller, Leroy Rambin, Bob Palmer, Dick Watson and C.W. "Scooter" Yeargain. Each rig package was designed to limit weight to 18,000 pounds. Each package also had to have outside dimensions of no more than 9 feet, 6 inches wide, 8 feet, 6 inches high, and 39 feet, 6 inches long, so that it could fit inside an L-382 or C-130 Hercules aircraft.

To survive the demanding conditions, workers fortified rigs so that the mast, substructure and mud pump enclosures could withstand winds of 100 mph. The heating system, consisting of two boilers and a direct-fired air heater, was designed to allow rig operations even at temperatures as low as

Above, inset: A Skycrane bringing in rig equipment at Prudhoe Bay, Alaska. Left: Rig No. 34, designed to be moved by helicopter, on location in late spring near Prudhoe Bay. *(Photos courtesy of Rielley Euper.)*

65 degrees below zero. The crew quarters and aux-iliary buildings also had an electrical heating sys-tem that would be comfortable at such low temper-atures.[25] The derrick and substructure were similar to other big land rigs, using a Lee C. Moore special Hi-Floor mast, 142 feet by 25 feet, with a 28-foot-high floor. The drawworks were mounted 4 feet, 6 inches above ground level.[26]

The Skycranes were delivered in April 1969 to Rowan Air Cranes in Anchorage. One of the Skycranes was under contract to Arco and the other to Standard Oil of California.[27] Not long after, a Skycrane took part in the first air-rig move in Alaska. The huge aircraft moved 1,229 tons of rig equipment and camp facilities to a new drilling loca-tion on the North Slope in July 1969. Over a nine-day period, the helicopter moved 174 loads averag-ing 14,126 pounds each over the tundra. Each trip to the new location more than eight miles away took about 20 minutes, and the operation was deemed "highly successful."[28] Indeed, Rowan noted that building a road to the site to move equipment and supplies would have cost about $200,000 a mile, and a surface move would have taken weeks instead of days.[29] The second air-mobile rig was moved by Skycrane the following month.

Rowan roughnecks vied to be the "hooker-upper." The first several workers who got the chance received a shock from static electricity when they touched the metal hook.

"Scooter" Yeargain, a 44-year Rowan veteran who officially retired in 1991 (he would continue as a consultant, member of the board of directors for Rowan Companies, as well as chairman of LeTourneau), said he was amused by the number of roughnecks who wanted to act as the "hooker-upper," the man on the ground who handled the hook as it dangled from the helicopter.

"The first man ran out there, where it was snowing, and he reached up and grabbed that hook — and the static electricity from the snow knocked him on his butt. He says, 'I'll fix that,' and gets him some welders' gloves. And the same thing happens. They learned they had to drop the hook on the ground first."[30]

But tragedy struck in September 1969 for Rowan and ERA. Three employees were killed when one of the Skycranes crashed on the North Slope.

An Alaskan roughneck saws and removes blocks of snow. The sun disappeared for three months during winter. *(Photos courtesy of Rielley Euper.)*

Killed were ERA pilots James Erwin, Jr., and Byron Davis and Rowan rig superintendent Allen Bryan, who had joined the company in 1956 as a floorman.[31]

Life Below Zero

Yeargain and other Rowan workers lived in the frigid temperatures before the advent of insulated clothing. "I'd have on five or six pairs of pants and seven or eight shirts at one time," he said in a 1997 interview. The heaters in the tents brought the temperature up to a relatively balmy zero, he added.

Pilots had to take extraordinary measures to keep their aircraft flyable. Yeargain recalled how one pilot, who had the great fortune to live in a house, would drain the oil out of his aircraft and put it in a can under his bed. The pilot would string up three or four 300-watt electric light-bulbs over his engine, covered with a blanket, to keep it warm.

Summers were short, and the sun never goes down on the North Slope, recalled Ernie Walston, who retired in 1986 as operations manager. During winter, however, the sun disappeared from December to February.

"Arco once brought in some people from a university who monitored the effect of working conditions in winter time versus summertime. If I remember correctly, productivity was about a third in winter as it was in summer."[32]

After the rush to get the rigs in place and begin drilling, the oil companies ran into another challenge. Due to the remote location, moving oil from the well to the market proved a formidable task. After much wrangling, the oil companies received permission from the federal government to build an Alaskan pipeline to the port of Valdez, where huge tankers would carry the oil to the United States and Japan. Oil companies rushed into production, buying pipeline and moving construction equipment to a staging area on the Yukon River.

But the pipeline was beset with problems before the first shovelful of dirt was turned. Conservation groups, worried about the environmentally sensitive Prince William Sound in Valdez, converged on the federal government to stop construction of the pipeline. A court injunction in 1970 stopped development of the pipeline and, for the next five years, the great Alaskan North Slope would lay dormant while the battles raged in court until the dispute was finally resolved by an act of Congress (Vice President Spiro Agnew cast the tie-breaking vote to end the land dispute).

A Strong Finish

By the end of the 1960s Rowan was active on many fronts. Between the company's offshore activ-

ities and its helicopter operation, the company was carving itself a highly specialized niche, which included adding new and more powerful equipment. Rowan purchased its first turbine-electric rig in the spring of 1968. At the time, Rowan knew of only two other turbine-powered rigs in existence.[33] The *Grapevine* noted that the turbine weighed only 1,250 pounds, while piston engines producing a similar amount of power weighed about 25,000 pounds. However, the turbine engine was not without its drawbacks for it "costs half again as much as its piston counterpart, and uses more fuel."[34]

Rowan workers tested the rig by using it for ultra-deep drilling in West Texas. Assembled and tested in Rowan's Odessa Yard, the turbine-powered Rig 9 was one of the largest land rigs in operation.[35] Power came from three turbines that burned gas or diesel fuel and produced a total of 3,300 horsepower. Its derrick was the same Lee

Below: An open house in Odessa, Texas, featured the turbine-powered Rig No. 9.

Inset: Officials from Rowan and National Supply Company look over the new Rig No. 9.

Powered by three turbine engines, Rig 9 was one of the largest land rigs in operation at the time.

C. Moore Hi-Floor cantilever mast that had been used on other deep-drilling Rowan rigs. The rig could drill to more than 25,000 feet.[36]

That same year, Bess Brants retired as secretary-treasurer of Rowan Drilling on March 31. She did not, however, immediately give up her office in the Rowan Building. The longtime employee was credited with engineering a smooth running office. The *Grapevine* noted that one of her greatest contributions had been serving as "liaison between management and the office force. Bess is the kind of person to whom you can talk freely, knowing that what you say will not be used against you, or passed on to others. This complete confidence from both sides and a rare sense of humor permitted Bess to settle most office complaints without involving the other members of management."[37] D.C. "Charlie" Anderson

was promoted from assistant secretary-treasurer to take her place.

By mid-1968, Rowan could boast that it had drilled three wells deeper than 20,000 feet. Only a few years earlier, such deep wells had been a rarity, but more and more rigs could reach below four miles, or 21,120 feet. Rig 7 drilled two of the "Four Milers," while Rig 30 completed one in late 1967 with a depth of 21,250 feet. The two Hi-Floor rigs, along with the new turbine rig, Rig 9, were busy drilling three more "Four Milers."[38] All of the wells were in West Texas.

In June, Rowan announced the Atomic Energy Commission had awarded the company a $804,536 contract to drill a nuclear test emplacement hole in Nevada. A special two-million-pound capacity derrick was built for the project. A beefed-up Rig 18 had a 1⅝-inch drill line to handle the 13⅜-inch drill stem to turn a 64-inch bit.[39] The hole was drilled to a depth of 4,150 feet, and 5 feet, 4 inches wide. The location at the Mercury Test Site was about 100 miles northwest of Las Vegas.

At 19 years old, Bill Person was a new Rowan employee when he helped dig the shaft. After finishing the job, Person and his crew were transported to a secured area by the military but close enough to feel the underground explosion.

"You'd actually see a swell coming across the ground just like a swell of water. I remember that Howard Hughes, who owned most of Las Vegas, was not keen on these tests because they would shake the hotels in Vegas. When the device goes off underground it forms a large cavern, as you can imagine, melting the material around it. Over time, the roof falls in until a big crater is formed."[40]

Also in 1968, Rowan created a 50-percent owned subsidiary, Rowan International Inc., specifically to carry out the company's offshore plans in foreign countries. Two men assigned to devote a large part of their time to the Panamanian subsidiary were Bob Palmer, executive vice president of Rowan International, and Charles Blanchard, vice president of sales. Palmer most recently had been assistant to the president; Blanchard, a 21-year employee, had been a sales representative in Rowan Drilling's various divisions. Other officers included Gilbert Rowe, president, and Scooter Yeargain and Cecil Provine, vice presidents. Palmer drew plans for a Twin Hull Column Stabilized Drilling Unit, while Blanchard traveled to the offices of prospective customers to let them know of Rowan International's plans.[41]

In 1969, Rowan ended its 42-year presence in Fort Worth. The Rowan Building had already been sold because of the company's plan to move its headquarters to Houston. It was later torn down and replaced with a Blockbuster Video Store. In Houston, Rowan leased the entire 19th floor (as well as half of the 18th floor) of the new 22-story Post Oak Tower Building in the Galleria area, just west of downtown Houston. The new offices would serve as the headquarters for its 575 employees worldwide. Arch Rowan moved his office to downtown Fort Worth where Hamilton Rogers, Rowan Oil's former president, had a private law practice.[42]

In October 1969, Arch resigned as chairman of the board but remained a company director and available for consultation. Still active, he hired Lynda Aycock as his bookkeeper in 1969 to help him with his affairs. "The first time I ever met him, I was sitting outside the secretary's office and he walked in wearing one of those little candy striped suits that looked like it was three sizes too big and he had his glasses on. He looked like a little old man."[43] Arch began devoting an increasing amount of time to his farm in Texas and pastimes like hunting.

To fill his conspicuous absence, the board named Rowe chairman and CEO. Cecil Provine was promoted from executive vice president to president of Rowan Drilling. In other corporate changes, Bob Palmer became president of Rowan International. Carl Brady was named president of Rowan Air Cranes, while remaining president of ERA. Rowan's longtime, versatile executive Mark Hart retired only a few months earlier following 33 years of employment.

Some of the old guard were gone and Fort Worth was no longer Rowan's headquarters. However, longtime employees like Rowe and Provine, as well as younger, rising executives like Bob Palmer and Scooter Yeargain, were there to carry on the company's goals and philosophy. During 1969, an industrywide decline in contract drilling in West Texas, Oklahoma and New Mexico idled rigs there, and Rowan sold five of its older land rigs. The sale was in line with Rowan's tried-and-true policy of shedding older units for newer, larger equipment. Rowan, which had revenues of more than $23 million in 1969, busily steamed ahead with its plan for increased offshore work. In July 1969, Rowan International ordered its first mobile offshore rig at a cost of $6.3 million.

The sudden halt of development in the Alaskan oilfield was a disappointment for Rowan and the entire oil industry. But just as the decade ended, a promising new area began to emerge — a region that again suited Rowan's expertise perfectly. Geologists were beginning to suspect huge reserves of oil under the North Sea, a brutally cold and violent stretch of ocean between Great Britain and Norway. Although the environment in the North Sea was at least as treacherous as northern Alaska, the two regions shared an important advantage. They were politically stable. More often, world politics were being driven by U.S. relations with the Middle East, where most of the world's oil was produced. Domestic companies, which were Rowan's customers, were increasingly frantic to find a reliable second source of oil in case the flow was interrupted for some reason. So despite the inclement weather, the rough seas and technical challenges, oil companies began developing new methods to extract oil from the North Sea.

By this time, Rowan International, which would soon be active in South America, had ordered its first Houston-Class offshore jack-up drilling rig, ushering in a new era of open-ocean drilling.

The *Rowan Louisiana* on location in the Gulf of Mexico.

CHAPTER EIGHT

BALANCE OF POWER

1970–1979

"[Palmer] had decided, 'Let's go out offshore. Let's do this. Let's do this.' And he's good with people. He's good with management. He's good with financing. Some of the boys, directors, used to tell me, 'Let's get us a financial officer.' I said, 'Hell, we don't need a financial officer. Palmer's the best financial officer you can hire.'"

— Cecil Provine, 1997[1]

U NTIL THE 1970S, THE MOST COMMON way to get oil from under the ocean was to build a platform on top of permanently fixed pilings and mount a rig on it, a setup very similar to the inland barges — except the platform couldn't move. In the seventies, however, the offshore drilling industry would be forever altered with the introduction of a simple but ambitious idea: a mobile, self-elevating offshore oil platform capable of drilling in ocean depths of up to 250 feet. The jack-up rig, as it would be known, offered the best of both worlds: it could be towed or motored to a location, yet it was set solidly on the sea floor.

The jack-up rig was an important element in Rowan's drive to position itself as an international offshore contractor. As oil exploration continued from the shores of South America to the glittering bays of southeast Asia, mobility and global reach promised to be deciding factors in the race for contracts. The globalization of the oil industry was important for another reason, as well. By the beginning of the decade, the Middle East was by far the world's largest producer of oil, home to more than 80 percent of the world's supergiant oilfields. Also by this time, oil's role in the daily life of billions of people had made a steady supply of the fuel a necessity. It was literally the lifeblood of the modern age, responsible for everything from the family sedan to the machines that erected skyscrapers.

Since World War II, American and British companies had comfortably dominated the Arab oil world. In the 1960s, however, Arab nationalism began to rise, provoked by America's support of Israel. The leaders of such major producers as Libya, Iran and Iraq were further goaded by the profits that U.S. companies took from the oil found in their territories. The situation quickly became politically tense, prompting countries like the United States, Britain and Germany to adopt voluntary "energy programs" whereby citizens were encouraged to conserve fuel. The Alaskan pipeline, which had been bogged down by environmental politics, was again put on the list of national priorities and construction began. Exploration efforts stepped up in the North Sea, South America and the Far East. And, still, tensions mounted.

The *Rowan Houston*

It was against this background that Rowan ordered construction to begin on Rowan's first

An illustration of Rig No. 4, Rowan's inland drilling barge.

mobile self-contained, self-elevating offshore drilling platform, known as the *Rowan Houston*, in August 1969. Rowan International awarded the contract to R.G. LeTourneau Inc., which had a plant and yard near Vicksburg, Louisiana.

The platform was designed to operate in water depths up to 200 feet. Its special leg footings, each 12-sided and 46 feet in diameter, allowed the huge structure to work in unusually soft bottom conditions. It featured air conditioned quarters for 78 people and a 90-foot-diameter heliport. The drilling platform was powered by three 750-horsepower propulsion thrusters.

The platform was a marvel on both land and in the water. If elevated next to the 22-story Post Oak Tower Building, where Rowan had its offices, the top of the 140-foot derrick mounted on the *Rowan Houston* would be 120 feet higher than the building. Also, the 13 million pounds of welded steel did not need to be shoved or tugged into the water: it used its own three feet. The gigantic platform "with about 15 well-versed men on board and several astute ground directors in the area, literally walks into the water by alternately jacking the bow and stern up and down."[2] On its first tow across the Caribbean, the platform moved more than five knots, or nearly six miles an hour, with only one 4,000-horsepower tug pulling it.

The new *Rowan Houston*, with a 20,000-foot drilling capacity, spudded its first well in 142 feet of water off the eastern coast of Nicaragua on May 9, 1970 for Shell.

By that time, Rowan had ordered a second rig, the *Rowan New Orleans*, from LeTourneau. In January 1971, the *Rowan New Orleans* rode out high winds and 15-foot swells in the Gulf of Mexico as she journeyed to her first work location. With "her three 290-foot long legs planted firmly on the ocean floor," the *Rowan New Orleans* began drilling for Mobil Oil Company.[3]

The *Rowan Houston* drilled seven wells off Nicaragua, Colombia and Honduras in 1971 for various oil companies. The platform finished the exploratory drilling in the Caribbean, and then Rowan towed it in the fall of 1971 to the Gulf of Mexico, off of Louisiana, to work for Sun Oil Company. Leg extensions were added so it could drill in water depths up to 225 feet.[4]

The following year, the *Rowan Houston* was again sent overseas to work in the oil-rich waters off Venezuela. From 1972 to 1974, *Rowan Houston* drilled 13 wells for the Corporacion Venezolana

January 4, 1972 — Gilbert Rowe steps down and C. Robert Palmer is named chairman and CEO.

1973 — OPEC embargoes oil to countries supporting Israel. The oil exploration boom begins.

1973 — Rowan acquires Merric, Inc.

1973 — Rowan President Cecil Provine retires.

del Petroleo. Rowan's American employees worked a 14-day on and 14-day off schedule with twice-a-month trips back to their families in Houston. The company's Venezuelan crews divided round-the-clock work over a seven-day period into shifts of eight hours on, four hours off, four hours back on and then eight off. In September, the *Rowan Houston* returned to the Gulf of Mexico, after a 13-day tow, to drill off the Louisiana coast.[5]

Active on Several Fronts

As the jack-up rigs began to make their mark in the industry, Rowan increased its development of all types of drilling rigs. On October 16, 1970, Rowan's newest inland drilling barge made its debut on the Sabine River in Orange, Texas, in a christening ceremony attended by more than 200 people. Arch's wife, Stella, broke a champagne bottle against Rig No. 4 as she christened the ship, "the queen of the Inland Fleet. May your dry holes be few and safety ride with you."[6] The slotted-type barge, built by Levingston Shipbuilding Company, was 210 feet long and 54 feet wide with a 14-foot lower hull and a 12-foot

Stella Rowan, Arch's wife, christens Rig 4 in 1970.

1975 — Arch Rowan dies.

1975 – The *Rowan III* is the first drilling tender to pass through the Suez Canal since its reopening that year.

1977 — The *Rowan Louisiana* unfurls the world's largest sail to harness wind power.

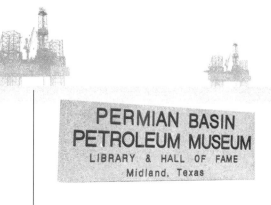

PERMIAN BASIN
PETROLEUM MUSEUM
LIBRARY & HALL OF FAME
Midland, Texas

1979 — Charles and Arch Rowan are inducted in the oil industry's Hall of Fame.

Above: Arch Rowan stands with members of Rig No. 4's christening body. They are, left to right, Joan Fleming, Carol Brady, Dena Cade, Stella Rowan, Arch, Heddie Rowe and Rebecca Palmer. (*Photo courtesy of Jean Rowan McNab.*)

Inset: After Rig 4's arrival at Bandjarmasin, a Kalimantan priest and priestess performed religious rites at an altar before blessing the rig and its workers.

posted-type raised deck. It could work in water depths to 20 feet and drill 30,000 feet deep.

The $2.5 million rig was designed to work in Louisiana's shallow waters and marshy areas. The rig, with air-conditioned quarters for 48 workers, also could be towed overseas for work in foreign waters. The barge rig worked briefly in Louisiana before heading to Indonesia to do exploratory drilling. After a transocean crossing of 67 days, Rig 4 tied up at Bandjarmasin on June 13, 1971.[7] The rig's move to a foreign country prompted the opening of a Rowan International office in Singapore.

That year Rowan engaged in an interesting side project when workers participated in a test of rescue operations in a simulated coal mine disaster. Westinghouse Electric Corporation, the prime contractor for the federal Bureau of Mines project, chose Rowan as a subcontractor. Under the estimated $966,345 cost-plus-fixed-fee contract, two drilling rigs were assembled at Rowan's Odessa Yard and then moved to Charleston, West Virginia. There, in the simulated test, the search and probe rig drilled an 8¾-inch diameter hole 776 feet to find the underground disaster area, add ventilation and provide medical and food supplies to trapped mine workers. Fifteen feet away from the probe rig, the larger rig, capable of drilling 2,500 feet deep, drilled a wide 28-inch hole for the rescue capsule.

Both holes came within a few feet of the underground targets in the coal mine. The test was "appraised as highly successful."[8] Bill Person, who was rig superintendent during the tests, recalled that the rigs were mobilized three times when explosions caused mines to cave in, but on all three occasions the miners had died from the initial explosion or the heat. Person, vice president of industrial relations in 1998, said Rowan no longer maintains the rigs for the Bureau of Mines.[9]

A New Name and a New Leader

On January 4, 1972, Gilbert Rowe stepped down and Bob Palmer was named CEO and chairman, less than a year after the company's name changed from Rowan Drilling to Rowan Companies. (The name change reflected the multiple roles the corporation played, particularly with its successful Alaskan airlift service.)

Rowe, who had been with Rowan since 1944, suffered from heart problems and was preparing to retire after a long and successful career. Known for his tenacity, Rowe had traveled to Norway several weeks prior to his retirement to talk with several potential customers about contracting for some North Sea drilling work. His wife, Heddie, said that "he got sick while he was over there, and do you

know he had those people come to his hotel room, and they came in his hotel room and sat around his bed while he was doing his business? He always worked. ... You couldn't slow him down."[10]

The board of directors announced the transition to ensure an orderly change in management "due to the retirement of M. Gilbert Rowe."[11]

Only 37 years old, Palmer had worked for Rowan since his college days, beginning as a roughneck, leaving briefly to earn his master's degree in engineering administration in 1966. Cecil Provine, in a 1997 interview, described Palmer as well-educated and the bearer of "young ideas."

"Some of the directors used to tell me, 'Let's get us a financial officer.' I said, 'Hell, we don't need a financial officer. Palmer's the best financial officer you can hire.' He fit right in as the executive officer. He's just an all-around good businessman."[12]

Tragically, Gilbert Rowe and his wife were not to enjoy retirement together. She remembered "the day he retired, he came home. He had a heart attack, went to the hospital and never came home."[13] He died January 18, 1972, at the age of

Bob Palmer was named chairman and CEO on January 4, 1972, succeeding Gilbert Rowe. Rowe suffered a heart attack two hours after the Rowan board of directors approved Palmer's appointment.

64. A company resolution described him as "sincere, concise, keen-of-mind, competitive in nature, ever seeking the new and alert to the needs of the industry, his creative designs for land and marine drilling rigs and equipment, plus his dynamic leadership as chief executive, guided the company to its present stature."[14]

The heart attack occurred on the same day the board approved Palmer's appointment. Upon hearing the news, Palmer rushed to the intensive care unit. "He waved at me through the glass and that is the last time we ever communicated," Palmer said in an interview with *Offshore Engineer*, a trade magazine. "[Fourteen] days later Rowe died and Palmer, feeling his leadership had been approved with the understanding he would remain under Rowe's tutelage for some period of time, offered to resign his post. The board unanimously rejected his offer."[15]

The Building Boom Begins

Palmer understood that Rowan's future was international in scope and "focused offshore while maintaining a strong domestic operations base. ... We're moving on and the pace is ever quickening."[16] Rowan sold its inland barges, modified other rigs, moved its Southern Division headquarters from New Orleans to the Morgan City Yard and purchased the *Jack Cleverley*, Rowan's third drilling tender. Five more offshore rigs were under construction, including the jack-up rigs, the *Rowan Anchorage* and the *Rowan Texas*, and a semisubmersible barge rig, named the *Rowan Morgan City*.

In February 1972, Rowan and Gotaas-Larsen, Inc., a Norwegian shipping company, announced the signing of a contract that made Rowan manager and operator of the two semisubmersible rigs under construction by Gotaas-Larsen. The semisubmersible rigs, worth $56 million combined, were designed to operate in the North Sea. Under the contract, Rowan initially received a 10 percent equity in the semisubmersibles with options to purchase additional equity. The rigs were built at two different sites in Norway with Rowan supervising the construction.[17] Ralph Coffman, formerly Alaska Division superintendent, went to Norway as operations manager.

Cecil Provine's wife, Lou, christens the *Rowan Anchorage* at a ceremony on August 6, 1972, in Singapore.

Meanwhile, another rig, the *Rowan Anchorage*, was completed and christened on a warm overcast day. About 300 people attended the ceremony in Singapore where the rig had been built by Marathon-LeTourneau. Cecil Provine's wife, Lou, christened the third jack-up rig in Rowan's fleet with a bottle of champagne. The rig, similar in design to the *Rowan Houston* and the *Rowan New Orleans*, went to work for Amoseas Indonesia, Inc. in the East Java Sea.

These jack-up rigs lived up to the company's expectations. Palmer remarked in a *Houston Post* article that by 1972, "our little three-rig division was making more money than all the rest of the company put together."[18]

Rowan also stayed busy onshore. In March 1973, Rig No. 18 drilled to a depth of 27,050 feet, or more than five miles, to create the third deepest hole up to that time in the United States. The well, spudded three years previously, was drilled in Washita County in Oklahoma. A *Grapevine* article noted that drilling such a deep hole had required not only leadership and determination but also "good iron, good people — people who exercise patience, perseverance, understanding of downhole drilling techniques and above all else, the exercise of extreme care at all times."[19]

International events drove this frenetic activity in the North Sea and off South America. The situation in the Middle East had grown more volatile, with Arab leaders speaking openly of unleashing the "oil weapon" to cut off supply to the United States, which continued to support Israel. Still seething from defeat in the 1967 Six-Day War, Egypt and Syria launched a massive offensive in October 1973, the beginning of the Yom Kippur War, so-named because it was launched on Judaism's holiest day.

Israel was taken by surprise. Following weeks of desperate fighting, the United States airlifted $2 billion in aid to counter the Soviet Union's support of the Arab nations. Incensed, the Organization of Petroleum Exporting Countries (OPEC) united behind Saudi Arabia in a complete embargo of oil supplies to the United States on October 20, 1973.[20]

The embargo made it painfully clear how dependent on oil the United States had become. Production elsewhere was stepped up, part of the reason Rowan was able to move so quickly and completely into the oilfields of Alaska, Venezuela and the North Seas.

Although in real terms, the flow of oil to the United States only declined nine percent in December 1973, the idea of an embargo touched off panic throughout the country. Automobiles lined up for blocks to receive gasoline, which skyrocketed in price because OPEC raised the price of oil from $2.95 to more than $11.65 a barrel. (The price had gone even higher as oil companies from around the world tried to outbid each other.)[21]

By the time the oil embargo ended in May 1974, the petro-political world had changed. OPEC, by asserting control over an individual nation's oil,

Rig No. 35, an air-mobile rig, at a drill site on the North Slope in Alaska in 1974.

had assumed a global importance that would continue so long as the world relied on oil.

Merric, Inc.

Against the backdrop of world politics and the crucial need for oil development, Rowan announced its purchase of Merric, Inc., an air taxi operator of rotary and fixed wing aircraft based in Fairbanks, Alaska. Rowan correctly predicted that the Alaskan pipeline, then under construction, offered opportunity in the air. Shareholders of Merric Inc. received a total of 40,593 shares of Rowan common stock with 4.2 shares of Merric stock exchanged for one share of Rowan stock.[22] Merric became a subsidiary of Rowan, and Merric's President Richard Wien and other key personnel retained their leadership positions. Merric operated a lodge and refueling facility at Bettles, just 35 miles from the pipeline route and south of the mineral-rich Brooks Range.

Merric, the fourth-largest aircraft service company in Alaska, had nine helicopters and four fixed-wing aircraft. The company provided helicopter support on ecological studies for pipeline work, and serviced government agencies and oil companies in geological surveying.

Left to right: Carl Brady, Cecil Provine, Bob Palmer and Arch Rowan in 1973. (*Photo courtesy of the* Anchorage Times.)

At the end of 1973, ERA and Merric together operated 36 helicopters and 12 fixed wing aircraft to make it the largest operator of charter aircraft in Alaska.[23] The combination of the two companies also would rank it as the largest helicopter operation in the state with bases at Anchorage, Fairbanks, Bettles and Deadhorse, near Prudhoe Bay.

Merric, like Rowan and ERA, had a pioneering history. Like Rowan, Merric had been founded by two brothers, Merrill Wien and brother Richard. Their father, Noel Wien, had come to Alaska in the 1920s and founded Wien Alaska Airlines. A *Grapevine* article noted that the "story of Noel Wien's life is the history of the development of Alaska itself. Against tremendous hazards of cold, mountains, and unmapped areas, he brought the first airplane service into many remote communities of Alaska."[24]

The two brothers grew up with aircraft and the dangers and excitement of a new frontier. As children, "barely old enough to hold a broom, they started sweeping hangars and loading aircraft to earn money for flying lessons. They each soloed

ERA's Anchorage facility housed 74 helicopters and 17 fixed-wing aircraft.

on their sixteenth birthday and had earned their commercial licenses by the time they were eighteen."[25] They majored in business management and engineering at the University of Alaska, while continuing to spend time flying for their father's airline. They got first-hand experience in aircraft and Alaska, flying from 1955 until 1965 into all areas of the vast state.

In 1959, the brothers bought a B-25 Mitchell bomber, using it for forest fire control for the Bureau of Land Management. A year later, they purchased a Hiller UH-12B helicopter, the beginning of its helicopter fleet.

On March 15, 1974, Merric, by then a Rowan subsidiary, welcomed more than 300 guests to a dedication ceremony of its new hangar at Fairbanks International Airport. The building housed the main offices for all Merric operations with a large section for both helicopters and fixed-wing aircraft, as well as a 2,500-square-foot shop and parts area. Merric, like ERA, was busy providing support for the construction of the Trans-Alaska Pipeline.

The facility opened at a fortuitous time. Bill Martin, administrative director for ERA, noted that the company operated nine fixed-wing aircraft and 11 helicopters "to accommodate more work than we had last year during our busy summer season. Although much of the demand is for pipeline work, we also have many requests for activities other than those needed for the pipeline."[26] ERA and Merric reported a revenue jump of 130 percent from $5.6 million in 1973 to $12.8 million in 1974.[27]

New Vessels Overseas

The building boom continued throughout 1973 as Rowan celebrated the launching of two new drilling vessels: the *Rowan Morgan City*, and its fourth jack-up rig, the *Rowan Texas*.

The christening of the $4.5 million *Rowan Morgan City* took place in Singapore. Bob Palmer described the *Rowan Morgan City* as "a very specialized type rig. It must rest on bottom in order to drill, thus its operating capabilities are extremely limited by water depth — the maximum being 24 feet. Further, water must be at least six feet deep for movement to each new drilling location."[28] The rig's first assignment was a five-well drilling program for Total Indonesie in Kalimantan, Indonesia, followed by a four-well extension.[29]

The *Rowan Texas* was built at the Marathon-LeTourneau yard in Vicksburg, Mississippi, under the supervision of "Scooter" Yeargain, vice president of operations, and the rig superintendent,

Tillman Jones. The jack-up rig could work in 225 feet of water and drill to 20,000 feet. Its platform had three 750-horsepower thrusters to move the unit between locations, and crew quarters for 78 workers, as well as a small hospital.[30] The *Rowan Texas* began work in the Gulf of Mexico where it drilled three wells.

The rig then set an industry record with a 13,550 statute-mile tow from the Gulf Coast to the Arabian Gulf in 98 days. The trip, with an 11,500-horsepower ocean-going tug pulling, began at Sabine Pass, Texas, on the morning of July 19, 1973, and ended off of Abu Dhabi on

October 24. Its propulsion-assist thrusters allowed the *Rowan Texas* to move an average of 136 miles a day at speeds up to six knots. A riding crew of workers made the trip, accompanied by three registered seamen and two caterers. The rig joined the *Rowan New Orleans*, which had already been drilling in the Arabian Gulf.[31]

Consolidation at the Top

Cecil Provine, who rose from water pumper on a steam rig to president of a global enterprise, retired on June 1, 1973, following 42 years with Rowan. To

Rowan consolidated the office of president and chairman following Provine's retirement. The 1975 board of directors is shown, left to right: William T. Fleming; J.C. Magner, standing; C.W. Yeargain; Thomas G. Kelliher, standing; C.W. Yancey; Carl F. Brady, standing; C.R. Palmer; Walter J. Hickel, standing; and Lawrence Cade. (*Photo courtesy of Jean Rowan McNab.*)

commemorate the occasion, the *Grapevine* reprint-ed an earlier biography published when he was a division manager, overseeing the company's 19 rigs in the Permian Basin. The biography chronicled his rising career with Rowan, and noted:

"He's no ordinary fellow — this man Provine. He bumped against it hard as an orphan but overcame difficulties nonetheless. He learned as a boy that he could do better than be a water pumper. As a rough-neck, his determination made him realize that he could be a driller or a superintendent. He learned as a superintendent and as an officer that he could be a leader. But more than all, he learned as a man that only the game fish swim upstream."[32]

Arch, Provine's mentor over the years, wrote that he would give Provine a "capital 'E' for effi-ciency" and that "he is more responsible than anyone I know for the fine success that this com-pany has made and for the many loyal and dedi-cated employees we have."[33] The company contin-ued to receive Provine's input; he was named vice chairman of the board.

Provine always showed faith in himself and in his workers. In a 1997 interview, given shortly before he passed away, he noted: "I always said if you turn a roughneck loose, he's going to figure out the easiest way to do it, and that's the way you come up with a lot of these ideas."[34]

At the time of Provine's retirement, the com-pany consolidated the offices of chairman of the board and president with Palmer in that position. The reorganization also created four operating divisions to be managed by a corporate vice pres-ident. C.W. Yancey was put in charge of domestic drilling operations, while Yeargain oversaw inter-national drilling operations. J.C. Magner's divi-sion was exploration and production, and Carl Brady was vice president of aircraft operations. Yeargain also was named assistant to the presi-dent. Charles Blanchard, vice president of Rowan International, also was named vice president in charge of international sales. D.C. Anderson, sec-retary-treasurer, became vice president for finance, accounting and administrative services.

In West Texas, welders were busy finishing two of the company's largest land rigs. Rig No. 5 was a jack-knife or "bulge-type" derrick, with the

Rig No. 5, shown here in Oklahoma in 1978, was powered using elec-trical and mechanical-drive trains.

largest derrick, rotary and set-back capacity of any rig built by Rowan, capable of drilling more than 30,000 feet. (It actually drilled a hole more than five miles deep.)[35]

Rig 5 operated using hybrid power, noted *The Oil and Gas Journal* in 1974:

"Rig No. 5 is neither a diesel/electric nor a straight mechanical-drive rig. But it uses both electrical and mechanical-drive trains in an unusual combination hookup that Rowan has used successfully on three similar rigs. The rotary table is driven with a generator/motor combina-tion and power for the rest of the rig components

is supplied by a mechanical drive which uses hydraulic, or fluid, couplings. According to a Rowan spokesman, the unique power-train arrangement improves operating flexibility.[36]

Rowan designed the new drilling giants for depth, expecting a demand for such deep drillers. "At present, there are few rigs capable of handling the extreme hook loads for running long strings of casing," Yancey said. "Mast, hoist and substructure capabilities would become overloaded on most rigs at the million pound level."[37]

Two years later, Rowan began construction in July 1976 at its Odessa Yard on another monster land rig. Rig No. 14 could drill 35,000 feet deep, and using a 25-ton drilling bit, drill out a hole 10 feet in diameter. The hole was a requirement of the rig's contract in the U.S. Department of Interior Bureau of Mines oil shale research and development program. The 120-inch diameter shaft was to be drilled 2,400 feet deep in the Piceance Creek Basin on the western slope of Colorado's Rocky Mountains. Trucked to Colorado, the rig became somewhat of a tourist attraction for people from the town of Rifle, 56 miles from the drill site. After Rig 14 completed its Colorado job, it headed to Texas to drill a 22,000-foot gas prospect for Pennzoil.[38]

50th Anniversary

Rowan celebrated its 50th year of business in 1973. "The company was founded on the principle that in any organizational endeavor men are more important than machinery and tools, and this emphasis on personnel has prevailed throughout the history of the company," wrote Arch.[39]

Palmer saw the company's position as unique in an energy-hungry world. Rowan possessed "the finest equipment, personnel and organization in the industry together with the financial strength to grasp opportunities as they develop. The challenge for the future is obvious — to protect the corporate heritage and to carefully allocate our manpower and financial resources while remaining in the forefront of a most dynamic industry."[40]

Over the preceding half-century, Rowan had drilled in Texas, New Mexico, Colorado, Wyoming, North Dakota, Alaska, Oklahoma, Mississippi, Florida, Georgia and Louisiana. Rowan International had expanded drilling operations to include Venezuela, Singapore, Norway, Sharjah, Kalimantan, Honduras, Nicaragua, Abu Dhabi and the Gulf of Arabia.

Rowan ordered two more jack-up rigs in 1973 and 1974 respectively. The gangly *Rowan Louisiana*, with 466-foot legs, was designed to drill in water depths up to 350 feet. After a two-

Rig No. 18, shown here drilling in Oklahoma in 1978, had drilled five miles — the third deepest hole in the United States up to that time — in 1973.

year construction program, it began working in the Gulf of Mexico.

In 1974, construction began in Vicksburg on the *Rowan Alaska*, which had 410-foot legs and could drill in waters 300 feet deep. Both the *Rowan Alaska* and *Rowan Louisiana* had drilling capacities of 30,000 feet. The estimated total cost of the two rigs was $31 million.[41] Their square-leg designs would differ from Rowan's four other jackups, which featured triangular-shaped legs.

In the North Sea

In Norway, the naming ceremony for Rowan's first semisubmersible drilling rig, the *Norskald*, was held on December 6, 1973, in Sandefjord, a sea town where craftsmen once built the small, wooden boats used in whaling. The semisubmersible rig was designed for use in deeper water over continental shelves. In these huge, floating vessels, the

Above: A high school band in Sandefjord played despite the blowing snow at the *Norskald* naming ceremony.

Left: E.H. Walston in front of the *Norskald*, still under construction. (*Photo courtesy of E.H. Walston.*)

hull was almost entirely submerged and the rig held in place by anchors and thrusters.

On a dark evening pummeled by blowing snow, the *Norskald*'s sponsor fired a bottle of champagne from a harpoon gun, shattering the bottle against a stability column on the 319-foot-high rig. More than 225 guests attended the ceremony, and the local high school band wore mittens to play such musical numbers as "Anchors Away."

The huge rig already had undergone sea tests to prove its sea-worthiness in the dangerous, surging northern seas. Winter storms in the North Sea, less than 500 miles below the Arctic Sea, and the neighboring Norwegian Sea to the north could stir up 90-foot waves and 100-mph gusts. During sea trials, the *Norskald*, under its own power, averaged 6.2 knots. It also passed tests showing it could survive even in waves of 100 feet.[42]

The *Norskald*'s first job was working in the Norwegian Sea for Mobil North Sea, Ltd. Rowan, which operated the rig under a management contract, had a 20 percent interest in the $31.5 million *Norskald*.[43] A truly international venture, the rig's roughnecks came from the United States, Norway, Scotland and other countries.

The *Norskald* towered over ocean tankers in the Sandefjord harbor, boasting awesome statistics. Its 12 supporting columns ranged in diameter from 12 feet to 24 feet, and were supported by massive 322-foot pontoons with a diameter of 28 feet. The deck, 128 feet above the pontoons, was 280 feet long and 277 feet wide, and the mast of the rig rose 167 feet above the deck. Each of the rig's two propulsion units had a capacity of 3,400 horsepower. Once on location, the platform would be held in place by eight 30,000-pound anchors, which were attached to 3,600-foot-long anchor chains. Each foot of chain weighed 100 pounds, which meant the chains themselves weighed 360,000 pounds.[44]

Sometimes, even more weight was needed in the wild seas. In a film made several years after *Norskald*'s completion, when the rig was at work in the North Sea 150 miles off Norway's coast, the narrator described how extra anchors had been added to ride out bad weather. The *Norskald* was being prepared to move to a new location when hurricane-force winds blew in with little warning. With 80 mph winds and 50-foot seas, the "*Norskald* stands alone in the savage sea bracing herself against pounding waves and howling winds. On the storm-battered bridge, a constant watch is maintained. *Norskald*'s propulsion capability assists in maintaining position. Storms like this may last a day or a week or more."[45] The storms finally abated, and with her propulsion

Left: The *Norskald* tests a well in the Norwegian sector of the North Sea.

Below: The *Norskald* nearing completion in Sandefjord in Norway.

Norjarl at work in the North Sea.

units to assist and a tug to guide, the *Norskald* moved to a new drilling location.

Rielley Euper, who retired from Rowan as senior electrical and mechanical supervisor, recalled seeing 70-foot waves in the North Sea and praised the massive semisubmersible rigs.

"You just used anchors to hold you in position. ... The operations were different from land or platform work because you're moving all the time. So we had motion compensators to hold the drill pipe so when the rig went up and came down, the compensator would go up and down to compensate for the movement. We had to learn about that and how to maintain it." [46]

Norskald's companion rig, the *Norjarl*, was launched in June 1974. The semisubmersible rig, designed and engineered by the Aker Group of Norway, took 15 months to build. Its twin hulls were built on the slipway at Aker's offshore yard in Verdal, Norway. The unfinished rig was then launched like a ship, and it built up a speed of 10 knots as it journeyed down the western Norwegian coast to Bergen for its final outfitting at the Lakesvaag yard. That final work was done under the direction of Bergens Mekaniske Verksted, a subsidiary of the Aker Group. [47]

Whereas the *Norskald* had four hulls, the *Norjarl* was a twin-hull rig. Rowan held a 20-percent interest in this latest semisubmersible. Both semisubmersibles were built at a total cost of $60 million. [48] With 75 crew members assigned to the rig on a 14-day on and 14-day off schedule, the *Norjarl*'s first assignment was drilling in the United Kingdom sector of the North Sea. As the *Grapevine* noted, "transplanted Texans, Oklahomans and Louisiana roughnecks will work alongside experienced

Norwegian mariners."[49] The *Norjarl* completed 220 days of drilling in the North Sea before it moved to the Celtic Sea, near Cork, Ireland, in late 1975. It was one of the first units to drill in the Celtic Sea.[50]

Arch Rowan Dies

Arch Rowan did not live to see these latest accomplishments. He died on January 19, 1975, at the age of 80. His survivors included his wife, Stella; two daughters, Sue and Jean; seven grandchildren; and a thriving company operating 31 rigs in five countries and 87 aircraft through ERA and

Merric in Alaska.[51] Rowan's consolidated profits from drilling and aircraft services in 1974 were $8.9 million, a 102 percent increase from 1973.[52]

At the time of his death, Arch was a director of Rowan and chairman of its executive committee. A company resolution referred to his "zest for life manifested through hard work and boldness of character," and described him as "a taskmaster who, as with himself, demanded the best of others."[53] In remembering the man who saw promise in a young man 45 years earlier, Cecil Provine said, "his friendship, his counsel and his example was priceless. We have lost a great coach and friend, but it is hoped the game plan originally prepared by the Rowan brothers will endure."[54]

In 1979, Arch and Charlie were posthumously inducted into the Hall of Fame of the Permian Basin Petroleum Museum in Midland, Texas. They were among those "whose careers have contributed substantially to the development of the petroleum industry in the Permian Basin and whose character has set a worthwhile example for the industry."[55] The brothers were among five peo-

Left: Cecil Provine at the time of his retirement in 1973. Like so many of Rowan's leaders, Provine rose through the ranks before he became president.

Below: Arch and Charlie Rowan were inducted into the Permian Basin Petroleum Museum's Hall of Fame in 1979.

PERMIAN BASIN PETROLEUM MUSEUM
LIBRARY & HALL OF FAME
Midland, Texas

ple so honored that year by the museum, which chronicled the history of oil drilling in West Texas and southeast New Mexico. The museum had been dedicated in September 1975 by President Gerald Ford.

Just as Charlie's death in 1961 came while Rowan dismantled its last steam rig, Arch's death occurred as the company marked the end of an era with the sale of two small land rigs. Rig 2 and Rig 10 could drill no deeper than 14,000 feet. Eleven of Rowan's 12 remaining land rigs had a nominal capacity of 18,000 feet to 25,000 feet, while its deepest land driller, mighty Rig 5, could drill more than 30,000 feet. But a *Grapevine* article reminded employees that small land rigs, like Rig 2 and 10, had been crucial to the company's development.

"It was just such rigs that created the worldwide drilling operations of Rowan Companies, Inc., today. In the 1940s such rigs were considered large and highly advanced. Gas and oil deposits were just beginning to be developed and could be found at much shallower depths than today when such 'easy' petroleum has been almost completely developed and new reserves can only be found in much deeper locations."[56]

The article recounted the rigs' histories. Rig 10, built in 1948, went to work in West Texas, briefly drilled in New Mexico, and then worked in Oklahoma except for a short foray into Arkansas. Rig 2, bought used and reconditioned in 1945, spent 30 years drilling in West Texas and New Mexico.

Through the Suez and Around the World

The drilling tender *Rowan III*, formerly known as the *Jack Cleverley*, made a historic trip in 1975. It became the first drilling tender to complete an ocean tow through the reopened Suez Canal. Egypt had closed the 101-mile canal to shipping for eight years after its defeat in the 1967 Six-Day War. The refurbished *Rowan III* left Morgan City, Louisiana, on July 3, and entered the canal August 13. As the vessel was towed through the Suez Canal, Rowan's marketing manager, R.E. Trout, recalled climbing into the derrick of Rig 11, which had been loaded on the tender's deck for the voyage, to catch the passing view:

Drilling Tender *Rowan III* at Rig 11. Rig and tender passed through the recently reopened Suez Canal, under Egyptian guns.

"Egyptian guns face us from the western bank ... tanks, guns, pill boxes and fortresses. Israelis on the eastern bank are in a trench with their guns, tanks and fortresses. We must go between them. ... We return the waves of those who wave at us. Moving at seven knots, we feel we are making good time. The desert stretches before us on both sides, baked to a bright tan, crisply sectioned by the stretch of blue water that is the Suez Canal."[57]

The tender arrived at Ras Al Khaimah in the United Arab Emirates and went to work servicing Rowan Rig 11 for Vitol.

The drilling tender would be followed through the Suez Canal by Rowan's sixth mobile offshore jack-up drilling rig, the *Rowan Alaska*. The rig, 247 feet in length and 200 feet wide, was the largest unit up to that time ever towed through the canal, and traced the route of *Rowan III* across the Atlantic, through the canal and then to Ras Tanura in Saudi Arabia to work for Aramco.[58] With four rigs in the Persian-Arabian Gulf, Rowan bought a huge, four-engine Convair 880 to fly from the Mideast to Houston every 28 days to change crews. Workers revamped the interior of the plane, cutting it down from the 120 seats it had for commercial flights, to 40 first-class style seats. The 18-hour trip was more comfortable for employees who previously had to change planes up to five times on the long trip home.[59]

In the Air

To improve efficiency and customer service, Anchorage-based ERA Helicopters and Fairbanks-

based Merric merged aircraft operations under the name of ERA Helicopters in mid-1975. Carl Brady became president and CEO of the combined companies, and Richard Wien, Merric's president, became executive vice president and chief administrative officer. Brady marked the occasion, saying, "We recognize the pride and esprit de corps that has developed within each company, and we respect that attitude. Our task now is to work toward the development of a similar attitude for the combined company."[60]

The aviation base at Fairbanks became the Northern Division and supervised North Slope operations at the bases of Deadhorse and Bettles. Fixed-wing and lodge operations at Bettles had been sold to Frontier Flying Services but ERA retained helicopter operating authority there.

Rowan bought Juneau-based Livingston Copters in late 1975.

Commissioning of the *Rowan Midland*, a semisubmersible rig. (*Photo courtesy of E.H. Walston.*)

The Anchorage base, now the Southern Division, was in charge of Cook Inlet helicopter operations at Nikiski and Rigtenders heliports. The combined fleet totaled 74 helicopters and 17 fixed-wing aircraft.[61]

In October 1975, Rowan acquired Livingston Copters, Inc., based in Juneau, Alaska. Rowan exchanged 25,840 shares of its common stock for all of Livingston's outstanding shares.[62] J. Arlo Livingston and other key company officials remained with Livingston as it became a Rowan subsidiary. Livingston, which had operated in Juneau for more than 15 years, had 11 helicopters and a "highly respected reputation for service to timber, mining and construction customers principally in the southeastern area of the state."[63]

With oil companies terrified of running out of crude oil inventory during this oil-crazed decade, Rowan continued to add marine rigs to match demand. The company launched its latest submersible rig, the *Rowan Fairbanks*, in November 1975. Built at the Marathon-LeTourneau shipyard in Singapore, the rig was "almost an amphibian," noted Bob Palmer. Dependent upon water to move from place to place, the rig required bottom support in very shallow water to drill. Along with its sister vessels, the *Rowan Morgan City* and *Rowan Rig 4*, the *Rowan Fairbanks* gave the company the ability to drill wells in areas where the water was too shallow for offshore rigs, and too wet for conventional rigs.[64]

Eighteen months after construction began, the $30-million *Rowan Midland*, a semisubmersible rig, began her maiden voyage in October 1976 from Levingston Shipbuilding Yard at Port Arthur, Texas, to a location in the Gulf of Mexico offshore Galveston. The steel giant rode high in the water on her three-day tow with one-fifth of her eight 100-foot stabilizing columns beneath the sea. Once on site, the columns were submerged to one-half their length by pumping sea water into ballast tanks located along each of the platform's supporting pontoons. The rig featured quarters for 94 crew members, and could drill to 25,000 feet in water depths up to 1,000 feet.[65]

Within two years, additional jack-up rigs were added. The *Rowan Odessa* and the *Rowan Juneau*, arriving in 1976 and 1977 respectively, were built at Marathon-LeTourneau's Vicksburg yard.

On its first job, however, the $20 million *Rowan Odessa* caught fire. The rig was drilling a well six miles off the coast of Louisiana when a gas leak ignited on September 26, 1977. Although crews worked to plug the leak, they were forced to evacuate the rig the following day because of the danger of a blow-out. The crew stayed on the nearby *Rowan Juneau* and work boats anchored a safe distance from the burning rig, returning every so often to try to relieve the high pressure from the well, as well as to prevent pollution to the waters of the Gulf of Mexico.

Famed oil well firefighter Red Adair and his crew quickly arrived to direct operations:

"The escaping gas finally ignited on October 1 and continued to burn until the morning of October 3 when the well 'bridged over,' [or sealed itself off], and stopped the fire. The gas was probably ignited by a spark from debris spewing out of the hole. Temperatures within the fire zone reached an estimated 1,700 degrees — hot enough to turn steel cherry red. Damage from the fire, however, was reduced as a result of large amounts of salt water and sand also blowing out of the hole and serving to cool the superheated metal."[66]

The searing heat from the burning gas melted a portion of the 147-foot derrick, collapsing it over the rig's control house. Damage was estimated at from $9 million to $12 million, fully covered by insurance.[67]

Fortunately, no one was injured nor was there any environmental pollution. The *Rowan Odessa* went to the Marathon LeTourneau facili-

ty in Brownsville, Texas, for repairs. Palmer said later that "while there was no actual injury to Rowan personnel, there was overriding injury to the company's pride from the first such occurrence in its 54-year history."[68]

Under Sail

Regrettable though the mishap was, the contract drilling business continued to improve, and Rowan showed $103.2 million in revenues at the end of 1977, a four-fold increase (from $24.7 million) since the oil boom began in 1973.[69] The company also scored an industry first when it unfurled the world's largest sail in an experiment to harness the wind to help move marine rigs. Palmer had envisioned such a sail assist back in 1970 during positioning of the *Rowan Houston* off the coast of Nicaragua in 30-knot winds. Asking himself, "why couldn't the force of the wind be used to aid in the transportation and stabilization of rigs," he later had sailing experts and engineers study the matter and test rigging up a sail on the *Rowan Juneau*.[70]

Finally, on March 18, 1978, 6,750 square feet of sail was hoisted and unfurled from the legs of the *Rowan Louisiana* during its tow from Galveston to the Bay of Campeche off Mexico. The rig, along with the *Rowan Texas*, was contracted to drill for Petroleos Mexicanos (PEMEX), the Mexican national oil company. Bess Brants' son, Clayton, whose firm was an insurance broker for Rowan, was a guest on the historic tow. He recalled the event in an article published in the *Grapevine:*

"As the yards and yards of Dacron caught the wind and began to blossom, big and billowy, Old Glory could not have looked better. All involved felt a quiet sense of pride and accomplishment. ... The furling gear was then tested, rolling the sail in on the spar then out again. The ease was amazing considering the enormous size. A tribute to the design and skill of the mechanics who put it all together, combining oilfield technology and the craft of sailmaking."[71]

The sail reduced the roll and pitch of the giant rig in the water. Now, calculations needed to be made on whether a sail-assist tow could save money. It cost up to $30,000 a day to move a rig

In March 1978, wind helped power the *Rowan Louisiana* to its drilling site using the world's largest sail.

150 miles, or an average of $200 a mile. However, an increase of only one-half knot towing speed could save $2,400 a day.[72]

Takeover Attempt

In the summer of 1978, a company called Chicago Bridge & Iron launched a hostile bid to take over Rowan by offering $26 a share for all of the company's common stock. Chicago Bridge, a maker of steel plate structures and tanks, owned about 4.9 percent of Rowan's 10.1 million shares of outstanding common stock when it tendered its offer.[73]

But Rowan's board unanimously recommended its shareholders reject the offer. The $26 offer was "inadequate and that the long-term interest of its holders would be best served if the company remained independent."[74] Rowan then sued in federal court in Houston to try to block the takeover attempt. Rowan claimed the offer violated federal securities laws and would inflict "substantial damage" on Rowan and its shareholders.[75] Chicago Bridge later filed a counterclaim.

As part of its strategy to defeat the hostile takeover attempt, Rowan announced in late June that it had reached an agreement to buy Armco's outstanding 50 percent interest in two Rowan affiliates, Rowan International and Rowandrill, in exchange for 1.9 million shares of Rowan preferred stock. This defense served two purposes: not only did Rowan get the remaining interest in four jack-up rigs, two submersible barges and a semisubmersible drilling rig, it also caused Chicago Bridge to reduce its tender offer to $24.50.[76]

Then on July 20, Schlumberger, Ltd. announced it had bought about 1.9 million shares, or about 18 percent, of Rowan's common stock in open-market purchases. However, the oilfield services and electronics concern said it would not seek control of Rowan and did not "intend, under the present circumstances, to increase its investment."[77] Five days later, Chicago Bridge withdrew its tender offer, saying "there is significant doubt that Chicago Bridge & Iron can gain effective control of Rowan."[78]

A 1980 article in *Forbes* magazine recounted how Palmer derailed the takeover attempt by appealing to the head of Schlumberger.

"[Palmer] grabbed a plane and flew to Paris, where he huddled with Jean Riboud, chairman of Schlumberger, Ltd., the $3.6 billion oilfield-service company. After thinking it over, Schlumberger agreed to be Rowan's protector. ... Palmer says that Riboud agreed to remain a passive investor, letting Palmer run the show. 'He didn't even ask for a directorship for Schlumberger,' Palmer says."[79]

The Aviation Center

In mid-1978, ERA broke ground on an aviation center at Anchorage International Airport. The 57,000-square-foot structure would be the largest fixed-wing base operation in Alaska with the space to service aircraft as large as a Boeing 707 or McDonnell Douglas DC-8. At about the same time as the ground breaking, ERA bought the assets of Jet Alaska, which had operated since 1968 from the airport and was

ERA's Aviation Center was the largest fixed-wing base in Alaska.

involved in med-evac and personnel transportation services. The purchase included Jet Alaska's six-place Learjet and 14-place Merlin Metroliner.[80]

On July 28, 1979, a grand opening was held at the new ERA Aviation Center at Anchorage. About 1,000 guests toured the facility, which was "the largest and most completely equipped fixed base facility under a single roof on the West Coast of the United States."[81]

ERA's director of marketing, Chuck Johnson, said the expansion came about as the company looked to keep its helicopters busy as work finished on the Trans-Alaska Pipeline.

"We started looking at the Gulf of Mexico which was in a real upswing at that point in time, in the late '70s, and we had a couple of Bell 205s working in the Gulf of Mexico for Exxon and some drilling programs, following the rigs around the Gulf, but we were not officially in business down there. ... So I made a couple of marketing trips down to the Gulf and came back and convinced Carl Brady that we should probably open

up our doors down there and start a real operation, which we did."[82]

ERA chose Lake Charles, Louisiana, because of its large commercial airport, as the site to build a maintenance hangar. In the meantime, a temporary office trailer and maintenance vans were located at the Lake Charles Municipal Airport.[83] By the end of 1978, six helicopters were at work in the new division.[84]

Next Generation of Rigs

In the waning years of the tumultuous 1970s, Rowan introduced yet another new design called the cantilever jack-up rig. The cantilever feature allowed the drill floor to extend over an existing offshore production platform for the reworking of existing wells or drilling additional wells. The first cantilever jackup, the $22.5-million *Rowan Fort Worth*, went to work in the Gulf of Mexico after its completion in late 1978. The rig could operate in water depths up to 300 feet and drill 30,000 feet deep. Two more cantilever-type rigs, the *Rowan Paris* and the *Rowan Middletown*, both similar to the *Rowan Fort Worth*, were under construction at Marathon's facility at Vicksburg. Their total estimated cost was $50 million.[85]

In 1979, Rowan, which already had 32 onshore and offshore rigs, announced that it was buying four additional cantilever-type jack-up rigs from LeTourneau-Marathon: the *Charles Rowan*; the *Arch Rowan*; the *Gilbert Rowe*; and the *Cecil Provine*.[86]

By the end of the decade, net income had risen 45 percent to $32.8 million from $22.6 million in 1978. Bob Palmer, in a speech to security analysts in mid-1979, discussed the ambitious building program that had prompted the company's rapid growth.

"I believe these rigs are tangible evidence of the philosophy that has guided Rowan's progress for 56 years — no long-range planning, just a strong army and strong treasury and an aggressive search for opportunities for conquest. We are pure opportunists dedicated to the strategy of inspiration, innovation and execution. We play a game termed free enterprise and feel that our profit and loss statement is our scorecard."[87]

Winds and machines: The *Charles Rowan*, on its way under sail, with an ERA helicopter on its landing pad.

CHAPTER NINE

A DIFFERENT BREED

1980–1990

"In the face of a severe and prolonged depression in contract drilling, [Bob Palmer] has demonstrated courage and determination, positioning Rowan to capitalize on any recovery. The basic stratagem here was a commitment to maintaining rigs and equipment in peak operating condition, manned with experienced, expert personnel."

— *The Wall Street Transcript*, 1987[1]

UNTIL 1980, ROWAN'S GROWTH had followed a smooth upward incline. Along with the fortunes of the oil industry, Rowan had profited from the world's increasing reliance on fossil fuel — even benefiting from the Arab oil embargo when new exploration sent Rowan's rigs around the world and deep offshore. By the dawn of the new decade, Rowan had staked out its expertise, and it was far from the dusty Texas oilfields that originally nurtured the company. The company had aggressively pursued the most difficult contracts anywhere in the world and developed into one of the industry's premier offshore drilling companies.

This transformation was accompanied by a rapid growth in the number of employees and rigs it operated. Between 1970 and 1980, the company had doubled in size to about 1,550 employees, with plans for additional growth. In the opening days of 1980, Rowan announced plans to build its eighth cantilever jack-up rig, the *Rowan Halifax*. Bob Palmer said construction of the rig, due to be delivered in three years from Marathon-LeTourneau's plant in Brownsville, Texas, showed "our confidence in a sustained long-range market demand for the deep-water jack-up type rig."[2]

Palmer was taking a calculated risk. An article in *Forbes* magazine went so far as to call him a "canny high roller," who was "betting the company"

on the new cantilever jackups, which the company first began ordering in mid-1978.

"These rigs do not come cheap, costing $27.5 million each. ... With oil at $30 a barrel, Palmer thinks there will be more demand than he can handle. 'We are betting the company that the business will be fantastic,' he says confidently. Now mark this: Palmer is paying $165 million for the new cantilever rigs. Rowan's total equity capital is only $133 million. You can see what he means about 'betting the company.' He plans to pay for them partly out of cash flow, partly with short-term bank loans."[3]

Rig Movement

In July 1980, the *Rowan Juneau* left Galveston to drill off Nova Scotia in the north Atlantic Ocean. The jack-up rig, a Gulf of Mexico veteran, had spent five weeks in Galveston undergoing winterizing procedures to toughen up for the icy work. The rig was assisted on part of its 2,400-mile journey by two sails, the fruit of Palmer's

---

The Rowan logo. Rowan Companies would double in size from 1980 to 1990.

The *Rowan Juneau* involved in a skid-off operation onto a platform.

1980 — Iraq-Iran War begins; OPEC loses control of prices and demand for oil drops.

1983 — ERA goes into passenger airline business.

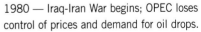

1981 — The *Gilbert Rowe* is launched, and begins work in the North Sea.

1983 — Third Gorilla rig is ordered from Marathon-LeTourneau in spite of the downturn. Profits fall to $21.9 million.

experiment years earlier. The sails were each 180 feet tall and 75 feet wide.[4] While the first use of sails had shown the idea was technically feasible, Rowan was trying to determine if it was economically worthwhile. Under sail, the *Rowan Juneau*'s speed went up one knot, so the savings, under reasonably favorable wind conditions, might vary between $6,000 and $9,500 a day. However, the sails seemed relegated to long moves since it took up to five days to erect and take them down.[5] With the work off Nova Scotia, Rowan opened an office in Dartmouth.

In 1979, Rowan had sold its 20 percent interest in the semisubmersibles *Norskald* and *Norjarl*. The move satisfied a new "corporate objective to divest assets not wholly-owned."[6] Also, North Sea drilling had slowed in 1978, causing an oversupply of rigs. The *Norskald* and *Norjarl* successfully had drilled more than 48 exploratory wells and accounted for several major discoveries, including the Statfjord, Murchison and Ula oil fields. The *Norjarl* also had

ERA's IFR Bell 212 prepares to take off from the helipad of the *Rowan Fort Worth*, off of the Louisiana coast.

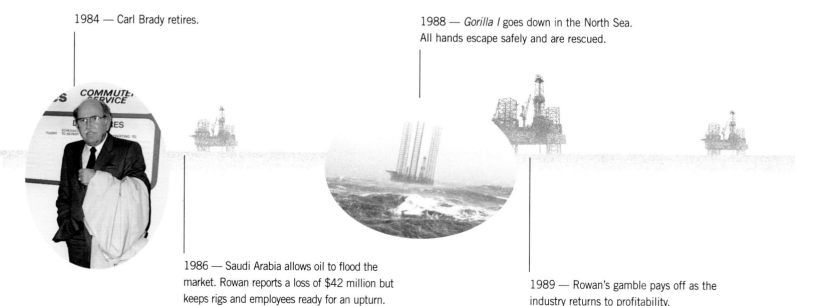

1984 — Carl Brady retires.

1988 — *Gorilla I* goes down in the North Sea. All hands escape safely and are rescued.

1986 — Saudi Arabia allows oil to flood the market. Rowan reports a loss of $42 million but keeps rigs and employees ready for an upturn.

1989 — Rowan's gamble pays off as the industry returns to profitability.

carried out the first successful sub-sea completions in 600 feet of water in the Beryl field in 1978.[7]

ERA was performing well, with its assets growing from $3.5 million in 1967 to more than $30 million by 1979. The company boasted the largest Twin Otter fixed-wing aircraft fleet in Alaska, and the only commercial private jet service. It also had the only round-the-clock Lear jet medical evacuation service. One-fifth of its helicopters operated out of Lake Charles, Louisiana, to serve the oil industry in the Gulf of Mexico.[8] In June 1981, Rowan held a ribbon-cutting ceremony for its newly constructed headquarters at Lake Charles Municipal Airport. That same year, ERA purchased its first BO105CBS and Bell 412 helicopters. The Bell 412s, a refinement of the Bell 212 with a new rotor system for better stability and increased air speed, were the first to enter commercial service.

For ERA, the years 1980 and 1981 were peak years in the Gulf of Mexico, despite stiff competition from 31 competitors, including one with several hundred aircraft, recalled Chuck Johnson, ERA's president in 1998. "Most of the competition came in after we cranked up down there in '78,

Above: The captain and co-pilot of a Twin Otter check out their aircraft outside ERA's hangar at Deadhorse on the North Slope.

Inset: Left to right: ERA Fairbanks manager Jerry Kocer, fixed-wing pilot Anders Ahren and maintenance coordinator Stan Halvarson with a Twin Otter at a North Slope hangar.

and when it all boiled out after the big oil bust in '86, we went down to about six."[9]

Johnson said that ERA, as a smaller company in the Gulf, could adapt to customer needs.

"We prided ourselves on staying close to the customer ... being able to react to their needs and taking care of them. Then with our financial strength from Rowan and their rigs offshore, we had over the period of time built up a fairly good infrastructure with fuel and communications and shore bases. So we were small enough to react and take care of them but we had the strength of the larger companies in that we had a good infrastructure and were financially strong."[10]

ERA had pioneered airborne radar approaches to rigs on the North Slope. "And we brought that skill to the Gulf of Mexico, and we certified the first airborne radar approach in the Gulf of Mexico (in April 1982) which was a big deal because we weren't exactly the biggest company down there," Johnson said.[11]

Rowan's new specialized arctic rig arrived in Prudhoe Bay in late 1981. The move prompted Rowan's largest trucking operation for a land rig as Rig 41 was carried to the North Slope in 131 tractor-trailer loads. Rig 41's 184-foot-tall derrick and substructure could move from one drill site to another on a wheel-mover that used a hydraulic jacking system similar to aircraft landing gear. The wheels, 11 feet tall, were retracted when crews prepared to drill and pushed down for towing to the next drill location.[12] The rig's initial assignment was development work for ARCO-Alaska, Inc.

Two new jack-up rigs, the *Arch Rowan* and the *Charles Rowan*, went to work in 1981 in the North Sea. Assisted by sail, the *Charles Rowan* was towed from New Orleans through the English Channel to a site off Britain's eastern coast. The *Arch Rowan* was towed from New Orleans to a site 25 miles off Grimsby, England, in 32 days. It had "walked" into the Mississippi River on the initial leg of its journey. Marathon-LeTourneau had come up with the method of "walking" rigs from its Vicksburg yard because of the temperamental Mississippi, according to the *Grapevine*.

"The Mississippi bank line can't be depended upon to stay the same. The river always is carrying away soil from some places and depositing it at others. The water levels change with the seasons. So LeTourneau engineers came up with 'walking' as a way to launch rigs without a permanent launchway. The longest distance a rig has been walked is eight hundred feet and the shortest is three hundred feet, according to a LeTourneau report."[13]

LeTourneau patented the launching pad, which consisted of a foot-like structure, an elevated hinge system and an upper structure rigidly attached near the rig's stern. The rig was "walked" by alternately lowering and raising the bow and

ERA Bell 412 helicopter with external fuel tank system developed by ERA employees.

stern legs in a see-saw fashion so the "foot," located between the legs, would swing forward to move the *Arch Rowan* down the river bank and into the water.

The Gamble

Bob Palmer's willingness to risk was acknowledged throughout the industry. He had been picked as the CEO of the Year in the category of oil services for 1979 by *Financial World* magazine. A few months later, *The Wall Street Transcript*, in its October 20, 1980, edition, had given him the Silver Award in the "Oil Services and Equipment Industry" category. The award by the weekly newspaper went to those CEOs who have taken "the proper steps to enhance the overall value of the enterprise for the benefit of the stockholders."[14]

On July 27, 1981, *The Wall Street Transcript* gave Palmer its Gold Award as the top CEO in the offshore drilling industry for 1980. The weekly noted that Palmer had "shown an extraordinary ability to anticipate market trends and to position

Rowan to take fullest advantage of these trends." One analyst, interviewed by the newspaper before making its selection, said Palmer "does not follow the crowd. In the last cycle in 1977 and 1978, everybody else was afraid of touching offshore rigs. Bob Palmer went ahead and ordered them."[15]

Rowan was reaping the rewards of its accelerated expansion. Rowan's growth during this period was nothing short of amazing. In 1979, the company had profits of $51.5 million before taxes. One year later that had doubled to $101 million before taxes. Consolidated revenues went up 45 percent to reach $369 million in 1981, compared to $255 million in the previous year. While buying new equipment, Rowan shed its outdated rigs. It sold one tender-assisted platform development rig in December 1981 and the other two tenders in January 1982 for a total of $25 million.[16]

Nearly 10 years after the death of Gilbert Rowe, Rowan's newest jack-up cantilever rig was named in his honor. The rig was towed from Belle Chasse, Louisiana, to the North Sea, off of the Netherlands, to work for British Petroleum. The location was fitting because Rowe's final achievement before his death "was the participation in

Inset: Cecil Provine and Bob Palmer at the dedication of the *Cecil Provine*, seen above, in the Port of Rotterdam in 1982.

Far left: The *Gilbert Rowe* at work in the North Sea.

negotiations for entry into the semisubmersible drilling market in the North Sea."[17] With the launching of the *Gilbert Rowe*, son Gilbert Edwin Rowe remarked that, "Gilbert Rowe is back in the oilfield again."[18]

It also was fitting that the *Arch Rowan, Charles Rowan* and *Gilbert Rowe* in the North Sea worked with the *Cecil Provine.* Cecil Provine, the man, climbed aboard his namesake for a look around before it left for the North Sea. Provine believed that Rowan, a veteran of both good and bad

FOOD FIGHT

IN JUNE 1981, ROWAN WON AN 11-YEAR battle with the Internal Revenue Service over social security and federal unemployment taxes on meals and lodging provided to employees on offshore rigs. Rowan took its argument before the nation's highest court. The 11-year fight came after a 1970 routine audit that spotlighted food and lodging provided to employees on 12 Rowan drilling rigs between 1967 and 1969. Employees weren't charged for the meals and lodging, but the IRS wanted Rowan to pay the payroll taxes on their value. Most Rowan employees already had paid the maximum amount that could be collected by the IRS for Social Security and unemployment taxes, so the audit included only those workers "who had left Rowan's employ during the year and, consequently, hadn't had that maximum deducted from their paychecks."[1]

The IRS calculated the value of meals and lodging at $42 a week, or $6 a day, a person between 1967 and 1969. That was based on the cost of a caterer who provided meals and maintained living quarters on a drilling tender. The IRS said the employees in question should have paid 4 percent of the value and Rowan the other 4 percent. Since the employees already had left the company, Rowan was to pay all 8 percent as a penalty.

Rowan Executive Vice President J.C. Magner said in an interview at the time that "the company was told by law firms and the IRS almost every step of the way that it had no case against the IRS. With the continuing support of both former Chairman of the Board M.G. Rowe, and present Chairman, C. Robert Palmer, the case was debated in administrative hearings and the courts for years."[2]

Then, in a 6-3 decision in June 1981, the Supreme Court said the value of meals and lodging could not be exempt from income tax and at the same time be deemed wages for Social Security and unemployment taxes. Justice Lewis F. Powell said, "we therefore hold that the Regulations are invalid, and that the (Internal Revenue) Service erred in relying upon them to include in the computation of 'wages' the value of the meals and lodging that petitioner provided for its own convenience to its employees on offshore oil rigs."[3]

The court ordered the IRS to refund Rowan $31,246.74 in Social Security and unemployment taxes, plus interest, that the company paid under protest before suing the federal agency. "That was something Jack was really happy about," recalled Elizabeth Magner.[4]

The Wall Street Journal reported that the decision "may force the Treasury to refund more than $17 million to taxpayers who have appeals pending before the IRS. The ruling applies in ... situations where employers, largely for ... convenience, provide meals or lodging to workers on the job. The ruling doesn't cover cash allowances for meals or lodging."[5] In the dissenting opinion, the justices said the "IRS regulations were a 'permissible interpretation' of federal tax laws."[6]

The Rowan emblem in the window of Rowan's new office in Aberdeen, Scotland.

stated that any "attempt by any outside force to gain control of the Persian Gulf region will be regarded as an assault on the vital interests of the United States of America."[20] The situation in the Middle East was becoming increasingly anti-American and the hostage crisis dragged on for more than a year, into Ronald Reagan's presidency. Oil prices rose steadily. When Iran and Iraq went to war with each other in late 1980, the price of a barrel of Arab oil jumped to its highest point to date — $42 a barrel.

With the sudden disruption of Middle Eastern oil, domestic companies like Rowan scrambled to increase supply. The American oil industry entered a glamour period of risky money, fast deals and unprecedented production, driving up revenue and profits. Dallas, Houston and New Orleans boomed. On television, Dallas introduced J.R. Ewing to the viewing public as the ultimate oil man. John Buvens started with Rowan as a young attorney in 1981, later rising to general counsel, and remembered the atmosphere across the company when he started.

> *"When I came to work at Rowan, we were at the tail-end of the construction boom for the jack-ups. It was a contractor's market, meaning people bought and took you lunch. When you went to negotiations, you could pretty much dictate what you wanted. Because there was a shortage of iron and a shortage of skill and technology and crews and experience, and Rowan had all that. So Rowan was kind of a Cadillac drilling company and very courted by customers."*[21]

But the boom didn't last long. A global network of unrelated forces handed the oil industry its biggest setback since the early 1970s. Inflation was rampant across the world. The number of oil exporting countries, including Malaysia, China and Angola, increased. The Alaskan pipeline increased its flow from the North Slope. Worse still, the combination of politics, higher prices and environmentalism dampened the demand for oil. Coal staged a comeback, nuclear energy emerged as a serious contender and some countries began using more natural gas.

At first, analysts had predicted a shortage in the world oil supply. But the decrease in demand

times, would grow even stronger. "I think I'd like to see the company grow larger still," he said. "The founders would be proud of where the company is today."[19] Awaiting delivery of Rowan's latest self-elevating jack-up rig, was the office staff at Rowan's new office in Aberdeen, Scotland. The offices were in a building more than 100 years old.

The Downturn Begins

These were good years for Rowan, but throughout this period, the world oil market was rumbling uncomfortably. In the Middle East, a group of Iranian religious zealots stormed the American Embassy and took 50 hostages. President Jimmy Carter responded with the Carter Doctrine, which and the increase in domestic production turned the shortage into a sudden glut. Oil prices slumped, and the market spun into a free-for-all. Instead of prices being determined by American oil companies or OPEC, oil was traded as a commodity.

Palmer, as president of the International Association of Drilling Contractors, spoke of the downturn at the group's annual meeting in October 1982. He linked the steep decline in rig work to "surpluses of oil and gas creating a soft price structure, tight cash flows of major oil companies, economic recession, high interest rates and uncertainty about tax policy." He added that also with "the tendency of our industry to over-build equipment, combined with over-optimism and periods of amnesia ... you have the ingredients for one of the sharpest downturns in the history of the drilling business."[22]

The overall effect of this was damaging to companies like Rowan. The number of rotary drilling rigs at work in the United States had dropped from an all-time high of 4,530 in December 1981 to less than 2,500 in September 1982. Palmer conceded the past year had been "perhaps one of the greatest periods of disorientation ever experienced in our industry," but acknowledged it was the free enterprise system at work.[23]

Rowan took advantage of a variety of money-saving measures, including the "dry" tow. Other companies had moved their drilling rigs to other sites by shipping them on barges but Rowan's first dry tow came in late 1982. In Saudi Arabia, a barge was ballasted down so the *Rowan Alaska* could be floated over it. Workers then raised the vessel under the rig and fastened it on. The tow to San Pedro, California, with stops in Singapore and Hawaii, lasted from July 29 to October 15, not as fast as hoped, but more economical, especially in the cost of insurance. It also gave the crew a smoother ride and the chance to prepare the rig for its next job. The *Rowan Alaska*'s rig superintendent, James Anders, described it as "a good way to go. ... We didn't experience the twisting sensation caused by the waves that I've noticed on other tows."[24]

The *Rowan Middletown* was the next rig to use the dry-tow method, but with a twist: The rig was moved on the back of a ship, not a barge. The *DYVI Tern*, owned by a Norwegian shipbuilder,

The *Rowan Alaska* being dry towed off the coast of California on its return from Singapore in 1982 aboard the barge *Marine Servant*.

was ballasted to position the *Middletown* could be over it. The rig was then moved from Brazil to Homer, Alaska, to begin a multiple well contract in Norton Sound.[25]

A dry tow has several crucial advantages over a wet tow for long hauls. The rig is essentially cargo on a ship during a dry tow, making the move safer and easier to manage in heavy weather. As a result, insurance rates are lower for a dry tow.

In the fall of 1983, Rowan undertook its first double dry tow, moving the *Rowan Anchorage* and *Rowan New Orleans* on the submersible cargo ship, *Sibig Venture*. The voyage, at an average of about 13 knots, from Saudi Arabia to the

Above: The *Rowan Middletown* under dry tow aboard the ship *DYVI Tern*, in 1983.

Below: One of ERA's 50-passenger Convair 580s at the Valdez airport in 1983.

Inset: Carl Brady at ERA's ticket counter in the Valdez airport in 1983 when ERA began scheduled airline service between Anchorage and Valdez.

Texas Gulf Coast, took 45 days.[26] A second double dry tow occurred in May 1985 when the *Rowan Middletown* and *Rowan Alaska* traveled from the California coast, around Cape Horn and to the Gulf of Mexico offshore Freeport, Texas. The 15,423-mile trip on the back of the *Sibig Venture* took 62 days.[27]

Rowan's latest land rig, No. 33, was completed in late 1982 and became the company's sixth rig in Alaska. Rig 33 was different from conventional land rigs, a reflection of the need to remain flexible and cost-conscious. Bruce Person, superintendent at the time, said it could do "exploration, development, conventional drilling ... just about anything we have to do in Alaska."[28] The rig floor was turned 90 degrees from its conventional position so the derrick could be raised or lowered from the side. The construction of its 190-foot-high derrick also made it able to work in remote wildcat locations. The rig, weighing more than 3 million pounds, could drill 25,000 feet deep.

ERA moved into the scheduled airline passenger business in May 1983 in a venture with Alaska Airlines. ERA began flying three trips a day between Anchorage and Valdez with a 50-passenger Convair 580 jet-prop plane.[29] The company

later added flights between Anchorage and Kenai, Bethel and 18 surrounding villages, using Convair 580s, Twin Otters and a leased "Dash-7" aircraft. The passenger flights, along with U.S. mail and freight handling, added to ERA revenues.[30]

The Gorilla Rigs

Before the downturn began, Rowan launched a new class of monster offshore rig when it purchased two of Marathon-LeTourneau's new Gorilla rigs. The mammoth structures, each nearly 40 percent larger than the conventional LeTourneau jackup, could work in waters up to 328 feet deep and drill 30,000 feet. Costing about $85 million each, the rigs could withstand 82-knot winds and seas as high as 90 feet.

In late 1983, Rowan announced plans to build a third Gorilla rig. Like the *Gorilla I*, it was to be built at Marathon-LeTourneau's Vicksburg Yard. This newest rig, 297 feet long and 292 feet wide, was nearly the length of a football field, and had a 30-foot deep hull, and quarters for 80 workers.

Gorilla Rig Manager Danny McNease, from his office at the rig's construction site in Vicksburg, remarked that *Gorilla I* was "not just a bigger piece of steel. Whether at the drilling end or the operations end — nothing can touch it. All Rowan's leaders have put their ideas into this rig."[31] The *Gorilla I* was considered by LeTourneau to be in the Super Gorilla class, since it was larger than the company's original Gorilla design. For example, *Gorilla I*'s three 503-foot legs were 43 feet taller than the original Gorilla design.[32]

The Gorilla incorporated ideas originating from Rowan, such as the Blow Out Preventer Scooter, Type SY. The portable, five-ton Scooter, which traveled on rails mounted on the rig's substructure, was named for Rowan International Vice President of Operations C.W. "Scooter" Yeargain, who gave input for the design to Varco Tools, which built the machine.[33] The machine, with a metal basket to carry workers, operated like a cherry picker. The basket could hold 1,000 pounds — two workers and their tools — and carry its human cargo to the rig's Blow Out Preventer Stack or surrounding equipment for maintenance or inspection work. It provided a safer method to service these areas of the rig.

With 503-foot legs, the *Rowan Gorilla I* was 40 percent larger than conventional jack-ups, and was considered part of the Super Gorilla class.

The *Gorilla I* eliminated dependence on semi-submersibles rigs, and was far more durable in bad weather. "When it gets too rough out here, the semisubmersibles have to go into survival mode and stop drilling," said *Gorilla I* Rig Superintendent Mike Moody. "We can stay in drilling mode. It would have to be awfully bad before we would have to shut down."[34]

The *Gorilla I* was the largest jack-up rig ever launched when it went into the Mississippi River in late 1983. Using Marathon-LeTourneau's "walking" method, the giant foot walked the rig, then weighing about 13,500 tons, more than 700 feet in 10 days.[35] The rig was taken to Belle Chase for final rigging, and then to the North Atlantic off Nova Scotia. It spudded its first well on February 5, 1984, for an exploration group managed by Husky/Bow Valley.

The Downturn Worsens

Meanwhile, the downturn steadily worsened. Rowan reported a huge drop in income for 1983 because of the lingering depression in contract drilling. Profits plummeted from $119.4 million in 1982 to $21.9 million. Total revenues went from $401.6 million in 1982 to $206.5 million in 1983. A few months earlier, Rowan had instituted an action-oriented plan that included moving the *Rowan Anchorage*, *Rowan New Orleans* and a half-dozen other rigs from overseas sites to domestic waters because of increased opportunities. Rowan's latest jack-up rig, *Rowan California*, also moved from its birthplace in Singapore to the West Coast after completion.

Another part of the plan was to concentrate on unique market segments: remote and harsh drilling environments. Palmer wrote that, "we are able to attack these severe environments more time and cost effectively than the competition because of the unique rig capabilities we have developed. We believe the decade ahead will provide high levels of offshore activity in the harsh environments of offshore Alaska, Canada and the North Sea."[36] The three Gorillas, expected to cost about $270 million, were part of that strategy, as well as upgrading five jack-up rigs to operate in more severe conditions. Palmer believed the "future success of Rowan is primarily dependent upon the economic success of the Rowan Gorilla."[37]

In spite of the industry recession, Palmer kept workers and equipment ready for when the market improved.

Palmer conceded that the new market strategy had risks but also potentially great rewards — if the company's assessment of the market place was correct. He noted that "investors are going to be required to exhibit some very unusual traits — faith, patience and staying power. ... Your directors and management are not simply trying to stay alive until '85. We are planning now for '95."[38] While carrying out its goals, Palmer said in 1983 that the company was "awaiting a stroke of good fortune — the precise moment when preparation meets opportunity. ... Rowan's intention is not only to survive but to emerge clearly as a victor."[39]

Unlike so many of the oil majors that laid off employees and stacked their rigs, Rowan staunchly stood by its workers. Palmer decided to "hot-stack" Rowan's out-of-work rigs by keeping crews on them to clean, repair and upgrade the equipment until new contracts came in.[40]

"These crews with their knowledge and experience with equipment and each other have been kept intact. They have not been laid off and scattered. ... The cost of hot-stacking is expensive. But it represents our commitment to be there first with the best in personnel and equipment."[41]

Rowan employees like Rielley Euper were grateful. "You didn't worry about losing your job," Euper recalled in a 1998 interview. "That makes for good morale, and when things do pick up, you have the people there you need."[42]

Rowan's *Gorilla II* was christened in September 1984 at Marathon-LeTourneau's Singapore shipyard. Amid bouquets of orchids, dancers dressed as lions performed the Lion Dance to block any evil spirits from interfering with the *Gorilla II*. Palmer, in a speech following the dance, described the rig as a "magnificent machine ... that represents the 23rd Rowan marine drilling rig, 20 of which have been built by Marathon-LeTourneau employees."[43]

Weeks later, the *Gorilla II* left for the North Sea on the back of a cargo vessel, the *Mighty Servant 3*, in the first tow of a Gorilla class rig. The *Gorilla II* would drill in 310 feet of water, the deepest North Sea location to be drilled by a bottom-supported rig.[44] The *Gorilla II*'s sister rig, the *Gorilla III*, built at Vicksburg, underwent a wet tow from the Gulf Coast to the Canadian North Atlantic. Extensions to give the *Gorilla III* a record 604 feet of legs were added at a cost of $3 million. Now able to operate in Gulf water depths of 450 feet, the *Gorilla III* drilled in 378 feet of water with 72 feet of penetration into the sea bottom, an industry record.[45]

Below: The *Rowan Gorilla II* in Singapore.

Inset: The Lion Dance was performed during the christening of the *Rowan Gorilla II*.

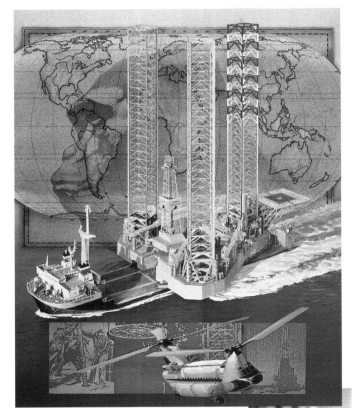

Above, right: Paul Kelly joined Rowan in 1982 and within three years opened the company's first office in England (inset).

Above, left: Illustration of the *Rowan Gorilla II* aboard the *Mighty Servant 3*, plus other Rowan operations.

In October 1984, Carl Brady retired as executive vice president of Rowan Companies and chairman of the board, president and CEO of ERA Helicopters. President Reagan sent him congratulations, noting that "yours has been a career marked by outstanding dedication and achievement."[46] ERA's new president David Baumeister described Brady as an innovator and a perfectionist. When Brady was named to the Alaska Business Hall of Fame in 1990, Baumeister described him as "a real entrepreneur."[47]

A year later, in October 1985, Rowan Drilling (U.K.) Ltd. opened a London office to be headed by Paul Kelly, vice president of Rowan Companies.

Kelly, a Yale-educated lawyer, had gone to work for Rowan in 1982, handling industry and government relations. In 1985, Rowan had seven jack-up rigs working in the United Kingdom and Dutch sectors of the North Sea. Kelly explained in a 1997 interview that while Rowan had drilled in the North Sea for years, it was mainly viewed as an American company since most of its employees in the United Kingdom came from the United States, which created some problems:

"In 1982, we came under pressure from both our customers and from the government to anglicize our operations. So I was sent over to the U.K. on a special mission to do just that, to open the company's first office in London so that we could improve our communications with both the government and with our major customers and to assist in the development of training programs

and to increase the United Kingdom employee complement in our operations over there. We have now achieved that, and we've been told now by the British government that in terms of relationships with the European Common Market, they consider us to be a British company."[48]

Kelly also would serve as managing director of British-American Offshore Ltd., a joint venture between Rowan and two other companies in which Rowan held 50 percent ownership. Rowan eventually owned 100 percent of British-American Offshore. The company is still considered "British" by the European business community.

In late 1986, Rowan took delivery of the $85.2-million *Gorilla IV*. Rowan had announced earlier that it would be building the *Gorilla IV*, a mightier version of its three existing Gorillas. It had three 605-foot legs for water depths up to

450 feet. Palmer described the *Gorilla IV* as Rowan's attempt to "build a better mousetrap."[49] The *Gorilla IV* went to work in the Gulf of Mexico, and later in mid-1988, it was towed to the United Kingdom sector of the North Sea. Rowan saw the *Gorilla IV* as the end of its major expansion program and had no plans to build further rigs. Palmer said that, as far as rig construction, "we are merely pausing, waiting on an improved economic environment."[50]

The Crash

Rowan experienced another year of declining profits in 1985, posting an anemic $3.8 million in profits, down from $4.2 million in 1984. The decline came on top of increasing revenues, from $198 million in 1984 to $272.5 million in 1985. The price of oil had leveled off somewhat, but the

The mighty *Gorilla IV* being towed to the North Sea.

A collage of Rowan drilling operations on and offshore in 1984.

prices fell through the floor. The Saudis had allowed something in the oil market that had never been seen before, not even in the early 1980s when Saudi Arabia had constricted its supply to keep prices up. Oil prices had become subject to the whims of the free market.

This dealt exploration companies, Rowan's biggest clients, a severe blow, which naturally trickled down to Rowan. That year, the company reported a loss of $42.1 million on revenues of $167.2 million.[51] Rowan ended up stacking all nine of its rigs in Texas for most of the year. To save money, Rowan closed its headquarters in Midland, Texas, and relocated personnel to the Odessa Yard.[52] In 1981, the oil industry had 1,450 drilling rigs working in Texas. By June 1986, only 219 rigs were operating in Texas, and the number of people working for drilling contractors there had dropped by 45,000 in the five-year period.[53]

Palmer described the drilling industry as being in a state of shock. Some companies went out of business, declared bankruptcy or were swallowed up by other firms. Palmer said, "the brutal fact is that the free enterprise system is working," as one-third of the drilling contractors left the Gulf of Mexico.

"At least another one-third are candidates for a fast departure. I believe Rowan to be a different 'breed of cat.' Our customer base is strong, our equipment modern and well-maintained. We have a capable, loyal and motivated workforce. Our financial plan is sound. I am confident that long-term opportunities are being created by the chaos and despair occurring within our industry. I believe Rowan is preparing for the future."[54]

He noted that Rowan owned four of the five existing Gorillas, giving the company an 80 percent market share, and had no long-term debt.[55]

The company sought out new customers and could report that, in 1987, its rigs worked for 31 customers, eight of them new ones.[56] Still, Palmer, in a 1988 speech to shareholders, described 1986 and 1987 as "lousy years, with 1987 the lousiest of them all."[57] In 1988, because of the depressed oil and gas prices, Rowan got out of the oil and gas exploration business. In 1989, all of its land rigs were idle.

industry was still unstable. In large part, Saudi Arabia was responsible for what little security there was. The country, which had the world's biggest oil reserves, was consciously varying its output to keep market prices stable.

This strategy served to prop up the price of oil, but was damaging to the Saudis, who found themselves underwriting increased production in other oil-producing areas like the North Sea, Alaska and Middle Eastern countries. In 1985, Saudi Arabia's imports to the United States had fallen from 1.4 million barrels a day to less than 30,000. The country issued warnings to other oil-producing nations that it would not continue to prop up the oil market. The warnings were ignored.

In 1986, Saudi Arabia announced that its patience had run out, and flooded the world market with cheap oil, precipitating the third serious oil shock, including the Arab oil embargo of the early 1970s, and the crisis in 1980 and 1981. Oil

The Industry Emerges

A staunch defender of the free market, President Ronald Reagan supported the recent developments in the oil market. His vice president, however, did not. George Bush was a Texas oil man himself and was determined to defend the domestic oil industry. He traveled to the Middle East and opened talks regarding setting quotas for oil producing countries and establishing a fixed price for oil. By late 1986, OPEC had agreed to a system of prices and quotas. There was only one snag: no one knew how to handle Iran and Iraq, which were still at war. In 1988, the United States brokered a cease fire, but it was one that favored Iraq.

Nevertheless, the end of the war signaled a new era. Oil prices began to rise again. Saudi Arabia announced a partnership with Texaco. The oil industry began to slowly pick itself up and dust itself off.

Palmer, who had stood by his employees as the industry collapsed around him, was once again honored for his bold management. He received the Gold Award in the offshore drilling industry category from *The Wall Street Transcript*. He was honored because "in the face of a severe and prolonged depression in contract drilling, [Palmer] has demonstrated courage and determination, positioning Rowan to capitalize on any recovery. The basic stratagem here was a commitment to maintaining rigs and equipment in peak operating condition, manned with experienced, expert personnel."[58] Palmer had been "willing to keep all of his employees except those lost through attrition when everybody else let go upwards of 40 percent of their staff. Albeit, he kept them at a wage freeze, but he kept them, and today, as a result of those efforts, his company is commanding more bids than he can actively take — and at premium rates."[59]

Rowan began to upgrade its equipment. Ten of its jack-up rigs had "top drives" and three more were to be installed so all of its cantilever-type rigs had the equipment. The top drive, which replaced the rig floor's rotary table, allowed for faster drilling while greatly reducing the hazard of sticking the drill string. The top drive "rotates the pipe from up in the derrick, rather than from the rotary table on the drill floor. It travels down a pair of rails as the bit advances down the hole."[60] Floor hands made less pipe connections, and hence worked faster, since the top drive drilled with 90-foot stands of pipe rather than 30-foot ones.

A Varco International official recalled how the company's top drive worked on a rig:

"The drill string is connected directly to the motor drive package. ... The traveling motor rotates the drill stem from the top — thus, top drive — with torque reaction taken through the guide rails. After the stand is drilled down, the connection is broken at the floor, the unit is hoisted to the top of the der-

Right: An ERA Bell 412 helicopter outfitted with the external fuel tank system, flying in the Gulf of Mexico.

Inset: The External Fuel System (EFS) development team poses with an EFS unit.

rick and another 90-foot stand is picked up, connected and drilled down."[61]

In July 1987, ERA obtained FAA approval for its auxiliary external fuel tanks for medium turbine helicopters. The company would get its first-ever company patent for the External Auxiliary Fuel System. The external tanks, which replaced the internal reserve tank and were attached below a helicopter's doors, meant two extra passenger seats and longer trips. By carrying an additional 155 gallons of fuel, the helicopter could fly at least 1½ hours longer at a normal cruise speed. The tanks were designed by ERA workers at their Lake Charles facility so helicopters could reach rigs up to 150 miles offshore while still retaining valuable passenger and cargo space.

As of January 1988, ERA changed its name from ERA Helicopters to Era Aviation, Inc. to better reflect its diverse fleet of aircraft. The company, with

Left: ERA Helicopters changed its name to Era Aviation, which celebrated its 40th anniversary in 1988.

Below: Era Aviation's facility in Lake Charles, Louisiana.

more than 750 employees, was operating 100 helicopters and 12 fixed-wing aircraft. It had expanded from Alaska and the Gulf Coast to the West Coast, Hawaii and overseas locations. Era flew sightseeing trips in Alaska and Hawaii. Its two major divisions were in Anchorage and in Lake Charles, Louisiana. In the Gulf Coast area, Era was the third largest helicopter operator.[62] The company celebrated its 40th anniversary in June 1988.

The *Gorilla I* Disaster

On December 8, 1988, the *Gorilla I* departed Halifax, Nova Scotia, under tow for the North Sea. The rig, which normally had a crew of about 98, was running a skeleton crew of 26, including maintenance workers, electricians and caterers. On land, Rig Manager Walter Couch prepared to shut down Rowan's single Halifax office, while Superintendent Jeff Cox traveled on the vessel.

For the first few days, the procedure went smoothly, similar to the many other times Rowan rigs had crossed and recrossed the Atlantic Ocean. Then, on the night of the 14th, the rig entered a low-pressure front so intense the barometer wasn't even capable of measuring atmospheric pressure. The following storm was huge. By the next day, the seas were surging at around 70 feet and the *Gorilla I* was in trouble.

Couch, who had traveled back to his home in Mississippi until the rig reached its new destination, boarded a plane and flew to Halifax as soon as he heard the news. He arrived the morning of the 15th. "I went over to the rescue center and they had some satellite photographs," he said. "The storm had a very defined eye just like a hurricane, only this was December, and they don't consider them hurricanes up there. We had pinpointed where the rig was relative to the eye, kind of right off the northwest corner of that storm."[63]

Since communication with the rig was impossible, constant surveillance was maintained by air, with military aircraft flying overhead to keep a constant vigil. Below, the situation wasn't improving. The tow line to the tug was severed. *Gorilla I* was adrift and beginning to take on water in the stern compartments.

On board the *Gorilla I*, Jeff Cox made the decision to abandon the sinking rig and sent the SOS signal that he was loading the crew onto one of the four 50-person rescue capsules. Four hours later, the $90 million *Gorilla I* capsized and went down in 16,000 feet of water.

After launching and then piloting away in the capsule, Cox recalled that "it was tense and quiet the first few minutes."[64] As the day wore on, they told jokes, sang songs and kept in contact with the outside world through radios. "They were trained how to load the capsule," Couch said. "You want to load it from the bottom up. The seats are in a circle, in a tier and you have to make sure all your weight is as low as you can get it. It's just a row of seats around."[65]

Throughout the night, the planes dropped flares on the water to light up the area around the capsule, but a rescue still wasn't possible due to high seas. Cox recalled that "those men kept flying over us all night long, talking to us and the boat and dropping flares. That helped morale as much as anything."[66] But the tiny capsule was subject to the rolling waves of a storm that would have been considered a hurricane had it hit one of the rigs in the Gulf of Mexico.

By daylight of December 16, the seas had calmed, with waves in the manageable 12-foot range. A life raft was launched from the *Smit London*, and the crew, three at a time, left the capsule for the tug. They had spent 22 hours in the capsule. There were no injuries, and the only close call was a diabetic crewman who had left his insulin aboard the *Gorilla I* and was dangerously close to a coma by the time the group was rescued.

After the ordeal was over, the crew and their families were put up at a Sheraton hotel in Halifax. Couch expected the crew members to want to go home as soon as possible. He was in for a surprise.

"Everything was very emotional. The group became very close in a short period of time and after a couple of days, when it was time to maybe shut some of this down, the people didn't want to depart. That was a reaction I didn't anticipate. They wanted to stay with one another. Even though their families were there with them, they didn't want to go home but wanted to stay with the people who were with them in the capsule. Actually, for some time there, they probably thought they weren't going to survive."[67]

Superior Training

That this dramatic story ended with no injuries was a testament to the crew's extensive training. Before crews went offshore, the company required them to pass a rigorous five-day training course, Couch said.

"They put a lot into five days of survival training, and we practiced that every week on the rig. Every Sunday, we would have drills, fire drills and abandon ship drills, which we tried to make it as real life as we could. In that situation, you had to wear a survival suit, which had safety devices on it like a light and rope to tie onto a buddy. It has a whistle, too. If you're in the dark and you can't see, you can blow the whistle."[68]

Even with all the precaution, it was the first time the Rowan safety program had been tested in a real emergency situation. Survival Systems International, manufacturer of the Whittaker capsule used in the evacuation, said it "was the first time a successful launch was made into seas over 40 feet high; the longest period spent in a capsule by a crew in a real emergency; and was the first evacuation crew with females (two women) aboard."[69] Rowan put out a full-page newspaper statement to thank all those who assisted and the crew members whose "training, courage, and high degree of teamwork in the final analysis was the reason they survived."[70]

In its report, the National Transportation Safety Board stated that structural failures, non-watertight ventilation openings, loose access hatches and unsecured cargo most likely had led to the flooding of compartments and tanks, which caused the rig to capsize and sink.

The high winds and seas lashed the rig so violently that equipment welded in various compartments broke loose, and cracks appeared in several tanks and two of the three legs. The report further stated that the structural failures "were the result of inadequate government and industry analytical methods during the design phase to assess the stresses imposed on the structure of self-elevating [mobile offshore rigs] while under ocean tow."[71]

The *Gorilla I*'s loss later was viewed by some as an unfortunate but timely event which, in a twisted way, helped Rowan survive the excruciatingly slow recovery of the industry. In a 1990 article, part of which was called "Rowan: A Storm Turned the Tide," *Business Week* noted the "catastrophe came just in the nick of time" when the company was recording its third consecutive year of losses and its stock had plummeted from 16½ in 1983 to 5¾ in 1988. "The $90 million insurance settlement for the accident, which caused no loss of life, helped tide the Houston-based company over in 1989."[72] (This is a view not shared by Bob Palmer, who never has considered the sinking as a positive event for the company.) Still, for 1989, Rowan lost $32 million on revenues of $217 million. This was still an improvement over 1988, when the company had losses of $69 million on revenues of $143 million.

Shortly following the *Gorilla I* incident, a major disaster struck the oil industry and the environment. When government and industry first proposed building an Alaskan pipeline to the port at Valdez, environmental groups reacted with outrage

---

Left: These dramatic photos on top and bottom of the page show the *Gorilla I* as waves and hurricane-force winds pummel it until it sank. The crew of 26 escaped to safety in a pod similar to the one shown at the left. *(Photos courtesy of Walter Couch.)*

Above right: Safety has been paramount for years at Rowan. Seen here is an ERA helicopter in 1983 rescuing three stranded Fish and Game workers who had been checking hibernating bears.

THE LAUNCHING PAD

ROWAN'S UNIQUE EXPERIENCES AND hardware led to several interesting and creative developments. One of these occurred in the late 1980s, during the height of the Cold War.

The company was approached with the novel idea of launching a rocket from an offshore Gorilla-type jack-up rig. The U.S. Air Force and NASA had begun discussing such launches from offshore pads with various petroleum industry companies, including Rowan and Houston-based engineering and construction giant Brown & Root. "The Air Force and NASA became concerned they didn't have enough launch capacity at Cape Kennedy and at Vandenburg Air Force Base," remembered Paul Kelly, who became involved with the project in the late 1980s.

"They began looking around for options and we were involved in a study that was done by Hughes Aerospace that looked at the feasibility of using offshore platforms as rocket launch platforms, and it would surprise a lot of people

to know that we could launch the shuttle off one of our Gorilla rigs with no problem."[1]

The concept had first been tested in 1967, when NASA and Italy had rocketed a satellite into orbit from a bottom-supported platform off South Africa. In a 1988 article, *Offshore Magazine* reported the "reason for looking offshore is economics. A Gorilla-type jack-up rig would cost $85 million to build and equip as a launching pad. A new land-based system similar to those in existence now would cost $400-600 million. Jackups, semisubmersibles, tension leg platforms and bottom-supported platforms are all being considered."[2]

Rowan suggested using a modified version of the Gorilla offshore rig. R.A. Keller, Rowan International executive vice president, said the Air Force and an aerospace contractor were confident the Gorilla could handle the weight and thrusts of a rocket. One version of the rocket would weigh about 5 million pounds and have 6 million pounds of thrust.[3] Keller said in a 1988 newspaper interview that

and stalled the project. It took the Arab oil embargo of 1973 and 1974 to begin construction on the pipeline. Environmental groups remained concerned about the Prince William Sound, a rich fishing ground and ecologically sensitive shipping port. All it would take, they said, was one big spill to destroy the Sound for generations to come.

Several minutes after midnight on March 24, 1989, that nightmare scenario came true. The *Exxon Valdez* supertanker hit a reef, spilling 240,000 barrels of oil into the pristine bay. Rowan's assistance to the $2 billion cleanup effort was tremendous. Era had the first helicopter on the scene, ferrying out U.S. Coast Guard workers to the crippled supertanker. Era committed 17 of its 26 civilian helicopters to carry government and oil company officials, news media, biologists and animal rescue workers from its Valdez hangar. The company tripled

its daily scheduled flights between Anchorage and Valdez, and assigned up to 42 employees to the Valdez hangar.[73]

The Coast Guard gave Era a Certificate of Merit in September 1989 for its service during the spill cleanup, citing the company for "immediate availability and continuous support of government- and private-sector air logistic requirements which contributed significantly to the effectiveness of the overall spill response. During the height of operations, you brought in additional aircraft and crews and maintained an extraordinary level of aircraft availability."[74]

More Plaudits

As the tumultuous 1980s drew to a close, it appeared that Palmer's bet would pay off. He had been criticized for "spending so much money acquir-

Rowan was first approached in 1987 by Air Force officials. "At first we thought it was a pretty far out idea, fun to fool with, but nothing to take too seriously," he said. "But looking at our rig was kind of enlightening to them."[4]

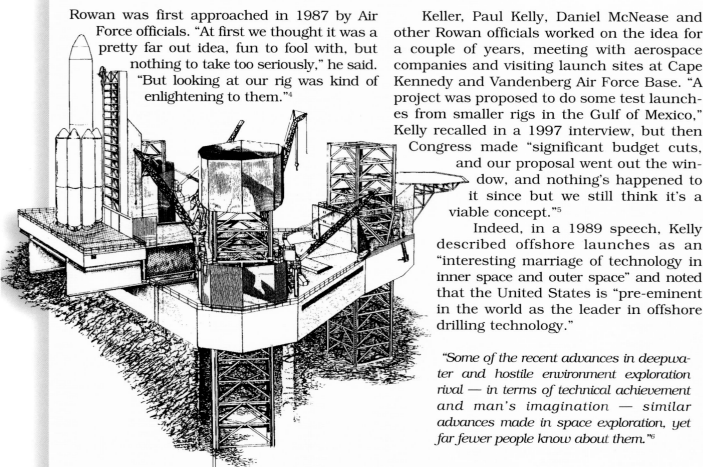

Keller, Paul Kelly, Daniel McNease and other Rowan officials worked on the idea for a couple of years, meeting with aerospace companies and visiting launch sites at Cape Kennedy and Vandenberg Air Force Base. "A project was proposed to do some test launches from smaller rigs in the Gulf of Mexico," Kelly recalled in a 1997 interview, but then Congress made "significant budget cuts, and our proposal went out the window, and nothing's happened to it since but we still think it's a viable concept."[5]

Indeed, in a 1989 speech, Kelly described offshore launches as an "interesting marriage of technology in inner space and outer space" and noted that the United States is "pre-eminent in the world as the leader in offshore drilling technology."

"Some of the recent advances in deepwater and hostile environment exploration rival — in terms of technical achievement and man's imagination — similar advances made in space exploration, yet far fewer people know about them."[6]

ing a top-notch rig fleet," noted *The Wall Street Transcript*, which again lauded Palmer with an award.

"Well, now it appears the bet has paid off. He's operating at 100 percent capacity when most of his competitors are running at 50 to 60 percent. His day rates are running 30 to 40 percent above the industry's. And although Rowan is still losing money, the prospects for profits now appear much closer."[75]

Indeed, one analyst would describe Palmer as a "visionary," and *Business Week* had this assessment:

"Instead of retrenching when the industry collapsed in 1986, Palmer refused to idle his rigs or fire employees. Instead, he worked them for whatever he could get, covering his losses by selling $60 million in new common stock. The move angered existing shareholders, whose stock was diluted by 17 percent, and Rowan still might have gone over the edge if not for the rig accident and the company's profitable business of providing helicopter service for offshore rigs."[76]

The Terminator crane became known for its ability to work in bad weather.

CHAPTER TEN

THE UPSWING BEGINS

1990–1992

"The demands of changing technology, customer requirements and regulatory compliance will eventually make obsolete the most perfect of our designs. Our recent acquisition ... of Marathon-LeTourneau will ensure that Rowan remains in the forefront of the offshore drilling industry."

— Bob Palmer, 1993[1]

AFTER MORE THAN A DECADE OF roller-coaster oil prices, war, and political maneuvering and profit losses, the industry began to turn around. But the atmosphere of renewed prosperity soon evaporated. On August 2, 1990, Iraqi dictator Saddam Hussein ordered 100,000 troops to invade neighboring Kuwait. The tiny country was quickly overrun, suddenly putting Iraq in control of more oil than any other single nation, including Saudi Arabia.

The world's reaction made it clear how important it was to protect the supply of oil. After a sharp spike in prices driven mostly by fear, production was stepped up elsewhere and prices actually dropped. Furthermore, Hussein had made a critical miscalculation. He had assumed he could split the U.S.-led coalition that formed in response to his annexation of Kuwait.

Coalition forces launched an unprecedented air war against Iraqi positions within Iraq and Kuwait. After a month of intensive bombing, ground forces swept into Kuwait and Iraq and easily overwhelmed the tattered Iraqi army. Throughout the entire conflict, gasoline prices remained steady, the world's oil supply remained basically unaffected and the coming prosperity wasn't damaged.

There was something unique about this latest turnaround in the oil industry. It was the first time that the fortunes of the industry weren't driven by the price of oil, but by technology. "The first boom resulted in gross over-building in the industry," said Mark Keller, Rowan's vice president of marketing.

"It was driven strictly from energy prices. People had no idea what their operating costs were and didn't care because of the amount of revenue they were generating. So much equipment was built during that time that it took so long for attrition and acquisitions to finally weed all this down to a market share that you could actually handle. I think a lot of us in this business cringe at the onset of an up cycle. You want to believe it but you don't really believe it. It's like watching a man climb out of a well. He gets almost to the top and gets kicked back to the bottom again and again."[2]

Yet Bob Palmer was convinced that Rowan, and the entire industry, was on the verge of a real recovery and embarked on another ambitious round of building — the construction of

In 1991, Rowan moved into the Transco Tower in Houston.

Super Gorillas. Rowan also moved to new headquarters and began a 401(k) savings plan for its employees.

The Return of Rig No. 4

Rowan's Rig No. 4, first christened in 1970, was reactivated in 1990 after eight years at the Morgan City Yard. The *Grapevine* recalled that "she was christened in 1970 the 'queen of our inland fleet.'"

"There was work in the Gulf of Mexico. Then the first and perhaps only wet trans-ocean tow of a barge to Indonesia. Later, she became a U.S. Gulf zero-discharge rig — again likely an industry first. Then the drilling market got brutal and Rowan's first posted barge rig was deactivated."[3]

With her return, she was renamed the *Rowan Fourchon*, and several of her crewmen were sent back to the familiar rig.

The *Rowan Fourchon* was smaller than many of the existing offshore rigs. However, W.W. "Pee Wee" Kebodeaux, the rig's former superintendent and her new manager, said "it does the same

duty as the big rigs. It's got power. You don't have to worry about overloading your engines in deep holes."[4]

After the rig's return from the Far East in 1977 to work off Texas and Louisiana, it was reconditioned at the Morgan City Yard and sent to drill in Mobile Bay, Alabama, so "that not even a drop of rainwater may pass to Mobile Bay if it falls on the rig first," thereby satisfying environmental concerns.[5] In returning to Mobile Bay, the rig was visiting a piece of its past. Rowan Vice President Robert Keller recalled that in 1979, "we drilled the first well in Mobile Bay. It turned out to be the discovery well — a 23,000-foot well."[6]

The *Rowan Fourchon* also ushered in another Rowan first. The barge rig worked along the African coast in 1991. The work was near the Gabonese capital of Libreville. Rowan Vice President Danny McNease described the new frontier for Rowan operations, saying that "in the location the *Fourchon* will work in, up the river from Libreville, the only accessible route by land must be with a four-wheel drive." Most of the crew would be drawn from the local population and live in nearby Port-Gentil.

1990 — A plane crash kills three, including Jack Keefauver, vice president of corporate aviation. Twelve others are injured.

1991 — Era President David Baumeister dies from cancer.

1990 — Rowan shows its first profit in five years, and the company gives its employees the first general pay increase in seven years.

Tragedy in the Air

On August 23, 1990, a Gulfstream twin turbo-prop, owned and operated by Rowan subsidiary, RDC Marine, Inc., crashed during takeoff from Houston's George Bush International Airport, killing three and injuring 12. The plane was en route to New Orleans to return rig crewmen from work in the North Sea. Killed were Jack Keefauver, 60, of Houston, Rowan's chief pilot and vice president of corporate aviation; co-pilot Wayne Kay, 49, of Katy, Texas, who had worked for Rowan over a 15-year period; and passenger Greg Hunter, 30, of Covington, Louisiana, a brother of Rowan employee Bill Hunter. All three men killed in the crash were in the cockpit, and "many of the injured, all-male passengers, were pulled from the burning aircraft by firefighters. Others found their way out through several holes in the plane."[7]

Keefauver had been vital to Rowan's corporate aviation department. The Air Force veteran had flown planes for 40 years. In his eulogy, CEO Bob Palmer told of Keefauver's impact on the company. He said:

"For 25 years Jack Keefauver and I dreamed the impossible dreams and together we made them happen. As Rowan's Aviation Department progressed from one Twin Beech — that was the ugliest airplane you ever saw, tan and black with red and white trim — to a fleet of magnificent aircraft, our business mission had as a primary purpose: to support Rowan's worldwide operations. And the drilling crews were first priority. ... Jack was more than a pilot. Some have said he was a pilot's pilot."[8]

Skyward to Profits

Even as individuals mourned, Rowan as a company was beginning to generate good news. In 1990, Rowan posted its first profit after five consecutive years of losses, driven in large part by the aviation business and the company's search for new sources of revenue. Net income was $1.9 million on revenues of $292 million, with aviation providing 38 percent of those revenues. Rowan poured nearly 60 percent of its capital expenditures for the year into aviation equipment, for, as Palmer remarked, "We know how to feed a winner!"[9]

The company also gave employees their first general pay increase in seven years. Ready to shake off the bruises but not the lessons of the

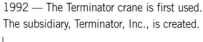

1992 — The Terminator crane is first used. The subsidiary, Terminator, Inc., is created.

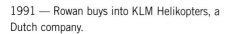

1991 — Rowan buys into KLM Helikopters, a Dutch company.

1993 — Rowan announces the acquisition of LeTourneau.

1980s, Palmer described Rowan as "confident and eager."[10] The *Gorilla IV* successfully drilled Shell Expro's first horizontal well in the North Sea. Horizontal drilling, which had just begun in the area, was used to drill both exploratory wells and to re-enter existing wells.

Tragedy struck again when Era President David L. Baumeister died on February 14, 1991, from cancer. The 46-year-old Baumeister, who was also a Rowan vice president, had joined ERA in 1974 as assistant operations director. Baumeister, like Charlie Rowan, was noted for his ability to

Rig No. 31 in Venezuela. The rig was part of a joint venture with a local company.

motivate others. Former Era President Carl Brady remembered that Baumeister "had a remarkable leadership ability. People who worked with him liked him. He had very good judgment. He had tenacity. He had 100-percent devotion to the company."[11] Wilbur D. O'Brien became Era's president, and following his retirement in late 1993, Chuck Johnson would be promoted from executive vice president to president.

While the aviation segment continued to attract new business, Rowan's six arctic land rigs in Alaska and its nine deep-well rigs in western Texas and Oklahoma remained idle, but Rowan landed a three-year contract in early 1991 to send five rigs to northeast Venezuela. The three smaller rigs were truck-mounted Cabot 900 rigs designed for mobility. They went to the Orinoco Basin to drill for heavy crude, while two larger rigs explored for medium-weight crude oil in the Furrial Trend, west of Maturin, in Venezuela.[12]

Rowan's return to Venezuela prompted the creation of a new joint venture called Rowan Drilling de Venezuela, C.A. Its three U.S. directors included Rowan vice presidents Paul Kelly, Danny McNease and Robert Croyle. Kelly, the former managing director of British American Offshore in the U.K., noted that "because of environmental reactionism in the U.S. Congress, domestic drilling is getting harder to do. A natural trend in our energy policy is to look for stable, foreign sources of oil in this hemisphere."[13]

After 23 years in the Post Oak Tower, Rowan in 1991 moved its corporate headquarters to the nearby 64-story Transco Tower, the tallest in the area. Rowan, with its reception area on the 54th floor, occupied a little more than two floors of the column-like black building.

The next year, Rowan announced that it would increase the number of scholarships awarded to children of employees from six to 10. The company also increased the value of the annual scholarship to $2,000. The *Grapevine*, in looking back over 37 years of the program, noted that 140 children of Rowan employees had received the scholar-

In 1991, Rowan purchased an interest in KLM Helikopters B.V., a subsidiary of KLM Royal Dutch Airlines.

ships. One of them was Bill Person, who in 1992 was a managing director of British American Offshore, Ltd.[14] Sharon Abbott, Rowan's first employee scholarship recipient, had become a special education teacher and activities coordinator at the Gillis W. Long Hansen's Disease Center, a noted leprosy hospital in Louisiana.

Era & KLM

In keeping with its increased focus on aviation, Rowan announced in 1991 that it was buying a 49 percent interest in KLM Helikopters B.V., a subsidiary of KLM Royal Dutch Airlines. The agreement provided for close cooperation between KLM and Era with the aim of not only strengthening KLM in its home market but also of international expansion for both companies. KLM, with headquarters in Amsterdam, the Netherlands, operated 12 aircraft consisting of seven Sikorsky S-61N and five Sikorsky S-76B helicopters. The helicopters principally served offshore platforms in the Dutch sector of the North Sea.

The $26 million initiative to buy a piece of KLM reinforced Era's position in the Rowan hierarchy. Palmer noted in a speech that his "heart is in the drilling business," and that "someday soon, I hope to tell exciting stories about drilling rig investments. But for now, those noisy, fuel guzzling,

vibrating, high-maintenance flying machines are the object of my affection. Era has been in the helicopter business 44 years and has made money 43 of those years. What else can I say?"[15] The joint venture, deploying Era equipment, expanded into Yugoslavia and Italy.

In the summer of 1991, Era sent two helicopters and an Alaska-based crew to Russia to support oil exploration and development. Era worked on Sakhalin, a 29,000-square-mile island off the east coast of Siberia, for Marathon Petroleum Sakhalin Ltd., which was to drill two offshore appraisal wells. Richard Larew, Era's vice president, said "conditions on Sakhalin are almost identical to Alaska and the Russians are turning to companies that have experience with offshore drilling in an arctic environment."[16] It was the first time a U.S. helicopter operator provided and flew U.S.-registered helicopters in Russia. Under the contract, Era's crew flew workers and supplies aboard its Bell 212 helicopters between the city of Okha and the offshore drilling rig.

A year later, five Alaska-based Era helicopters were flown to Croatia as part of United Nations peacekeeping and relief efforts for the embattled republic of Bosnia. In Anchorage, the helicopters were quickly painted white with U.N. markings, disassembled and flown to Amsterdam aboard a cargo plane. After test flights, the aircraft, carrying 20 Era employees and two KLM Era radio officers, flew to Zagreb, the capital of Croatia. The helicopters began ferrying U.N. personnel on briefing missions and to refugee camps. In the summer of 1993, KLM Era was the successful bidder and added two 20-passenger S-61N helicopters, staffed with Dutch crews, to work with Era's five Bell 212s already in Zagreb.

Wishing for the Long-Term

In the drilling market, however, the business was slow to increase, resulting in a $44.4 million loss on $272.2 million in revenues for 1991. Palmer noted in a 1992 speech that the cause of the current plight for drilling contractors was too much oil and not enough demand. He expected a return to profitability for Rowan, and "I assure you the long-term outlook for Rowan is exciting. I just wish the long term would hurry."[17]

To compensate, Rowan executives sought out other business niches. They created Terminator, Inc., a new subsidiary of Rowan Energy Investments, Inc., to remove abandoned platforms and perform other salvage and construction activities offshore. Rowan also patented a skid-off process that enabled workers to skid off the drilling packages of non-can-

tilevered jack-up rigs onto fixed production platforms, and drill or rework wells.

Danny McNease, Terminator's executive vice president, described it as "a way to maximize the value of some of our older rigs. Projections indicate there will be at least 1,500 platforms abandoned in the 1990s just in the Gulf of Mexico. Somebody's got to take them all down."[18]

Rowan's slot rig, the *Rowan New Orleans*, was converted, at a cost of $5 million, so it could skid a giant marine crane, rated for 550 tons. Now, the rig could not only drill but also operate as a crane barge. Terminator's first contract was with Hall-Houston Oil Company. The job called for the crane and crew to cut, plug and abandon 16 pipelines and

Above: Unloading freshly painted helicopters for the U.N. in Amsterdam in 1992.

Inset: U.N. helicopter lifts off in Holland to eventually join the international peacekeeping mission in Croatia.

Above: The *Rowan New Orleans* uses the Terminator crane on its first job in 1992.

Inset: The Terminator crane helped clear wreckage caused by Hurricane Andrew.

23 wells, as well as remove and dispose of five platforms and 14 single-well structures. After Hurricane Andrew struck in late August 1992, the *Rowan New Orleans* and Terminator crane cleared offshore structures damaged from the huge storm. It became known for working in bad weather, for "when the seas get rough and crane barges shut down, the Terminator offshore crane keeps going."[19]

In March 1991, the *Gorilla III* had left the Gulf for a site in the North Atlantic 160 miles off Nova Scotia near Sable Island to work on a long-term drilling and production project for LASMO Nova Scotia, Ltd. and its partner, Crown Corporation-Nova Scotia Resources, Ltd. There, in about 145 feet of water in June 1992, the Gorilla, as related by the *Grapevine*, "provided Canada's first offshore oil production and — in a first for our industry — began the first dual drilling-production operation on a jackup in a harsh environment."[20] The rig's production facilities, operated and maintained by LASMO employees, could process 40,000 barrels of a light, high-quality oil called Scotia Light each day and drill at the same time. Once processed, the oil was pumped to a storage supertanker and later transferred to a shuttle tanker that would take it to market.

New Customers

The drive for new customers also led Rowan away from its historical focus on oil. In late 1992, a surge in natural gas discovery in the Gulf of Mexico prompted Rowan to move the cantilever jack-up rig, the *Charles Rowan,* and the slot jack-up rig, *Rowan Juneau,* from the North Sea to the Gulf. Palmer told office employees, "I see a light at the end of a tunnel and it's not a freight train. It's the flicker of natural gas."[21] Indeed, by early 1994, more than 80 percent of Rowan's offshore rigs would be drilling for gas.[22] Rowan closed its Southeast Asia offices and moved its barge rigs, *Rowan Morgan City* and *Rowan Fairbanks,* to the Gulf. The *Gilbert Rowe* already had been moved from Singapore to Alaska's Cook Inlet, where it began drilling for ARCO in the summer of 1993.

Rowan also found new customers in the many independent companies now operating in the Gulf. Major oil companies had virtually ceased exploration work but numerous independents had

cropped up because of government procedures that allowed them to farm-in on existing offshore leases. Palmer, in a 1993 speech, said that:

> *"The problem with these new customers is that many are short of two vital ingredients, expertise and money; but they were long on ideas and guts. In due course, we have developed a program that can assist with the first problem. ... Last year, Rowan started a program of Total Project Management by becoming the General Contractor for the planning, drilling and completion of wells in the Gulf of Mexico. Utilizing Rowan rigs and personnel, we are offering fixed-price contracts for the first time in over 20 years."[23]*

That year, under the new program, Rowan drilled 13 turnkey wells. The group was involved in 28 projects, 26 of which were turnkey drilling wells, that produced $90 million in revenues.[24] Rowan drilled its first turnkey well in the North Sea within a year.

The *Rowan Juneau* at work in the Gulf of Mexico.

Above: The external tanks added flight time and space for personnel.

Inset: Soldiers from the Arkansas National Guard check the fit of an Era external fuel system.

In 1993, Era Aviation Services, an Era division, won a major contract with the U.S. Army Reserve and Army National Guard for External Auxiliary Fuel Systems. The fuel systems were to be produced at Era Aviation's facility in Lake Charles. The 140-gallon fuel system added 1½ hours of flight endurance, while retaining cabin space for passengers or cargo. Era Aviation, over a three-year period, was to deliver 53 sets of external auxiliary fuel tanks and 75 airframe kits. The tanks could be removed, replaced or swapped between aircraft as needed.[25] The first helicopter with the fuel system was presented to the Louisiana National Guard.

In 1993, the company recorded a loss of $13 million on $353 million in revenues, something of an improvement as compared to a $74 million loss on $250 million in revenues the year before.

Buying LeTourneau

Things were clearly turning for the better when, in November 1993, Rowan announced it was buying the long-time builder of its jackups, Marathon-LeTourneau Company, for $52 million. Under terms of the agreement, Rowan paid $10.4 million in cash and the balance through promissory notes due in five years. Marathon-LeTourneau, a subsidiary of Highland Park, Kentucky-based General Cable Corporation, had more than $95 million in revenues in 1993.

Marathon-LeTourneau, based in Longview, Texas, had three major product lines: a steel mill that recycled scrap and produced alloy steel and steel plate; a manufacturing shop that manufactured huge heavy equipment for the mining and timber industries; and a marine division that built more than one-third of all mobile offshore jack-up drilling rigs, including all 20 of Rowan's jackups. It had not, however, built a jackup in years.

The idea to buy LeTourneau originated completely from Palmer, according to General Counsel John Buvens. "At the time we bought it, nobody was talking about building any drilling rigs, but he always has his own vision," Buvens said.[26]

The announcement took the industry by surprise. William Provine, son of retired Rowan President Cecil Provine, and head of Rowan's investor relations and international marketing, recalled in a 1997 interview that "Everybody said, 'What in the hell is this drilling contractor doing buying a company that has a steel mill and makes mining equipment? ... Boy, we got some really bad press. Our stock went down, but it's turned out that it's been a stroke of genius."[27]

No one was more thrilled than LeTourneau itself. Jack McElroy, LeTourneau's vice president of finance, said, "It was almost miraculous that Rowan came along. It was a company that we knew. ... It meant that the marine part of our business, which was such a rich tradition, would continue."[28] Ronnie Neihaus, whose father and son had both worked for LeTourneau, was the logistics coordinator at LeTourneau's Vicksburg plant. He said in a 1998 interview that "the best thing that happened to LeTourneau in the last few years was when Rowan purchased us. Rowan is known worldwide to be a fair company, a good company. They take care of their people."[29]

It was a smooth acquisition according to most involved, with some humorous instances. Ed Thiele, Rowan's vice president of finance at the time

of the acquisition, remembered that when Rowan's team went over LeTourneau's books, they turned up assets that LeTourneau management wasn't aware the company owned.

"One that came to light was part ownership in a country club. It wasn't on the books. Apparently, they performed some services like grading work for the country club, and took partial ownership instead of getting paid. Years after we closed the transaction, we found that we had that asset because somebody wanted to buy it. But while we were in the process of closing the sale, well, it burned. Anyway, the sale went through and the guy got the insurance money to rebuild it. So he probably came out ahead."[30]

Dan Eckermann, LeTourneau's president and CEO, described LeTourneau as a maverick builder of unique machines powered by electromechanical drive. "They're all very large. They're all off-road. They're all, in their own way, in harsh environments. The jackups perform in ... big waves, big currents, big winds. There is no textbook that you can go to, to design those kind of things, because they're so rare."[31] He said the company is the only one in the world that does turnkey jack-up rig from design and construction through servicing and support.

Eckermann said that at LeTourneau's Longview plant, "there may not be another place on the face

LeTourneau's base of operations in Longview, Texas.

of the earth, where you will see scrap steel being put into a pot and melted, and then you'll follow it through the process and see a finished product drive out the back door."[32] But the company was beginning to look at outsourcing those items it could get at lower costs.

"LeTourneau has a capability brochure that has a title on it, and it says 'Yes, we can.' This organization has a tremendous can-do attitude. I mean unmatched can-do attitude, and most presidents and CEOs yearn for that can-do attitude. ... We're glad we have it, and I want to keep it. So what's the 'but?' The 'but' is we've learned there's another part of that you should ask, 'Can you do it,' and if the answer is 'Yes,' you should then ask the next question: 'Should we do it?' ... It's not realistic to be able to manufacture everything for everybody all the time and expect to do that well."[33]

A Mover of Mountains

The company was founded by R.G. LeTourneau, an inventor, industrialist and self-described Christian businessman. His uncle, Albert W. Lorimer, wrote a book that encompassed R.G.'s spirituality and working experience in the title and subtitles: *God Runs My Business: The Story of R.G. LeTourneau: Farmhand, Foundry Apprentice, Master Molder, Garage Mechanic, Laborer, Inventor, Manufacturer, Industrialist, Christian Business Man, and Lay Evangelist.*

He described his nephew as "a man's man — big and husky, hale and hearty. He has the bluffness of the outdoors and the roughness of the shop about him. Coat off, sleeves rolled up, hat pushed back, he thoroughly enjoys his physical tasks. He likes to get around and know people."[34]

Born in 1888, R.G. was similar to Arch Rowan in that he was a self-educated man. He never made it past the seventh grade, ending his formal education at 14 when he was already 6 feet tall. He loved moving the earth with big machines, and when he died in 1969, he held more than 250 U.S. patents. His son, Richard, professor emeritus of LeTourneau University and former chief executive officer of R.G. LeTourneau Inc., would say that "if there was ever a 'father' or pioneer of modern day earthmoving

R.G. LeTourneau described himself as a "Christian businessman." He was also an inventor and industrialist.

equipment, it was my own father, Mr. Robert G. LeTourneau."[35]

In his 1960 autobiography, *R.G. LeTourneau: Mover of Men and Mountains*, R.G. LeTourneau wrote, that "as a mechanic, I like my machinery because I learned early that man is worth what man produces, and good machines help him produce more. [I] built an eight-wheeled digger that out-produces the work of thousands of men at the time I was born."[36] Regarding his company, he pronounced it "unique in that we never use a bolt where a weld will do."[37] He believed there were "no big jobs; only small machines."[38]

In an article after his death at the age of 80, *Roads and Streets* magazine noted that "in building his company, LeTourneau made and lost several fortunes.

"Rather than being discouraged by loss, he was spurred to greater innovation, and his successes far outweighed his losses. Hitting on a popular earth scraper design, he built factories in Stockton, California; Peoria, Illinois; Toccoa, Georgia; and Vicksburg, Mississippi. In 1946, he built the plant at Longview, Texas."[39]

It was just a short hike down the street from the Longview plant that he and his wife, Evelyn, began LeTourneau University.

LeTourneau and his company were responsible for many industry firsts including the electric-wheel drive system, rubber tires on heavy equipment, fork lifts that could unload up to 50 tons of logs from a truck with one bite, portable bridges and the electrically controlled Tournapull, a two-wheel tow unit.[40] During World War II, the company also built machines for the military.

"LeTourneau and his employees shipped, from Pearl Harbor to V-J Day, 28,600 different powerful earth-moving machines. The military said one of LeTourneau's bulldozers, alone, in World War

Above: A D5 tractor in Italy in 1943. *(Photo courtesy of LeTourneau University.)*

Left: R.G. LeTourneau with rubber tires. LeTourneau was among the first to put rubber tires on heavy earth-moving machinery. *(Photo courtesy of LeTourneau University.)*

II did the work that 1,000 men with shovels accomplished in World War I. On D-Day in Europe and on Pacific Islands, the LeTourneau dozers destroyed tank traps, diverted machine gun bullets and stormed pill boxes."[41]

During the Vietnam War, LeTourneau added two domed buildings at his Longview plant for a bomb assembly line and produced 2.3 million bombs for the military between 1965 and 1973.[42]

Erwin LaBaume, who went to work for LeTourneau in 1950, said R.G. was a "great believer in making his own equipment as opposed to buying it from a manufacturer. At one time, he made just about everything we used, including brass, steel and aluminum hex-head cap screws."[43] Price Stratton, who began as a welder for LeTourneau in 1947, said R.G. "never wanted

Above: The Tournavista Evangelical Church in Peru, a missionary and development center. *(Photo courtesy of LeTourneau University.)*

Right: Price Stratton shows off his catch.

to build two machines alike. By the time we'd get one developed, he'd have an upgrade for it."[44]

Stratton, who referred to R.G. as "Pop," also spent time in the 1950s at Tournavista, R.G.'s missionary and development venture at the headwaters of the Amazon River in Peru. He remembered the crew there killing a 7-foot long anaconda with a 40-foot pole. "About a year later, I brought a 16½-foot anaconda back to the house alive. (R.G.) said, 'You got no sense, Price.' I said, 'Well, I wanted the skin.' I had to laugh. I told him, 'One thing about it, Pop, I didn't have no 40-foot pole to get it with.'"[45] He had hit the 115-pound snake with a stick as it waited in the river for an alligator and then dragged it from the water.

R.G. knew how to work. Bart McCoy, who later headed LeTourneau's Operation Improvement Group, said that R.G. "would come to work at seven every morning. He would go home at noon for an hour. He would come back at one, and work to five, then go home for two hours. He'd come back from 7 o'clock to 9 o'clock."[46] He did a lot of his conceptual work on the weekends, McCoy recalled, and "it was not uncommon for him to come in on a Monday morning and have a new idea. He might come and say, 'Bart, get out a clean piece of paper.'"[47]

Jim Golden, who worked more than 45 years for LeTourneau, described R.G. as a stern taskmaster.

"If you were a 'yes' man and you nodded your head at everything he said, you'd last two or three months. ... He wouldn't have men working around him that agreed with everything he did. So you had

to learn to argue with him . ... He was ready to quarrel over how to engineer something. He figured a good quarrel would improve what he was doing."[48]

Golden recalled a time in 1962, when the company was in financial trouble, that "the only telephone that had a listing as R.G. LeTourneau Incorporated was a pay phone, and that phone was in R.G.'s office. ... So when the phone would ring, he would answer it, and if he wanted to make an outside call, he had to put a 10-cent coin in that phone just like anybody else. I mean it got that bad, and he set there on that phone for the whole month of February in 1962 and kept his creditors off his back. Then along came a company ... and they made a deal with R.G." to build a drilling rig in Vicksburg.[49]

A *Scorpion* at Sea

Some years before, LeTourneau recounted in his autobiography how he got the idea that led to the creation of the three-legged jack-up rig, the *Scorpion*, which he began to build in 1954. He and his engineers took what they knew about heavy equipment and sought out information on hurricane winds and tidal waves.

"In the end, after building scale models and loading them to the breaking point, we were not much better off than the little boy who told his father, 'I guess I won't go to school today.' 'Guess again, son,' replied the father.'" ... We sounded out some oil companies drilling offshore and got this answer: 'Go ahead and build it. If it works, come see us again.'"[50]

The cost, though, for LeTourneau to build the platform, with no guarantee of success, was $3 million.

LeTourneau and Zapata Off-Shore Company, headed by future U.S. President George Bush, joined together in the risky birth of jack-up rigs.

ZAPATA OFF-SHORE CO.
HOUSTON, TEXAS

You are Cordially Invited . . .

... to the Christening of Zapata Off-Shore Company's Drill Barge SCORPION Tuesday, March 20, 1956 Pier 12 Galveston, Texas

George H. W. Bush
President
Wayne H. Dean
Vice President

"Drilling Ahead"

R.S.V.P. 2218 City National Bank Building

Invitation to christening of the *Scorpion*, a joint venture between LeTourneau and Zapata, which was headed by future president George Bush. *(Photo courtesy of LeTourneau University.)*

Bush described LeTourneau in his autobiography, *Looking Forward*.

> *"A kind of George Patton of engineering. ... He'd come to us with a proposition: he'd build the Scorpion at his own expense. We'd advance him $400,000 — refundable if the completed rig didn't work; if it did, he'd get an added $550,000 and 38,000 shares of Zapata Off-shore common stock. Our feeling was that any-body who had that much confidence in himself was worth the gamble."[51]*

LeTourneau wrote that "we made a deal that I believe is unique for untested equipment running into so many million dollars."[52]

The three-legged *Scorpion*, christened in New Orleans, was outfitted in Galveston. In its initial attempt, Bush wrote, the 9-million-pound rig "didn't work — at least, not at first. Put out to sea on its first assignment, the *Scorpion*'s jacking system failed and the Gulf saltwater got into its gear boxes."[53] LeTourneau, though, was unfazed. Bush wrote that "LeTourneau didn't go back to the drawing board, he came over to the deck itself. We watched incredulously as he looked at his monster's legs, then at the rack-and-pinion gears. Then right there on the steel deck, he pulled out some chalk and sketched the changes that had to be made. No engineer's drawings, not even a slide rule. But it worked."[54]

The rig drilled its first well for Standard Oil Company of Texas and then moved to other locations. Author Philip G. Gowenlock, in his book on LeTourneau equipment and company history, wrote that the "*Scorpion* set a world record for relocation of a drilling rig when, in June 1956, the platform was moved off one well location, towed approximately one mile, and commenced drilling a new well — all within 8½ hours. In comparison with other types of offshore platforms, which required a spud penetration depth of up to 100 feet, the LeTourneau platforms were capable

R.G. LeTourneau and George Bush. Bush described LeTourneau as a "George Patton of engineering." The man in the dark suit is Dick LeTourneau, R.G.'s nephew and president of LeTourneau in the late sixties and early seventies. *(Photo courtesy of LeTourneau University.)*

of stabilizing within 5 to 7 feet of penetration of the sea floor."[55]

Nearly 40 years after construction began on the *Scorpion*, Rowan saw its purchase of LeTourneau as important to its drilling future. Palmer wrote to stockholders that while Rowan's offshore rigs were "adequate for any of today's challenges ... the demands of changing technology, customer requirements and regulatory compliance will eventually make obsolete the most perfect of our designs. Our recent acquisition ... of Marathon LeTourneau will ensure that Rowan remains in the forefront of the offshore drilling industry."[56]

The *Rowan Midland* semisubmersible rig joined the *Gorilla II* in the search for oil in the Gulf of Mexico.

CHAPTER ELEVEN

A FEEL FOR THE DEAL

1993–1998

"We have drilled a helluva lot of holes in the ground, which in the final analysis, is why we have survived. Our customers like the way we perform."

— Bob Palmer, 1997[1]

ROWAN'S HISTORY IS STUDDED with examples of the drive to do things on a grand scale, from building an entire fleet of mammoth offshore oil rigs to spending millions of dollars just to keep its workforce employed.

These are not the traits of a corporation driven only by the bottom line. Rowan's business ethos is dictated by the company's deeply ingrained sense of integrity and loyalty. Its strength has lay always in the company's willingness to pursue a contract anywhere, and branch out into related businesses that fit and fall within Rowan's expertise. "It's for sure a 'can do' company," said Corporate Secretary Mark Hay. "The founders were the kind of people who were very innovative, and they came up with a lot of neat ideas in the early stages of the business. Their attitude created an atmosphere for everybody to be creative."[2]

After almost 14 years of struggle, it was all the more satisfying when the turnaround that had begun in the early 1990s finally arrived in full force. Rowan anticipated the future with the acquisition of LeTourneau, completed in early 1994. According to William C. Provine, Rowan's vice president of investor relations and son of Cecil Provine. "The reason Rowan bought LeTourneau was not that we wanted to get into the steel or manufacturing business. We bought this company to give us an option on the future, to build new, innovative drilling rigs."[3]

Rowan continued to move and upgrade existing rigs, such as the 10-year-old *Gorilla II*, which received longer legs to drill in deeper waters. At the Sabine Pass yard in Texas, sections were added that gave the rig, when raised, a record air-gap of 429 feet. With its 605 feet of legs, the *Gorilla II* settled into its first location in "397 feet of water, probably a record depth for jack-up rigs in the Gulf of Mexico."[4] It had just returned from the North Sea to the Gulf, joined by Rowan's semisubmersible rig, the *Rowan Midland*.

LeTourneau's Mega-Machines

LeTourneau was known for more than building among the best offshore rigs in the world. The subsidiary produced and sold the largest wheel loader ever operated. The L-1800, with a 50-ton capacity, was LeTourneau's latest generation wheel loader, used for mining and quarry work in among the harshest operating conditions. It was one of the first new products to be marketed after Rowan's acquisition of the company. LeTourneau was the first and only company to design, build and install individual-drive electric motors inside the huge wheels.

Welding work on LeTourneau's pipeline in Vicksburg.

LeTourneau's powerful and huge L-1800 loader. Each wheel contains an electric motor, an industry first.

1993 — The L-1800 is introduced.

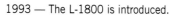

1995 — Era buys assets of Alaska Helicopters.

1994 — Rowan buys yard at Sabine Pass, Texas and sold three submersible rigs.

"This means no power-robbing drive shafts, transmissions or gear-shifting to distract the operator — instead, only variable electric power and control, coupled with full hydraulic power."[5]

LeTourneau began building an electric-drive loader in 1967, matched with a 12-cylinder diesel L-500. For the later L-700, the *Grapevine* disclosed that R.G. LeTourneau had Goodyear create a 39-inch tire mold, "so the loader could have the proper-sized rubber under foot. 'Goodyear was reluctant to build 39-inch tires because they were not sure equipment of this size would sell,' reports John McDonald, LeTourneau application engineer."[6] LeTourneau used the mold to build its own huge tires. Ed Thiele, chief financial officer, remembered the first time he saw the giant machine he was "thinking like an accountant, not an engineer."

"The thing that fascinated me the most was the size of the equipment. It's basically a 50-yard scoop on the big one, and when you stand in it, you can put 10 to 12 people in the bucket, and there's still a lot of room around the edges. When you look in the tires, you have to kind of stretch to see inside the wheel well and the sidewall of the

tire is about eight inches thick. It's kind of staggering when you see that."[7]

The first L-1800 went to work at a coal mine in Wyoming's Power River Basin. The monstrous 33-cubic-yard machine, with a 2,000-horsepower diesel engine, could lift 100,000 pounds and featured a dump height of 23½ feet. At the mine, it worked two 12-hour shifts every day, loading coal and digging overburden. Its maximum speed was a dizzying 11 miles an hour. The 45-cubic-yard bucket could fill up in as little as 38 seconds. McDonald described the L-1800 as a "surprisingly nimble machine."[8] Each 13-foot diameter tire cost about $25,000.[9]

The L-1800 joined more than 300 of LeTourneau's large electric wheel-loaders working around the world. Dan Eckermann, LeTourneau's president and CEO, said that the company had sold about 20 L-1800s (with a price tag of about $3 million each) as of March 1998. The machine has proven itself and "it's moving very well in diversified applications," Eckermann said.

"We have it in copper. We have it in gold. We have it in coal. We have it in iron ore ... and we have it all over North America, including Canada.

1997 — The *Gorilla II* is selected to drill for the Sable Offshore Energy Project.

September 1995 — Work begins on the *Gorilla V*, requiring the reopening of LeTourneau's Vicksburg yard.

1997 – Profits hit a record $147 million.

We have it in South America, including Chile, Brazil and Argentina, and we have it in Australia, and we have it in Europe."[10]

Era Overseas

Era expanded its international operations by signing a $17 million, three-year contract, to work in the South China Sea. Working as a subcontractor to China Southern Airlines Zhuhai Helicopter Company, Era provided four pilots, one Super Puma Helicopter and maintenance for the first year. In the second year, it added a second Super Puma and crew. Era flew equipment, supplies and passengers between Shenzhen, China, and Amoco Orient

Petroleum Company's offshore oil production platform. Bryan Blixhavn, Era's vice president of marketing, said, "this is the first time a U.S.-based helicopter company has landed a Super Puma contract in China."[11]

The company also bought the assets of Alaska Helicopters, Inc. for $11 million in 1995, including hangar and office space at Anchorage International Airport and 17 Bell helicopters.[12] The purchase was a strategic move to consolidate the Alaskan helicopter business similar to those undertaken in the sixties and seventies with the Merric, Wein and Livingston.

Like its parent company, Era was diversifying. When the decade began, nearly all of Era's revenues were derived from the oil and gas business. By 1993, however, that industry would account for only 30 percent of its business, said Rowan Vice President William Provine.

Air crews inspect an Era Super Puma in China.

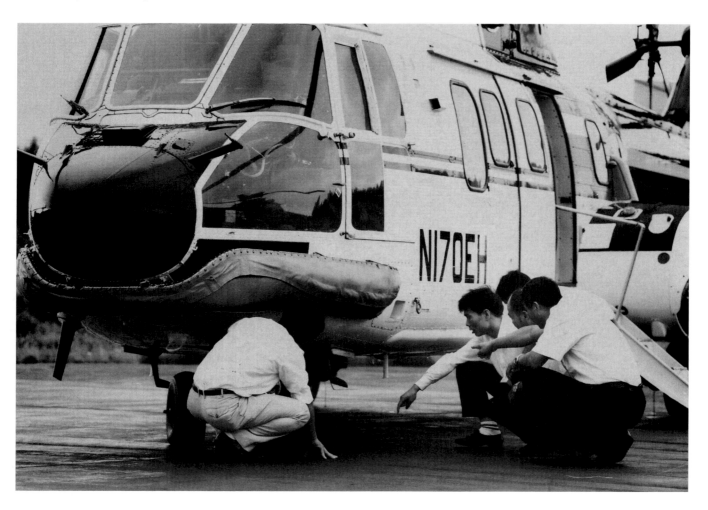

Above: An Era helicopter is ready for service as part of the air ambulance program at Anchorage's Providence Hospital.

Right: Era Classic Airllines' DC-3 Skyliners, the *Spirit of Alaska* (white) and the *Spirit of the North* (silver).

"We are flying tourists in Alaska to Mount McKinley, the glaciers and the Juneau area. In 1994 we carried 34,000 passengers, a 15 percent increase over 1993. We had 25 helicopters fighting forest fires in California. We are providing medivac services in Alaska, and we have manufactured external fuel tanks for the Army and Air National Guard."[13]

The company also founded Era Classic Airlines, a 1940s-style sightseeing charter service on two Douglas DC-3 Skyliners. Mike Doebler, pilot for Classic Airlines, started flying for Era in 1994. "When I came to Era, I thought, boy, I used to fly a DC-3 and that is the one thing I regret leaving," Doebler said. "I probably will never get another chance to fly a DC-3, and then these showed up."[14]

Those flying the tours were greeted by crew members wearing 1940-style uniforms, serenaded by Big Band music and surrounded by period decor. Both Era Classic aircraft were modified with large picture windows, so each of the 28 passengers was provided enhanced views of the Alaskan landscape. The *Grapevine* noted that "in contrast to the original 1940s editions, the aircraft have up-to-date instruments, including color radar, navigational equipment and radio communications. That way, Era ensures '90s safety for travelers enjoying the '40s atmosphere."[15]

The planes, the *Spirit of the North* and the *Spirit of Alaska*, were originally military

Above: Crews serving aboard Era Classic Airlines wear uniforms from the 1940s to add authenticity to the excursion. Background image: Mount McKinley. *(Photos by Karine Rodengen.)*

aircraft. As part of Era Classic Airlines, they began making twice daily flights from Anchorage to Mount McKinley and Prince William Sound between May and September. Era President Chuck Johnson said the idea for Era Classic Airlines was prompted by changing market conditions. "We were primarily an oilfield service company. But as things changed, our market shifted, and now our tourism revenues exceed our oilfield revenues in Alaska," he said.[16]

Era later added Alaskan adventure trips called heli-hiking tours, designed for those who did not just want to fly over but also wanted to get their feet on the ground. The heli-hiking tours included helicopter drop-off and pick-up, a guide, snacks, water bottles and outdoor gear. The tours were offered in Denali National Park and Valdez. In the park, tourists could view Mount McKinley and Mount Deborah and also look for caribou, moose and birds. In Valdez, there also was wildlife, along with views of glaciers, alpine lakes and waterfalls.

The tour in Juneau included flights over gold mines, mountains, alpine lakes, blue glaciers and the Juneau Icefield. An option on the Juneau tour was for a sled dog ride with Iditarod Trail Sled Dog Race veteran Libby Riddles, the event's first female champion in 1985. As an Era newsletter noted, "Where else can you hike on a glacier, soar over

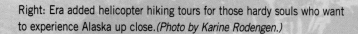

Right: Era added helicopter hiking tours for those hardy souls who want to experience Alaska up close. (Photo by Karine Rodengen.)

Rowan's Sabine Pass yard provided 20,000 square feet of office space and 30 acres of yard, dock, parking space and helipads.

majestic mountains, ride on a dog sled through snow fields in the summer and meet ... Libby Riddles, all within the stretch of two hours?"[17] Dennis McDonnell, Era's director of tourism, sales and marketing, said that those taking the hiking/flying tours were "the baby boomers who are a little more adventurous than sightseers in the past."[18]

In late 1994, the company bought the riverside yard at Sabine Pass, Texas. The purchase provided 20,000 square feet of office space and 30 acres of yard, dock, parking and helipads. The huge Terminator crane was put to work there, and some of the office space was rented to commercial tenants. In 1995, Richard Fornea, chief of the Sabine Pass yard, said the facility was "paying for itself. We've done rig-ups, rig-downs, two leg-ups on Gorilla rigs, and shipyard repair."[19] LeTourneau used the site for some jobs, while Era staged helicopter operations from it.

Rowan shed some equipment as well, selling off three submersible barge rigs, the *Rowan Fourchon*, the *Rowan Morgan City* and the *Rowan Fairbanks* for $12 million to Falcon Drilling Company.[20]

The Gorilla Fleet

After almost a decade since delivery of the mammoth *Gorilla IV* in 1986, Rowan announced plans for the world's largest bottom-supported offshore unit, the $175 million *Gorilla V*. Palmer said that once completed in 1998, the *Gorilla V* would be the most competitive jack-up rig in the North Sea and the only one that could work in 400 feet of water. At the time, all Gorilla-class rigs enjoyed 100 percent utilization. When the *Gorilla V* arrives in the North Sea, Mike Marcom, who runs the North Sea operation from Rowan's London office, said the rig will be staffed by existing Rowanites.

"We have a philosophy on the employee front of not laying people off. So we tend to have employees that have been on the rig for a good while, and they tend to come over with the rig. Those guys will keep the other four rigs functioning, and when what we do is borrow permanently some of the hands from the other rigs to make up that leg force so we can get experienced crews."[21]

The *Gorilla V* in under construction during the summer of 1997 (top photos) and under tow in July 1998 (above).

The only risk was the volatility of oil and gas prices, but Palmer said that "after 72 years of surviving and sometimes prospering in this crazy business, we are confident we possess the ability to deal with whatever problems may arise. The final issue is one of timing — Why now? All we can offer by way of explanation is a feel for the deal."[22]

The construction of *Gorilla V* meant the reopening of LeTourneau's Vicksburg yard for full-scale rig

work, a most happy occasion. The yard had closed in August 1992, 50 years after R.G. LeTourneau opened it to build equipment for World War II. When it closed, the company was forced to sell the equipment in the machine shop at auction. Only a few employees, including a maintenance man, remained at the site during those quiet years. However, with the reopening, several long-time employees returned. Don Cross, vice president of the yard, said that "the first 12 people that were hired back in here had a 29-year per man average with this company in this yard."[23]

Groundbreaking for the $20 million refurbishing project occurred on September 26, 1995, at the yard 10 miles south of downtown Vicksburg. Mississippi Governor Kirk Fordice, who spoke at the ceremony, said "one Gorilla leads to another and each is greater than the last."[24]

Compared to the *Gorilla IV* (with 504-foot-long legs), the *Gorilla V* was designed with 562½-foot legs that were triangular shaped, replacing the square-truss type, for even better durability and jacking efficiency. It has quarters for 120 workers, whereas *Gorilla IV* can handle 86 workers. *Gorilla IV*'s hull was 297 feet long, 292 feet wide and 30 feet deep. The *Gorilla V* was designed to be 306 feet long, 300 feet wide and 36 feet deep. *Gorilla V* is also able to both drill and produce wells at the same time. Rowan Senior Vice President Paul Kelly described the *Gorilla V* as "not just another jack-up rig to replace one retiring from the fleet. What we are talking about is a seriously new and improved product."[25]

Besides its toughness, *Gorilla V* was built with enhanced hoisting capacity and greater automation. Robert Rimlinger, who works for Rowan as the rig's project manager, said that "most jack-up rigs are normally rated for one and a quarter million pounds to a million and a half pounds, and we can pick up two million pounds. ... We've also got some automated pipe handling and racking systems. You're not standing up as we've had in the past and operating the drilling equipment. You're actually sitting down in a chair with joystick controls and switches."[26]

The *Gorilla IV* under dry tow to the North Sea.

As of March 1998, with work coming to an end on *Gorilla V*, the yard employed about 750 full-time workers and about 200 contract laborers. The shipyard was "once again a beehive of activity."[27] The *Gorilla V* also meant more work at the Longview plant. Rudy Harris, vice president of operations in Longview, said that much of the steel going into the 54 million pound rig "comes from our mill. All of the gear units that raise the platform up and down, we design and build here. ... The cranes that are on board the rig were built here. Anchor winches, all that type of thing."[28]

Edgar "Ish" Loflin reminisced just how far offshore technology had grown. Loflin was head of LeTourneau's engineering group at Vicksburg when the first jack-up rig was launched in 1956. "Our first rig was the first designed to operate in water deeper than 40 feet," he said. "We really grew."[29] The *Scorpion* was the first of 77 offshore rigs built at Vicksburg. In 1982, at the peak of its rig construction, the yard employed about 1,700 workers. LeTourneau built 92 additional rigs in Brownsville, Texas; the Republic of Singapore; Quebec; Hong Kong; and Scotland.

The Good Times Roll

The *Gorilla V* was the clearest indication of Rowan's hope that more prosperous days were on the horizon. Palmer, quoted in a 1996 article, described how Rowan had been preparing for economic reward for 14 years by keeping its employees skilled, its rigs primed and its balance sheet strong. "We are positive for the future, and we believe the future of Rowan is currently under construction. We call it *Gorilla V*."[30]

The *Gorilla V* began its journey down the Mississippi River July 20, 1998 for final outfitting and leg extensions because its full design height, like past rigs, would not fit under the river's bridges. George Cupstid, manager of the Vicksburg yard's engineering group, said that, "Historically, we've always stopped at a little town just below New Orleans called Belle Chasse for final leg erection but now that we have ownership of a dock at Sabine Pass, we want to take it to that facility and use that."[31]

Gorilla V will soon be joined by sister rigs. Construction on two similar units, the *Gorilla VI* and

Rowan once again gambled when Rowan ordered three more Gorillas. But orders arrived even before the rigs were finished.

Gorilla VII has already begun, and the units are scheduled for delivery in 2000 and 2001 respectively.

The announcement that Rowan intended to build two more Gorillas was made around the time the company announced second-quarter profits of $12.7 million, its best quarter in 13 years, with a joyful "let the good times roll" pronouncement in the company's news release.[32] By the end of the year, the company showed its first year-end profit since 1990, a healthy $61 million on $571 million in revenues. Palmer reflected Rowan's optimism for the future.

"We believe the disastrous business cycle of the recent past is over — and we have arrived at a new strategic inflection point. We are ready because we have stayed ready. Our customers are making money and, more importantly, they are beginning to increase expenditures in an

effort to add to oil and gas reserves with a drill bit. As a result of increased rig utilization and day rates, Rowan's financial performance has improved dramatically. We believe the time is right to once again focus upon an expansion of the enterprise.[33]

Since then, Rowan has ordered a third Gorilla. Speaking one morning during a corporate breakfast meeting, Palmer was more direct: "Management's job is significantly more demanding than milking the maximum cash from an aging asset base. We believe there are but two choices for a business enterprise: grow or die."[34]

The total cost of the three latest *Gorillas* is estimated at $555 million. Three leading markets for huge jackups are the Gulf of Mexico, eastern Canada where *Gorilla III* had been drilling since 1992, and the North Sea.[35]

In March 1997, Mobil Oil Canada and its partners announced that the *Gorilla II* would drill for the Sable Offshore Energy Project, which was expected to deliver a daily average of 460 million cubic feet of market-quality gas and 20,000 barrels a day of natural gas liquids. The gas fields were about 140 miles off the Novia Scotia coast, and their gas reserves were estimated at 3 trillion cubic feet. A groundbreaking ceremony for the construction phase of the project was held in early 1998.

To service exploration and production operations in the deep water sector of the Gulf of Mexico, Era introduced the newest addition to its Gulf fleet in late 1997: the 19-passenger Sikorsky S61N helicopter. It was the first of its type in the Gulf and only one of 75 S61N helicopters in the world providing commercial offshore transportation and civil search-and-rescue operations. The helicopter could fly 400 nautical miles, and with its unique boat-hull airframe, take off or land in the water. It was ideal for companies transporting personnel and supplies to drilling locations more than 150 miles off the coast. Era President Chuck Johnson said a helicopter as large as the S61N had not worked in the Gulf since the 1980s.[36]

By 1997, however, the Gulf Coast had become the largest helicopter market in the world, according to Al Meyer, who became senior vice president and manager of the Gulf Coast Division. "The way the Gulf has evolved, it started out as marshes in the fifties and then went offshore in the sixties through seventies and into the eighties," he said.

"Now in the nineties, they've started what they call deep water operations. The furthest operation we've ever supported has been 200 miles out of Fuchon, which is south of Houma, Louisiana."[37]

A Record Year

For 1997, Rowan recorded a profit of $147 million on $695 million in revenues, of which drilling accounted for 63 percent. It was the best

The Gulf of Mexico continues to be one of the three leading markets for jack-up rigs, such as the *Rowan Paris*.

Era's first Sikorsky S61N in the Gulf of Mexico lands on the *Rowan Paris* in early 1998.

year in the company's history. That included a $9.8 million charge for early debt reduction, and a $20.2 million charge to conclude its turnkey drilling operations, no longer really necessary since rigs were busy and the program had been plagued by a long-running problem well. In early 1998, Rowan ended its joint venture with KLM Era Helicopters in return for cash and equipment approximating its 49 percent interest. The equipment included two Sikorsky S-61N helicopters to be used by Era in the Gulf of Mexico.[38]

R.G. Croyle, Rowan executive vice president, said intense price competition and decreased hours flown by North Sea oil companies caused KLM Era to lose revenue and market share. "KLM decided that the helicopter business was so small and such a non-core part of their overall business strategy that they desired to get out of the helicopter business. We could not take it over because of the fact that a U.S. company is prohibited by European ... laws from owning more than 49 percent of a European aviation company."[39] Rowan looked at some possible partners but could not "work out an arrangement that we felt preserved the same relationship we had with KLM ... and so to expedite their ability to sell their

interest, we sold our interest out to KLM, and they immediately sold the entire company" to a Dutch competitor.[40]

Gorilla V already has landed a one-year contract for North Sea work. Rowan had announced in September 1997 that Amoco Corporation's U.K. exploration unit had signed a letter of intent for the rig.[41] An article published in *Offshore Engineer* in January 1998, noted that Rowan was again benefiting from the risky proposition of ordering three huge Gorilla rigs when "dayrates were barely hinting at an upward direction."

"Two years of meteoric dayrate and rig demand increases have vindicated Palmer's judgment. 'They thought we were crazy when we ordered three Gorilla rigs,' says Palmer through a broad grin. 'We figured it would require $85,000 per day to payout. We have announced a contract [for Gorilla V] *for [$67 million] of dollars that translates into about $183,000 per day. So that is a little better than break-even."[42]*

Indeed, the *Gorilla V* one-year contract was valued at $67.4 million.[43] Meanwhile, the *Gorilla II* was headed to eastern Canada on a 600-day con-

Gorilla II under dry tow from Sable Island to the North Atlantic, off the coast of Nova Scotia.

tract, while *Gorilla IV* received a one-year extension on its North Sea contract.

Rowan's land rigs were even enjoying a revival after years of hot-stacking. During 1997, seven of the company's 14 land rigs achieved an 84 percent utilization rate. All of Rowan's offshore rigs were at work, with 13 of the 21 rigs working at rates averaging $67,000 a day. Of the 608 mobile offshore drilling rigs in the world as of March 1998, 585 were under contract, 20 were out of service and only three rigs were ready and available for work.[44] It was a far cry from the tough 1980s. Paul Kelly, senior vice president, remarked on the globalization of drilling in a 1997 interview. "In just the past two years, we have had 39 countries that have never had offshore exploration before, award licenses or leases to encourage oil companies ... and gas companies to come in and explore for oil and gas in those countries."[45]

In Rowan's 75 years, it had grown from a tiny family firm with one rig to an aviation, rig construction and international drilling conglomerate with more than 5,000 employees and $1.2 billion in assets.[46] The bedrock to this success has been — and always will be — the family-like relationships that span the company, noted Paul Kelly:

"There is a strong culture of honesty and team work. ... Because we function as a team, the relationships among the management are fairly informal, and it's a company that is not bureaucratic. ... We try to keep things simple and to communicate directly with one another more than by sending memos."[47]

A quotation that appeared in Rowan's employee handbook in 1957 is still a part of the handbook today:

"If you work for a man, in heaven's name work for him; speak well of him and stand by the institution he represents. Remember an ounce of loyalty is worth a pound of cleverness. If you must growl, condemn, and eternally find fault, why, resign your position and when you are on the outside, damn to your heart's content. As long as you are part of the institution, do not condemn it. If you do, the first high wind that comes along will blow you away, and you will never know why."[48]

In a speech to the Pioneer Oil Producer Society, Palmer summed up Rowan's history and why the company will continue to thrive: "We have drilled a helluva lot of holes in the ground, which in the final analysis, is why we have survived. Our customers like the way we perform."[49]

APPENDIX

Director	Tenure as Board Chairman	Tenure as Board Member
Charles Rowan, Chairman	May 26, 1924 to June 12, 1961	May 26, 1924 to June 12, 1961
Arch Rowan, Chairman	June 12, 1961 to Oct. 24, 1969	May 26, 1924 to Jan.19, 1975
Spencer F. Rowan*		May 26, 1924 to Oct., 7, 1926
Bess Brants		Feb. 17, 1930 to March 31, 1968
F. Weldon Brigance		March 13, 1935 to Jan. 27, 1954
A.C. Allen		March 9, 1946 to Dec. 7, 1949
Gilbert Rowe, Chairman	Oct. 24, 1969 to Jan. 4, 1972	Oct. 1, 1948 to Jan. 4, 1972
Mark Hart		Oct. 1, 1948 to May 1, 1969
Elton M. Hyder, Jr.		Jan. 30, 1950 to Feb. 6, 1962
Cecil Provine		Dec. 18, 1952 to April 26, 1985
Hamilton Rogers		Jan. 27, 1954 to March 4, 1958
Arch H. Rowan, Jr.*		Jan. 26, 1955 to August 7, 1962
C.W. Yancey		Sept. 26, 1958 to April 27, 1984
J.C. Magner		March 17, 1964 to April 27, 1984
R.H. Huey		May 24, 1967 to June 30, 1970
Lawrence Cade*		June 23, 1967 to April 26, 1985
William T. Fleming*		July 28, 1967 to April 28, 1989
Carl Brady, Sr.		Oct. 25, 1968 to Oct. 31, 1984
		Oct. 23, 1987 to April 24, 1992
C.R. Palmer, Chairman	Jan. 4, 1972 to present	Jan. 24, 1969 to present
Harold Decker*		August 15, 1978 to April 25, 1986
		July 24, 1970 to April 28, 1972
Thomas G. Kelliher*		April 28, 1972 to April 27, 1979
F. Frank McCollum, Jr.*		April 28, 1972 to July 23, 1976
C.W. Yeargain		April 25, 1975 to present
Walter J. Hickel*		July 23, 1976 to Dec. 6, 1990
Robert W. Baldwin*		April 27, 1984 to April 23, 1993
J.C. Walter, Jr.*		April 27, 1984 to April 23, 1993
Kenneth E. Montague*		April 26, 1985 to April 22, 1988
Peter Simonis*		April 26, 1985 to April 25, 1997
James R. Lesch*		April 25, 1986 to April 24, 1992
Henry O. Boswell*		April 22, 1988 to present
H.E. Lentz*		April 27, 1990 to present
Charlies P. Siess, Jr.*		April 26, 1991 to present
Wilfred P. Schmoe*		April 24, 1992 to present
Ralph E. Bailey*		April 23, 1993 to present
Lord Moynihan*		April 26, 1996 to present
R.G. Croyle		Jan. 22, 1998 to present
D.F. McNease		Jan. 22, 1998 to present
Hans M. Brinkhorst*		July 14, 1998 to present

Denotes non-Rowan employee

NOTES TO SOURCES

Chapter One

1. Arch H. Rowan, 1973 interview: 3.
2. "Fifty Years of Growth," Grapevine Winter 1973: 2.
3. C.L. Rowan, "Mr. C.L. Rowan Reviews 25 Years of Contracting," Grapevine Oct.-Nov. 1948: 1-2.
4. Ibid.
5. Arch H. Rowan, 1973 interview: 1-2.
6. Charlie Rowan, "Mr. C.L. Rowan Reviews 25 Years of Contracting," Grapevine, Oct.-Nov. 1948: 2.
7. "Two Brothers and a Rig," Grapevine, Sep.-Oct. 1957: 3.
8. "Fifty Years of Growth," Grapevine, Winter 1973: 2.
9. Arch H. Rowan, 1973 interview: 2.
10. "Charter of Rowan Drilling Co.-Houston," Texas Secretary of State documents, May 10, 1924.
11. "Minutes of First Meeting of Directors," Rowan Drilling Co. Corporation Record: 2.
12. Charlie Rowan, "Mr. C.L. Rowan Reviews 25 Years of Contracting," Grapevine, Oct.-Nov. 1948: 2.
13. "Wortham Producers Usher in New Oil Boom," Houston Post-Dispatch, Nov. 28, 1924.
14. "Unusual Activity is Prevalent in Mexia," Houston Post-Dispatch, Nov. 27, 1924.
15. "Wortham Producers Usher in New Oil Boom," Houston Post-Dispatch, Nov. 28, 1924.
16. "Humble to Lay Additional 8-inch Line to Wortham," Fort Worth Star-Telegram, Dec. 3, 1924.
17. "50 Rigs to Be Drilling Soon," Houston Post-Dispatch, Nov. 29, 1924.
18. Charlie Rowan, "Mr. C.L. Rowan Reviews 25 Years of Contracting," Grapevine, Oct.-Nov. 1948: 2.
19. Carl Coke Rister, Oil! Titan of the Southwest (Norman: University of Oklahoma Press, 1949): 178.
20. Walter Rundell Jr., Early Texas Oil: A Photographic History, 1866-1936, The Montague History of Oil Ser. 1 (College Station: Texas A&M University Press, 1977): 183.
21. Charlie Rowan, "Mr. C.L. Rowan Reviews 25 Years of Contracting," Grapevine, Oct.-Nov. 1948: 2.
22. Arch H. Rowan, 1973 interview: 3.
23. "40 Years in the Same Family," Grapevine, Oct.-Nov. 1964: 3.
24. "40 Years in the Same Family," Grapevine, Oct.-Nov. 1964: 3.
25. Charlie Rowan, "Mr. C.L.Rowan Reviews 25 Years of Contracting," Grapevine, Oct.-Nov. 1948: 2.
26. Walter Rundell Jr., Early Texas Oil: A Photographic History, 1866-1936 (College Station: Texas A&M University Press, 1977): 36.
27. "Fifty Years of Growth," Grapevine Winter 1973: 3.
28. "The Rowan Oil Co.," Grapevine, Sept.-Oct. 1957: 8.
29. "Charter: Rowan Oil Co.," Texas Secretary of State documents, filed May 18, 1927.
30. "Charter: Rowan Oil Co.," Texas Secretary of State documents, filed 18 May 1927.
31. "The Rowan Oil Co.," Grapevine, Sept.-Oct. 1957: 8.
32. Arch H. Rowan, 1973 interview for 50th anniversary of Rowan: 7.
33. Cecil Provine, interviewed by the author,
34. "Oldest ??? Employee," Grapevine, March-Apr. 1949: 2.

Chapter Two

1. The Historical Committee of The Fort Worth Petroleum Club, Oil Legends of Fort Worth (Taylor Publishing Co., 1993): 193.
2. John Henry Brown, Indian Wars and Pioneers of Texas (1896; Easley, S.C.: Southern Historical Press, 1978): 519.
3. The Liverpool History Book Committee, The History of Liverpool, Texas and Its People (Houston: D. Armstrong Book Printing Co., 1996): 111.
4. Sue Rowan Pittman, interview by Joan Thompson, April 6, 1998. Transcript: 29.
5. Ibid: 1.
6. John Henry Brown, Indian Wars and Pioneers of Texas (1896; Easley, S.C.: Southern Historical Press, 1978): 519.
7. The Liverpool History Book Committee, The History of Liverpool, Texas and Its People (Houston: D. Armstrong Book Printing Co., 1996): 111.
6. Ibid.
7. John Henry Brown, Indian Wars and Pioneers of Texas (1896; Easley, S.C.: Southern Historical Press, 1978): 518.

8. Archibald Hamilton Rowan and Charles Louis Rowan Files, The Petroleum Hall of Fame Records, Midland, Texas.
9. The Historical Committee of The Fort Worth Petroleum Club, Oil Legends of Fort Worth (Taylor Publishing Co., 1993): 193.
10. C.L. Rowan, "Europe Thru an Oil Man's Eyes," Grapevine Nov.-Dec. 1949: 4.
11. Arch H. Rowan, interview, 1973: 1.
12. "Arch H. Rowan Receives One of Oil Industry's Highest Awards," Grapevine, Sept.-Oct. 1951: 10.
13. Arch H. Rowan, 1973 interview: 7-8.
14. The Historical Committee of The Fort Worth Petroleum Club, Oil Legends of Fort Worth (Taylor Publishing Co., 1993): 193.
15. Ibid.
16. Martha Rowan Hyder, interviewed by Joan Thompson, April 18, 1998. Transcript: 3.
17. "Mr. Charles Bids Us Farewell," Grapevine, May-June 1961: 2.
18. Arch Rowan, 1973 interview, 8.
19. Ibid.
20. Charles Gardner, interviewed by Joan Thompson, March 25, 1998. Transcript: 4.
21. "The Will to Fight," Grapevine, Nov.-Dec. 1962: 2.
22. "Peace Troubles His Soul," Grapevine, Spring 1975: 1.
23. Ibid.
24. Ibid.
25. The Historical Committee of The Fort Worth Petroleum Club, Oil Legends of Fort Worth (Taylor Publishing Co., 1993): 193.
26. Ibid.
27. "Peace Troubles His Soul," Grapevine, Spring 1975: 2.
28. Leroy Menzing, "Arch Rowan: He's Been Practicing Law Without a License for 25 Years," Petroleum Independent Nov.-Dec. 1973: 37.
29. James A. Creighton, A Narrative History of Brazoria County (Waco: Brazoria County Historical Commission, 1975): 305-06.
30. "Peace Troubles His Soul," Grapevine, Spring 1975: 3.
31. Sue Rowan Pittman, interviewed by Joan Thompson, April 6, 1998. Transcript, p. 27.

Chapter Two Sidebar

1. The Liverpool History Book Committee, The History of Liverpool, Texas and Its People (Houston: D. Armstrong Book Printing Co., 1996) 113.
2. Ibid.
3. Ibid.: 117.
4. Ibid.: 114.

Chapter Three

1. "Cecil Provine — 42 Years with Rowan," Grapevine ,April-June 1973: 2.
2. Walter Rundell Jr., Early Texas Oil: A Photographic History, 1866-1936 (College Station: Texas A&M University Press, 1977): 224.
3. Grapevine, Spring 1975: 2.
4. Daniel Yergin, The Prize, (New York: Simon & Shuster, 1992): 264.
5. Ibid.
6. Charlie Rowan, "Mr. C.L. Rowan Reviews 25 Years of Contracting," Grapevine, Oct.-Nov. 1948: 2.
7. Wayne Gard, The First 100 Years of Texas Oil and Gas (Dallas: Texas Mid-Continent Oil and Gas Association, 1966): 26.
8. Ibid.
9. "Charter: Rowan and Nichols Oil Company, Fort Worth, Texas," Texas Secretary of State documents, filed Sept. 8, 1930.
10. "The Rowan Oil Company," Grapevine, Sep.-Oct. 1957: 8.
11. Cecil Provine, interviewed by Joan Thompson, October 7, 1997. Transcript: 4.
12. Bess Brants, personal statement on Cecil Provine's retirement, Grapevine, April-June 1973: 4.
13. A.H. Rowan, personal statement on Cecil Provine's retirement, Grapevine, April-June 1973: 4.
14. "Lacy Boyd Doesn't Have to Imagine Our Early Days," Grapevine, Fourth Quarter, 1988: 17.
15. Ibid.
16. "Cecil Provine — 42 Years with Rowan," Grapevine, Apr.-June 1973: 2.
17. Mark L. Hart, personal statement on Cecil Provine's retirement, Grapevine, April-June 1973: 4.
18. "Rowan Oil Company, San Antonio, Texas: Application for Dissolution of Corporation," Texas Secretary of State documents, received Jan. 2, 1934.
19. "The Rowan Oil Company," Grapevine, Sep.-Oct. 1957: 8.
20. "Foreign Permit of Rowan Drilling Company, Wilmington, Del.; Fort Worth, Texas," Texas Secretary of State documents, filed April 23, 1934.

21. "Charter of Rowan Drilling Company: Certificate of Dissolution," Texas Secretary of State documents, filed April 23, 1934.
22. Grapevine, Sep.-Oct. 1949: 3.
23. "Fifty Years of Growth," Grapevine, Winter 1973: 3.
24. L.J. Hartmangruber, "Rowan Pioneers in Barge Drilling," Grapevine, Sept.-Oct. 1953: 6.
25. Ina Yancey, interviewed by Joan Thompson, March 31, 1998. Transcript: 2.
26. Ibid.
27. C.L. Rowan, "Venice Housing," Grapevine, July-Aug. 1953: 10-11.
28. "Fifty Years of Growth," Grapevine, Winter 1973: 4.
29. "Rowan Tracks," Grapevine, March-April 1966: 7.
30. Charlie Rowan, "Mr. C.L. Rowan Reviews 25 Years of Contracting," Grapevine, Oct.-Nov. 1948: 2.
31. C.A. Warner, Texas Oil and Gas Since 1543 (Houston: Gulf Publishing Co., 1939): 218.
32. F.W. Brigance, "F.W. Brigance Compliments Drilling Organization," Grapevine, Jan.-Feb. 1949: 1.
33. "Foreign Amendment: Foreign Permit of Rowan Drilling Company, Delaware," Texas Secretary of State documents, filed December 30, 1938.
34. Railroad Commission of Texas et al. v. Rowan & Nichols Oil Co., Supreme Court Reporter, vol. 60 (St. Paul, Minn.: West Publishing, 1940) 1022-23.
35. "Oil Proration: Supreme Court Rules States Have Full Power to Set Allowables," The Wall Street Journal, June 4, 1940.

Chapter Four

1. Charles Rowan, "Mr. C.L. Rowan Reviews 25 Years of Contracting," Grapevine Oct.-Nov. 1948: 3.
2. A. H. Rowan and H.E. Dralle, "Barge Mounted Diesel Electric Rigs," World Petroleum June 1941: 84.
3. Cecil Provine interview with Joan Thompson, Oct. 7, 1997. Transcript: 4.
4. Grapevine, Spring 1975: 3.
5. Daniel Yergin, The Prize, (Simon & Shuster: New York, New York, 1992): 385.
6. Arch H. Rowan, 1973 interview: 5.
7. "Statement of Assets and Receipts," Renewal Permit: Foreign Permit of Rowan Drilling Company, Delaware, Texas Secretary of State documents, filed March 17, 1944.
8. Grapevine Spring 1975: 3.
9. "Fifty Years of Leadership," Grapevine, Winter 1973: 9.
10. William Clements, Jr., interviewed by Joan Thompson, April 30, 1998. Transcript, pp. 1-2.
11. Daniel Yergin, The Prize (Simon & Shuster, New York, New York): 410-411.
12. "Announcing the Reorganization of the Rowan Drilling Company," Grapevine Oct.-Nov. 1948: 3.
13. "Rowan Oil Company Balance Sheet, Aug. 31, 1948," Application for Permit to Do Business in the State of Texas, Texas Secretary of State documents, filed 1 Oct. 1948.
14. "The Rowan Oil Company," Grapevine, Sep.-Oct. 1957: 8.
15. "Rowan Drilling Company, Inc., Balance Sheet, Aug. 31, 1948," Application for Permit to Do Business in the State of Texas, Texas Secretary of State documents, filed Oct. 1, 1948.
16. "Two Brothers and a Rig," Grapevine, Sep.-Oct. 1957: 4.
17. A. H. Rowan, "Birthday Greetings," Grapevine, Sep.-Oct. 1949: 2.
18. "Mark Hart Retires After 33 Years Service," Grapevine, June-July 1969: 6.
19. Ibid.: 7.
20. A.H. Rowan, "Mark Hart Elected Vice President of Rowan Drilling Company, Inc.," Grapevine May-June 1952: 2.
21. "From the Desk of M.G. Rowe," Grapevine , June-July 1969: 2.
22. "From the Desk of M.G. Rowe," Grapevine, June-July 1969: 2.
23. "It's Your Baby, You Name It!" Grapevine, Oct.-Nov. 1948: 1.
24. "257 Contest Entries Sent in by 85 Employees," Grapevine Nov.-Dec. 1948: 1.
25. "The Winner! Dorice Swanson of the Houston Office Wins Grand Prize in Paper Naming Contest," Grapevine, Nov.-Dec. 1948: 2.
26. Ibid.
27. Ibid.
28. "A Publication is Born," Grapevine, Oct.-Nov. 1948: 1.
29. Charles Rowan, "Mr. C.L. Rowan Reviews 25 Years of Contracting," Grapevine, Oct.-Nov. 1948: 3.
30. Ina Yancey, interviewed by Joan Thompson, March 31, 1998. Transcript: 1.
31. Ibid: 7.
32. Clayton Brants, interviewed by Alex Lieber, March 31, 1998. Transcript: 16.

33. *Ibid.*
34. Charley Wharton, interviewed by Alex Lieber, April 2, 1998. Transcript: 4.
35. *Ibid.*
36. F.W. Brigance, "F.W. Brigance Compliments Drilling Organization," *Grapevine*, Jan.-Feb. 1949: 1.
37. "The Fruits of Free Enterprise," *Grapevine*, May-June 1949: 1-2.
38. "Twenty Years in the Field for Rowan," *Grapevine*, May-June 1949: 1.
39. *Ibid.*: 2.
40. Mrs. Paul Holland, "Our Newest Baby — Rig No. 22," *Grapevine*, Nov.-Dec. 1949: 6.
41. "The 1940s," Rowan Companies, Inc. 1988 Annual Report: 6.

Chapter Five

1. "Arch Rowan Honored as 'Roughneck of 1957,'" *Grapevine*, May-June 1957: 8.
2. John A. Boatman, "Rowan's Barge Rig 13," *World Oil*, Nov. 1951: 119.
3. John A. Boatman, "Boatman's Boastings from Louisiana," *Grapevine*, May-Jun 1950: 9.
4. F.G. Anderson, "Andy's Amblings Around Venice," *Grapevine*, May-Jun 1950: 8.
5. John A. Boatman, "Boatman's Boastings From Louisiana," *Grapevine*, July-Aug. 1950: 12.
6. Heddie Rowe, interview with Joan Thompson, Nov. 6, 1997. Transcript, 20-21.
7. "Barge 'M.G. Rowe' Launched," *Grapevine*, Sep.-Oct. 1950: 12.
8. "Rowan Expands for Marine Drilling," *Grapevine*, May-June 1951: 3.
9. John A. Boatman, "Rowan's Barge Rig 13," *World Oil*, Nov. 1951: 124.
10. "Louisiana Rigs Now Outnumber W. Texas Rigs," *Grapevine* May-June 1957: 15.
11. "Rowan Offices Will Be Moved to Fair Bldg.," *Fort Worth Star-Telegram*, May 13, 1950.
12. "Rowan Occupies New Offices in Fair Building," *Grapevine* Jan.-Feb. 1951: 3.
13. *Ibid.*
14. "Notes From North Dakota," *Grapevine*, Jan.-Feb. 1952: 12.
15. "Rowan Pioneers in Winterizing Rigs," *Grapevine*, Nov.-Dec. 1952: 5.
16. Reilley Euper, interviewed by Joan Thompson, February 10, 1998. Transcript: 8.
17. "Rowan to Move into Deep Water," *Grapevine*, Nov.-Dec. 1954: 3.
18. "Shades of Robinson Crusoe," *Grapevine*, Jan.-Feb. 1955: 9.
19. C.L. Rowan, "Rowan in Retrospect — 1950," *Grapevine* Nov.-Dec. 1950: 3.
20. Charlie Rowan, "Mr. Charlie Rowan Reviews 30 Years of Contracting," *Grapevine*, Sep.-Oct. 1953: 9.
21. "Rowan Offers Pension Plan," *Grapevine* Nov.-Dec. 1952: 3.
22. *Ibid.*
23. "C.L. Rowan Introduces Vacation Plan," *Grapevine*, July-Aug. 1950: 1.
24. "Service Pin Awards to Be Made at Crew Meetings," *Grapevine*, Jan.-Feb. 1951: 2.
25. Ibid.
26. "Rowan Offers Pension Plan," *Grapevine*, Nov.-Dec. 1952: 3-4.
27. "Two Brothers and a Rig," *Grapevine*, Sept.-Oct. 1957: 5.
28. John Jackson, interviewed by Alex Lieber, April 16, 1998. Transcript: 5.
29. Mildred Rucker, interviewed by Alex Lieber, March 25, 1998. Transcript: 6-7.
30. "Co-Op. Student Chooses Rowan On Graduation," *Grapevine*, May-June 1957: 2.
31. Heddie Rowe, interview with Joan Thompson, Nov. 6, 1997. Transcript: 18.
32. "Second Generation of Management," *Grapevine*, Jan.-Feb. 1955: 2.
33. *Ibid.*
34. "Rowan Companies Make Progress," *Grapevine*, Jan.-Feb. 1955: 5.
35. "Arch H. Rowan Receives One of Oil Industry's Highest Awards," *Grapevine* Sep.-Oct. 1951: 10.
36. *Ibid.*
37. "Arch Rowan Chosen Outstanding Citizen," *Grapevine*, March-April 1956: 9.
38. Arch H. Rowan, acceptance speech for the Golden Deeds Award, April 12, 1956, transcript: 2.
39. *Ibid.*
40. "A.H. Rowan Selected As 'Outstanding Citizen,'" *Fort Worth Star-Telegram*, Feb. 22, 1956.
41. "Rowan Pleased With Results of Policy to Encourage Education," *Grapevine* Sep.-Oct. 1959: 6.
42. "Arch Rowan Honored as 'Roughneck of 1957,'" *Grapevine* May-June 1957: 8.
43. "Texas Pacific Coal Buying Rowan Oil Assets For Stock," *The Wall Street Journal*, May 28, 1958: 9.
44. "Rowan Oil Company Assets Sold to T.P. Coal & Oil Company For Stock," *Grapevine*, May-June 1958: 3-4.

45. "Rowan Oil Management Personnel Valuable Asset to T.P.C.&O.," *Grapevine*, May-June 1958: 4.
46. "Rowan Oil Company Assets Sold to T.P. Coal & Oil Company For Stock," *Grapevine*, May-June 1958: 3.
47. "Rowan Sells Assets to Texas Pacific Coal & Oil in 89,639,000 Stock Deal," *The Oil and Gas Journal*, June 2 1958: 65.
48. "When It Takes Gas to Get Gas," *Grapevine* March-April 1954: 10.
49. "Ten Years of Safe Drilling With Gas," *Grapevine*, June-July 1964: 3.
50. "Rowan Pioneers Gas Drilling in New Mississippi Area," *Grapevine*, Jan.-Feb. 1960: 7.
51. "Rowan Brings in Discovery Well in Borden County, Texas," *Grapevine*, Nov.-Dec. 1959: 6.

Chapter Five Sidebar

1. "Hadacol Corner: Spraberry Metropolis," *Grapevine*, Nov.-Dec. 1951: 4.
2. Roger M. Olien and Diana Davids Olien, *Wildcatters: Texas Independent Oilmen* (Austin: Texas Monthly Press 1984): 105.
3. Roger M. Olien and Diana Davids Olien, *Wildcatters: Texas Independent Oilmen* (Austin: Texas Monthly P, 1984): 106.
4. Leroy Menzing, "Arch Rowan: He's Been Practicing Law Without a License for 25 Years," *Petroleum Independent* Nov.-Dec. 1973: 38.
5. "Spraberry Plaintiffs Gain Permanent Injunction," The Associated Press, published in the *Fort Worth Star-Telegram* April 25, 1953.
6. "Some Exceptions: Production in Spraberry Halted Today," The Associated Press, published in the *Fort Worth Star-Telegram*, April 1, 1953.
7. "Spraberry Order Called Assault Against Waste," The Associated Press, published in the *Fort Worth Star-Telegram* April 22, 1953.
8. "Spraberry Order Void," *The Oil and Gas Journal*, June 15, 1953: 79.
9. Roger M. Olien and Diana Davids Olien, *Wildcatters: Texas Independent Oilmen* (Austin:Texas Monthly Press, 1984): 106.

Chapter Six

1. Bob Palmer, interviewed by the author, July 21, 1998. Transcript: 6.
2. Martha Rowan Hyder, interviewed by Joan Thompson, April 18, 1998. Transcript: 38.
3. "Arch H.Rowan Jr. Dies of Burns from Kerosene Blast," *Fort Worth Star-Telegram*, Aug. 7, 1962.
4. Horace Craig, "Rowan Worked to Perfect Fire Protection for Fliers," *Fort Worth Star-Telegram*, Aug. 12, 1962.
5. *Ibid.*
6. Jean Rowan McNab, interviewed by Joan Thompson, February 2, 1998. Transcript: 12.
7. "Arch Rowan Presented Honorary Degree," *Grapevine* , May-June 1962: 11.
8. "Citation of Arch H. Rowan for the Degree of Doctor of Laws," ts., News Bureau files, Bethany College, Bethany, W.Va.: 1.
9. "Indian Territory: Rowan's New Area of Operations," *Grapevine*, May-June 1962: 6-7.
10. "Executive Offices Move to Houston," *Grapevine*, Jan.-March 1963: 3.
11. "Rowan Acquires First Drilling Tender," *Grapevine*, April-May 1963: 6.
12. "Brighter Drilling Outlook for 1964," *Grapevine*, Dec.-Jan. 1964: 2.
13. "Morgan City Yard: Increasing Emphasis on Offshore Drilling," *Grapevine*, Dec.-Jan. 1964: 3.
14. "Morgan City Yard Now Operative," *Grapevine*, Dec. 1964-Feb. 1965: 4.
15. "One Platform, Two Rigs!" *Grapevine*, Dec. 1964-Feb. 1965: 5.
16. Sarge Welch, "Morgan City Vignettes," *Grapevine*, July-Sep. 1965: 12.
17. "Secured and Abandoned Rig," *Grapevine* July-Sep. 1965: 3.
18. "Two New Rigs to Alaska," *Grapevine*, Jan.-Feb. 1966: 3.
19. "Alaska Now Full Fledged Rowan Division," *Grapevine*, Aug.-Sept. 1966: 3.
20. "Rig Seven Goes Split Level," *Grapevine* July-Sep. 1965: 6.
21. "Rig Seven Drills Fastest Well in Delaware Basin," *Grapevine*, March-April 1966: 4.
22. Archibald H. Rowan, interview, transcript, October 1973: 10.
23. "Rowan Keeps One Jump Ahead of the Trend," ts., undated, attached to 22 Nov. 1967 letter from M.L. Hart, vice president of Rowan Drilling Company: 2.
24. "Rowan Stock Gains 61% on First Trading," *Houston Chronicle*, Sept. 7, 1967.
25. "Rowan Drilling Company, Inc. Registers 300,000 Common Shares for Offering," *Grapevine*, May-June 1967: 2.
26. C.R. Palmer, address, ts., Lehman Brothers Oil Service/Contract Drilling Conference, New York, Sept. 23, 1992: 4-5.

27. Bob Palmer, interviewed by the author, July 21, 1998. Transcript: 6.
28. "Profile: Rowe Sees U.S. Rigs Held by Fewer, Larger Companies," *The Oil and Gas Journal*, Oct. 9, 1967: 220.
29. *Ibid.*
30. "How We Are Doing," *Grapevine*, Oct.-Dec. 1967: 2.
31. "Profile: Rowe Sees U.S. Rigs Held By Fewer, Larger Companies," *The Oil and Gas Journal*, Oct. 9, 1967: 220.
32. *Ibid.*
33. "Rowan to Raise Rig Crews' Pay By 5 Percent," *Tulsa Daily World*, Dec. 1, 1967.
34. "Drilling-crew Pay Hike of 5% Mulled," *The Oil and Gas Journal*, Dec. 11, 1967: 86.
35. *Ibid.*
36. *Ibid.*

Chapter Six Sidebar

1. "First Invention Patented," *Grapevine*, Sept.-Oct. 1961: 2.
2. "Rowan Gets First Patent," *Grapevine*, Jan.-March 1963: 4.

Chapter Seven

1. C.W. Yeargain, interviewed by the author, July 21, 1997. Transcript: 7.
2. "Rowan Acquires Largest Alaskan Helicopter Operation," *Grapevine*, Jan.-Feb. 1968: 3.
3. *Ibid.*
4. *Ibid.*
5. "First Annual Meeting Since Going Public," *Grapevine*, May-June 1968: 4.
6. Carl Brady, interviewed by the author, July 13, 1998. Transcript: 2.
7. Beth Burgos, "Carl Brady: Working Hard Makes Success Look Easy," *Alaska Flying*: 30-31.
8. Jeffrey Richardson, *Alaska Business Monthly*, Jan. 1990: 34.
9. Beth Burgos, "Carl Brady: Working Hard Makes Success Look Easy," *Alaska Flying*: 31.
10. Jeffrey Richardson, "Carl F. Brady," *Alaska Business Monthly*, Jan. 1990: 34.
11. *Ibid.*: 35.
12. "Rowan Acquires Largest Alaskan Helicopter Operation," *Grapevine*, Jan.-Feb. 1968: 4.
13. *Ibid.*
14. Beth Burgos, "Carl Brady: Working Hard Makes Success Look Easy," *Alaska Flying*: 31.
15. *Ibid.*
16. *Ibid.*: 7.
17. Cecil Provine, interviewed by Joan Thompson, Oct. 7, 1997. Transcript: 45.
18. "Another Rowan First," *Grapevine* Jan.-Feb. 1968: 6.
19. *Ibid.*
20. *Ibid.*
21. Rowan First Civilian Buyer: Huge 'Copter Scores Offshore," *Tulsa Oil World* of the *Tulsa Daily World*, March 24, 1968.
22. Cecil Provine, interviewed by Joan Thompson, Oct. 7, 1997. Transcript: 47.
23. "Rowan Readies Two 'Air Mobile' Rigs," *Grapevine*, July-Aug. 1968: 7.
24. "Rowan Gets Arctic Slope Job," *The Houston Post*, Sept. 20, 1968.
25. "Odessa Send-off Party for Rig 35," *Grapevine*, Jan.-Feb. 1969: 4.
26. John L. Kennedy, "Helicopter Will Move Deep Rig, Offshore Service Unit," *The Oil and Gas Journal*, Aug. 26, 1968: 121.
27. "Two Skycranes Now in Alaska," *Grapevine*, March-May 1969: 12.
28. "Skycrane Moves Rig on North Slope," *Grapevine*, Aug.-Sep. 1969: 5.
29. "Aircraft Operations," 1969 Annual Report of Rowan Drilling Company, Inc.
30. C.W. Yeargain, interviewed by the author, July 21, 1997. Transcript: 7.
31. "Rowan Mourns Loss of Three," *Grapevine*, Oct.-Dec. 1969: 12.
32. Ernie Walston, interviewed by Alex Lieber, April 15, 1998. Transcript: 7.
33. "Rowan Assembles Turbine Rig," *Grapevine*, Jan.-Feb. 1968: 7.
34. *Ibid.*
35. "Rowan Buys Rig for Deep Texas Work," *Tulsa Daily World*, April 1, 1968.
36. "Rowan Assembles Turbine Rig," *Grapevine*, Jan.-Feb. 1968: 7.
37. "Bess Brants Retires ... Sort of !" *Grapevine*, March-April 1968: 3.
38. "Four Mile Club," *Grapevine*, May-June 1968: 14.
39. "Big Hole in Nevada," *Grapevine*, July-Aug. 1968: 3.
40. Bill Person, interviewed by the author, July 22, 1997. Transcript: 2.
41. "Rowan's Newest Subsidiary," *Grapevine*, March-May 1969: 3.

42. "Now, Houston Is Our Home," *Grapevine*, March-May 1969: 4.
43. Linda Aycock, intervied by the author, July 22, 1997. Transcript: 4.

Chapter Eight

1. Cecil Provine, interviewed by Joan Thompson, Oct. 7, 1997. Transcript: 30-31.
2. Leroy Rambin, "International Awakening," *Grapevine*, May-June 1970: 15.
3. "On the Job," *Grapevine*, Jan.-Feb. 1971: 4.
4. Rowan 1971 Annual Report: 8.
5. "Rowan-Houston Returns to Gulf Coast," *Grapevine*, Winter 1974: 11.
6. "Christening of a Queen," *Grapevine*, Sep.-Oct. 1970: 4.
7. "A Journey to Bandjarmasin," *Grapevine*, July-Sep. 1971: 7.
8. Rowan 1970 Annual Report, 1970: 7. "Mine Rescue System Highly Successful," *Grapevine*, Jan.-Feb. 1971: 4.
9. Bill Person, interviewed by Alex Lieber, July 30, 1998, by phone.
10. Heddie Rowe, interviewed by Joan Thompson, Nov. 6, 1997. Transcript: 51.
11. "C. Robert Palmer Named Board Chairman," *Grapevine* Jan.-March 1972: 3.
12. Cecil Provine, interviewed by Joan Thompson, Oct. 7, 1997. Transcript: 30-31.
13. Heddie Rowe, interviewed by Joan Thompson, Nov. 6, 1997. Transcript: 46.
14. "Minutes of the Regular Quarterly Meeting of the Board of Directors," Rowan Companies, Inc., Jan. 28, 1972: 2.
15. Rick von Flatern, "Reinventing Rowan," *Offshore Engineer* Jan. 1998, reprinted in Rowan brochure.
16. Bob Palmer, "From the Ship's Log," *Grapevine*, April-June 1972: 1.
17. Rowan 1972 Annual Report: 5.
18. John Ira Petty, "Cautious Approach Paying Off Over Long Term," *Houston Post*, May 4, 1992.
19. "Rowan Rig No. 18 Drills Record Hole," *Grapevine*, Jan.-March 1973: 2.
20. Daniel Yergin, The Prize, Simon & Shuster, New York, NY, 1991: p. 625
21. *Ibid.*
22. "The Merric, Inc., Merger," *Grapevine*, Jan.-March 1973: 5.
23. Rowan 1973 Annual Report: 11.
24. "Meet Merric: Wien Brothers Realize a Dream," *Grapevine*, Spring 1974: 8.
25. *Ibid.*
26. "Merric Opens Fairbank's Finest Hangar," *Grapevine*, Summer 1974: 7.
27. Rowan 1974 Annual Report, 1974: 9.
28. "Making History: Rowan-Morgan City," *Grapevine*, Jan.-March 1973: 9.
29. Rowan 1973 Annual Report: 8.
30. "Making History: Rowan-Texas," *Grapevine*, Jan.-March 1973: 9.
31. "Rowan Completes Record Rig Tow," *Grapevine*, Winter 1973: 15.
32. "Pumper to Division Manager," *Grapevine*, March-April 1950: 8.
33. A.H. Rowan, personal statement on Cecil Provine's retirement, *Grapevine*, April-June 1973: 4.
34. Cecil Provine, interviewed by Joan Thompson, Oct. 7, 1997: 36.
35. "Two Rigs Near Completion in West Texas," *Grapevine*, Fall 1973: 7.
36. "New Rigs Built For Superdeep Drilling," *The Oil and Gas Journal*, Feb. 18, 1974: 94.
37. "Land Giant Completed in West Texas," *Grapevine*, Spring 1974: 2.
38. "Rig 14 Wrap Up," *Grapevine*, Winter 1977: 15.
39. Arch Rowan, "From the Ship's Log," *Grapevine*, Winter 1973: 1.
40. "Fifty Years of Leadership," *Grapevine*, Winter 1973: 10.
41. Rowan 1973 Annual Report: 7.
42. "Norwegian Sea: No Place for the Timid," *Grapevine*, Spring 1974: 5.
43. Rowan 1973 Annual Report: 9.
44. "Norwegian Sea: No Place for the Timid," *Grapevine*, Spring 1974: 6.
45. "Saga of the Semis," sound filmstrip, by Carolyn Ramsey, Carolyn Ramsey Productions, 1977, transcript: 4-5.
46. Rielley Euper, interviewed by Joan Thompson, Feb. 10, 1998. Transcript: 14.
47. "Norjarl to Challenge North Sea," *Grapevine*, Winter 1974: 3.
48. Rowan 1974 Annual Report: 7.
49. "Norjarl to Challenge North Sea," *Grapevine* Winter 1974: 2.
50. "On the Move Offshore," *Grapevine* Fall 1975: 3.
51. "Peace Troubles His Soul," *Grapevine* Spring 1975: 1.
52. Rowan 1974 Annual Report: 2.

53. "Rowan Companies, Inc., Minutes of Organizational Meeting of the Board of Directors," April 25, 1975: 2.
54. "Peace Troubles His Soul," *Grapevine* Spring 1975: 4.
55. 1979 Hall of Fame Dinner (Midland: Permian Basin Petroleum Museum, Library, and Hall of Fame, 1979), program guide, Feb. 15, 1979: 1.
56. "Rowan Ends Another Era," *Grapevine* Spring 1975: 9.
57. R.E. Trout, "Between Two Worlds," *Grapevine* Winter 1975: 9.
58. "On the Move Offshore," *Grapevine* Fall 1975: 5.
59. "Destination Dubai," *Bit & Rotor* Fall 1975: 1.
60. "Alaska Aircraft Operations Merge Under One Name," *Bit & Rotor* Fall 1975: 2.
61. Rowan 1975 Annual Report: 10.
62. *Ibid.* 16.
63. *Ibid.* 10.
64. "Singapore Ceremony Marks Addition to Rowan Offshore Fleet," *Grapevine* Spring 1976: 14.
65. "Saga of the Semis," sound filmstrip, by Carol Ramsey, Carol Ramsey Productions, 1977, transcript, 7.
66. "Rowan-Juneau Assists Rowan-Odessa," *Grapevine* Winter 1977: 16-17.
67. Rowan 1977 Annual Report: 9.
68. "Rowan-Juneau Assists Rowan-Odessa," *Grapevine* Winter 1977: 17.
69. Rowan 1977 Annual Report: 3.
70. "Sailing ... Rowan Style," sound filmstrip, by Al Rubio, MPA Inc., 1982, transcript.
71. "Rowan Sails to Mexico," *Grapevine*, Summer 1978: 18.
72. *Ibid.*: 20.
73. "Chicago Bridge Sets Bid for Rowan Cos. Of $26 a Share," *The Wall Street Journal*, June 13, 1978.
74. "Rowan's Directors Vote Against Offer of Chicago Bridge," *The Wall Street Journal*, June 16, 1978.
75. Susan L. Hedding, "Commentary," *Grapevine* Summer 1978: 1.
76. "Rowan Cos. Agrees to Buy Armco Stake in 2 Drilling Firms," *The Wall Street Journal*, June 26, 1978.
77. "Schlumberger Buys 18 percent of Rowan Cos. On the Open Market," *The Wall Street Journal*, July 21, 1978.
78. "Chicago Bridge Bid For Rest of Stock in Rowan Cos. Ends," *The Wall Street Journal*, July 1978.
79. "A Canny High Roller," *Forbes*, Jan. 21, 1980: 50.
80. "ERA Buys Jet Alaska," *Grapevine* Summer 1978: 29.
81. "ERA Aviation Center Opens," *Grapevine* Three/1979: 22.
82. Chuck Johnson, interviewed by the author, Nov. 11, 1997. Transcript: 7-8.
83. "Gulf Birds Added to Alaska Fleet," *Grapevine* Three/1979: 5.
84. Rowan 1978 Annual Report: 8.
85. "New Construction," *Grapevine* One/1979: 11.
86. Rowan 1979 Annual Report: 1
87. "Rowan Today," *Grapevine* Three/1979: 19.

Chapter Nine

1. "Rowan Recognized for the Right Moves," *Grapevine* Third Quarter, 1987: 6.
2. "Growing With Rowan," *Grapevine* One/1980: 2.
3. "A Canny High Roller," *Forbes*, Jan. 21, 1980: 50.
4. "Rowan Juneau Leaves Galveston for Nova Scotia," *Grapevine* Three/1980: 12.
5. Donald M. Taylor, "Sails Assist Jackup Rig on 2,400-mile Tow," *Ocean Industry* September 1980: 12.
6. Rowan 1980 Annual Report: 13.
7. "Rowan in the North Sea," *Grapevine* First Quarter, 1982: 7.
8. "Growing With Rowan," *Grapevine* One/1980: 4-5.
9. Chuck Johnson, interviewed by the author, Nov. 11, 1997. Transcript: 9.
10. *Ibid.*: 10.
11. *Ibid.*: 13.
12. "Rig Moves: The Walk of the Arch Rowan," *Grapevine* Three/1981: 4.
13. "Rig Moves: The Walk of the Arch Rowan," *Grapevine* Three/1981: 6.
14. "Palmer Receives The Wall Street Transcript Award," *Grapevine* Four/1980: 12.
15. "C. Robert Palmer Receives Gold Award," *Grapevine* Three/1981: 19.
16. Rowan 1981 Annual Report: 3.
17. "Gilbert Rowe Returns to the Drilling Industry," *Grapevine* First Quarter, 1982: 11.
18. "Gilbert Rowe Returns to the Drilling Industry," *Grapevine* First Quarter, 1982: 10.
19. "Cecil Provine — the Man and His Namesake," *Grapevine* Second Quarter, 1982: 7.
20. Daniel Yergin, *The Prize*, (New York: Touchstone, Simon & Shuster, 1996).
21. John Buvens, interviewed by the author, July 21, 1997. Transcript: 6.
22. "C.R. Palmer Addresses Meeting," *Grapevine* Fourth Quarter, 1982: 4.
23. "C.R. Palmer Addresses Meeting," *Grapevine* Fourth Quarter, 1982: 4.

24. "Dry Tow of the Rowan-Alaska," *Grapevine* Fourth Quarter, 1982: 6.
25. Rowan 1983 Annual Report: 7.
26. "Rowan's First Double Dry Tow," *Grapevine* Fourth Quarter, 1983/ First Quarter 1984: 12.
27. "Another Fine Dry Tow," *Grapevine* Third Quarter, 1985: 9.
28. "Rowan's Rig No. 33: Unique in the Industry," *Grapevine* Fourth Quarter, 1982: 13.
29. "ERA Helicopters, Inc., Has a First, a Second and a Couple of Heroes to Crow About," *Grapevine* Second Quarter 1983: 8.
30. Rowan 1983 Annual Report: 11.
31. "Rowan Gorilla Rigs," *Grapevine* Third Quarter, 1983: 12.
32. "Gorilla Tackles North Atlantic," *Grapevine* Fourth Quarter, 1983/First Quarter, 1984: 14.
33. "A Rich Drilling History," *Grapevine* Fourth Quarter, 1984: 2.
34. "Gorilla I and Juneau: Stars of North Atlantic," *Grapevine* Second Quarter, 1984: 14.
35. "Gorilla Possible Candidate for World Record," *Grapevine* Fourth Quarter, 1983/First Quarter 1984: 16.
36. "Letter to Stockholders," Rowan Companies, Inc., 1983, Annual Report, 2-3.
37. "Moving Ahead to '95," *Grapevine* Second Quarter, 1984: 3.
38. *Ibid.*: 4.
39. "Rowan's Business Strategy: Preparation Meets Opportunity," *Grapevine* Third Quarter, 1983: 5.
40. Larry Gardner, "'Hot-stacking' Idle Rigs," *Grapevine* Second Quarter, 1984: 8.
41. *Ibid.*: 9.
42. Rielley Euper, interview with Joan Thompson, 10 Feb. 1998, transcript, 22.
43. "Fueled by Good Omens: Rowan Gorilla II," *Grapevine* Fourth Quarter, 1984: 12.
44. Rowan 1985 Annual Report: 2.
45. *Ibid.*
46. "Brady's Service Lauded," *Grapevine* Fourth Quarter, 1984: 16.
47. Jeffrey Richardson, "Carl F. Brady," *Alaska Business Monthly* Jan. 1990: 35.
48. Paul Kelly, interviewed by the author, Oct. 24, 1997. Transcript: 7-8.
49. "A Better Mousetrap," *Grapevine* First-Second Quarter, 1985: 11.
50. "A Strong Future We Have Built," *Grapevine* First Quarter, 1987: 2.
51. Rowan 1986 Annual Report: 1.
52. *Ibid.*: 7.
53. "Our Future Is Before Us: Industry Must Be Prepared," *Grapevine* First Quarter, 1987: 3.
54. Rowan 1986 Annual Report: 2.
55. *Ibid.*: 3.
56. Rowan 1987 Annual Report: 4.
57. C.R. Palmer, "Rowan's 1988 Shareholders' Meeting: An Aspect More Favorable," *Grapevine* Second Quarter, 1988: 16.
58. "Rowan Recognized for the Right Moves," *Grapevine* Third Quarter, 1987: 6.
59. *Ibid.*
60. "Big Yellow Machines Find Place on Rowan Rigs," *Grapevine* First Quarter, 1988: 22.
61. M.E. Jacques, Varco International, Inc., "Top Drive: Surviving the Growing Pains," *Offshore*, April 1988: 38.
62. "Era Gives New Name to Aviation Excellence," *Grapevine* First Quarter, 1988: 6.
63. Walter Couch, interviewed by Alex Lieber, May 20, 1998. Transcript: 6.
64. "Professionalism, They Call It," *Grapevine* Fourth Quarter, 1988: 15.
65. Walter Couch, interviewed by Alex Lieber, May 20, 1998. Transcript: 10.
66. "Professionalism, They Call It," *Grapevine* Fourth Quarter, 1988: 15.
67. Walter Couch, interviewed by Alex Lieber, May 21, 1998. Transcript: 13-14.
68. *Ibid.*
69. "Professionalism, They Call It," *Grapevine* Fourth Quarter, 1988: 14.
70. "Professionalism, They Call It," *Grapevine* Fourth Quarter, 1988: 16.
71. "NTSB Outlines Cause of Rowan Gorilla I Sinking," *Grapevine* Oct. 16, 1989: 90.
72. Mark Ivey, "Rowan: A Storm Turned the Tide," in "Survival Stories From the Oil Patch," *Business Week*, March 12, 1990: 81.
73. "NOIA, Rowan Group View Alaskan Oil Spill," *Grapevine* First Quarter, 1989: 8.
74. "Coast Guard Honors Era," *Grapevine* Third Quarter, 1989: 11.
75. "Palmer Wins Bronze Award," *Grapevine* Second Quarter, 1989: 3.
76. Mark Ivey, "Rowan: A Storm Turned the Tide" in "Survival Stories From the Oil Patch," *Business Week*, March 12,1990: 84.

Chapter Nine Sidebar: Rowan vs. IRS

1. "Rowan vs. the IRS," *Grapevine* Four/1981: 2.
2. *Ibid.*
3. Rowan Companies, Inc., Petitioner, v. United States," 452 US 247 (U.S. Supreme Court, 1981).
4. Elizabeth Magner, interviewed by Joan Thompson, July 14, 1998. Transcript: 4.
5. "Fringe Benefits Aren't Taxable, Top Court Rules," *The Wall Street Journal*, June 9, 1981.
6. Rowan Companies, Inc., Petitioner, v. United States," 452 US 247 (U.S. Supreme Court, 1981).

Chapter Nine Sidebar: Platform Technology

1. Paul Kelly, interviewed by the author, October 24, 1997. Transcript: 8-9.
2. Jeff Littleton, technology ed., "Offshore Missile Launch Sites Under Study," *Offshore*, May 1988: 28.
3. *Ibid.*: 29.
4. Donald Woutat, "'Star Wars' Goes to Sea: Air Force Considers Using Offshore Oil Rigs to Launch Rockets," *Los Angeles Times*, July 6, 1988.
5. Paul Kelly, interviewed by the author, Oct. 24, 1997. Transcript: 9-10.
6. Paul L. Kelly, "From Inner Space to Outer Space: New Developments in Offshore Drilling Technology For Environmentally Sensitive Areas — Offshore Platforms as Rocket Launch Systems," adapted from an address to The Sixth Symposium on Coastal and Ocean Management in Charleston, S.C., July 1989, pamphlet: 15.

Chapter Ten

1. Rowan 1993 Annual Report: 2.
2. Mark Keller, interviewed by the author, July 21, 1997. Transcript: 4.
3. "Queen of the Inland Fleet Returns to Reign," *Grapevine* Second/Third Quarter, 1990: 15.
4. *Ibid.*
5. *Ibid.*: 16.
6. *Ibid.*
7. "Fourchon Takes On New Frontier," *Grapevine* Second Quarter, 1991: 10.
8. Earnest L. Perry and R.A. Dyer, "3 Killed in Crash at Airport," *Houston Chronicle*, Aug. 24, 1990.
9. C. Robert Palmer, "Do They Hear What We Hear?" adapted from speech at PaineWebber Conference, March 7, 1991, *Grapevine* Second Quarter, 1991: 1.
10. Rowan 1990 Annual Report: 3.
11. "His Bright Spirit Benefitted Many," *Grapevine* First Quarter, 1991: 12.
12. "Gone to Argentina," *Grapevine* First Quarter, 1995: 10.
13. "Venezuela Venture Takes Off," *Grapevine* Second Quarter, 1991: 8.
14. "Rowan Program Grows Through Three Decades," *Grapevine* First Quarter, 1992: 16.
15. C. Robert Palmer, "Rowan Is the One to Buy," *Grapevine* Third Quarter, 1991: 6.
16. "Era to Fly Russian Project," *Grapevine* Second Quarter, 1992: 5.
17. C. Robert Palmer, "Looking at Rowan For the Long-Term," adapted from a speech at PaineWebber's Energy Conference, 4 March 1992, *Grapevine* First Quarter, 1992: 7.
18. "Terminator, Inc., Aims at Platform Removal Business," *Grapevine* Second Quarter, 1992: 10.
19. "Terminator Inc. Now Established Offshore Power," *Grapevine* First Quarter, 1995: 8.
20. "Gorilla III Sets Records in Canada," *Grapevine* Third Quarter, 1992: 20.
21. "Seeing the Light," *Grapevine* Fourth Quarter, 1992: 6.
22. William C. Provine, "Rowan Stays Ahead of the Curve," adapted from speech at the Howard Weil Energy Conference, 23 March 1994, *Grapevine* First Quarter, 1994: 1.
23. C.R. Palmer, "The Value of Developing a Feel For the Deal," *Grapevine* First Quarter, 1993: 6.
24. Rowan 1993 Annual Report: 2.
25. "Era Wins Contract for External Auxiliary Fuel Systems," *Grapevine* Third Quarter, 1993: 7.

26. John Buvens, interviewed by the author, July 21, 1997. Transcript: 8.
27. William C. Provine, interviewed by the author, Oct. 15, 1997. Transcript: 11.
28. Jack McElroy, interviewed by the author, March 9, 1998. Transcript: 8.
29. Ronnie Neihaus, interviewed by the author, March 10, 1998. Transcript: 3.
30. Ed Thiele, interviewed by the author, July 22, 1997. Transcript: 6-7.
31. Dan Eckermann, interviewed by the author, March 9, 1998. Transcript: 8.
32. *Ibid.*
33. *Ibid.*: 19.
34. Albert W. Lorimer, *God Runs My Business: The Story of R.G. LeTourneau* (New York: Fleming H. Revell Co., 1951) 150-51.
35. Richard H. LeTourneau, introduction, *The LeTourneau Legend: The History of R.G. LeTourneau Inc., 1920-1970*, by Philip G. Gowenlock (Brisbane, Australia: Paddington Publications, 1996): x.
36. R.G. LeTourneau, *R.G. LeTourneau: Mover of Men and Mountains* (Chicago: Moody Press, 1960) 2.
37. R.G. LeTourneau, *R.G. LeTourneau: Mover of Men and Mountains* (Chicago: Moody Press, 1960): 50.
38. *Ibid.*: 143.
39. "R.G. LeTourneau, 'Mr. Earthmover' ... Christian Businessman," *Roads and Streets*, July 1969: 94.
40. "Rowan and LeTourneau Open New Historical Chapter," *Grapevine* First Quarter, 1994: 8-9.
41. "Success By Another Name," *Grapevine* First Quarter, 1995: 12.
42. "Success By Another Name," *Grapevine* First Quarter, 1995: 13.
43. "Helping Move the Earth," *Grapevine* First Quarter, 1995: 14-15.
44. Price Stratton, interviewed by the author, March 9, 1998. Transcript: 7.
45. *Ibid.*, 12.
46. Bart McCoy, interviewed by the author, March 9, 1998. Transcript: 4.
47. *Ibid.*, 5.
48. Jim Golden, interviewed by the author, March 9, 1998. Transcript: 7.
49. *Ibid.*: 9-10.
50. R.G. LeTourneau, *R.G. LeTourneau: Mover of Men and Mountains* (Chicago: Moody Press, 1960): 120.
51. George Bush, with Victor Gold, *Looking Forward* (New York: Doubleday, 1987): 72.
52. R.G. LeTourneau, *R.G. LeTourneau: Mover of Men and Mountains* (Chicago: Moody Press): 121.
53. George Bush, with Victor Gold, *Looking Forward* (New York: Doubleday, 1987): 72.
54. Ibid.: 72-73.
55. Philip G. Gowenlock, *The LeTourneau Legend: The History of R.G. LeTourneau, Inc., 1920-1970* (Brisbane, Australia: Paddington Publications, 1996): 272.
56. Rowan 1993 Annual Report: 2.

Chapter Eleven

1. C. Robert Palmer, speech to the Pioneer Oil Producers Society, April 21, 1997. Transcript: 10.
2. Mark Hay, interviewed by the author, July 22, 1997. Transcript: 7.
3. William C. Provine, "Rowan Stays Ahead of the Curve," adapted from speech at the Howard Weil Energy Conference, 23 March 1994, *Grapevine* First Quarter, 1994: 3.
4. "Gorilla II Moves to Gulf to Work Sub-Salt Areas," *Grapevine* Second Quarter, 1994: 12.
5. "LeTourneau Loaders Carry Company Name Worldwide," *Grapevine* Third Quarter, 1994: 14.
6. "LeTourneau Loaders Carry Company Name Worldwide," *Grapevine* Third Quarter, 1994: 14.
7. Ed Thiele, interviewed by the author, July 22, 1997. Transcript: 11-12.
8. "LeTourneau Loaders Carry Company Name Worldwide," *Grapevine* Third Quarter, 1994: 14.
9. *Ibid.*
10. Dan Eckermann, interviewed by the author, March 9, 1998, transcript, 7.

11. "Era Makes Strides in Operations," *Grapevine* Third Quarter, 1994: 18.
12. "Era Purchases Assets," *Grapevine* Third Quarter, 1995: 2.
13. William C. Provine, "Our Potential As Driller, Aviator and Manufacturer," adapted from speeches at two conferences, *Grapevine* Second Quarter, 1995: 3.
14. Mike Doebler, interviewed by the author, July 13, 1998. Transcript: p. 2.
15. "Era Puts Favorite Aircraft in Tourists' Skies," *Grapevine* Second Quarter, 1995: 10.
16. Clifford Gerhart, "Classic Craft Returns to Alaska Skies," *Alaska Business Monthly*, June 1995: 14.
17. Anna Palmore, "Dog Gone Tour," *Eranautics*, Aug. 1997: 4.
18. "Era Spells Adventure for Active Travelers," *Grapevine* Third Quarter, 1997: 19.
19. "Terminator, Rowan Yard Give a Lift on the River," *Grapevine* Fourth Quarter, 1995: 9.
20. "Rowan to Sell Barge Rigs," *Grapevine* Second Quarter, 1995: 3.
21. Mike Marcom, interviewed by the author, June 2, 1998. Transcript: 12-13.
22. "New Gorilla Jackup Due 1998," *Grapevine* Second Quarter, 1995: 12.
23. Don Cross, interviewed by the author, March 10, 1998. Transcript: 5.
24. "LeTourneau Business Back on the River," *Grapevine* Third Quarter, 1995: 16.
25. Paul L. Kelly, "Building for the 21st Century," speech to NOMADS-Houston Chapter, 24 June 1997, transcript, 14.
26. Robert Remlinger, interviewed by the author, March 10, 1998. Transcript: 10-11.
27. Paul L. Kelly, senior vice president, Rowan Cos., "Contractors Reacquaint Themselves With Optimism," *World Oil*, December 1996: 45.
28. Rudy Harris, interview by the author, March 9, 1998. Transcript: 14.
29. Edgar "Ish" Loflin, interviewed by the author, March 10, 1998. Transcript: 7.
30. C. Robert Palmer, "How Never to Lose Time in the Drilling Industry," adapted from a speech to the Lehman Brothers Energy Conference, 10-11 Sept. 1996, *Grapevine* Third Quarter, 1996: 1.
31. George Cuspid, interviewed by the author, March 10, 1998. Transcript: 12.
32. Michael Davis, "Rowan Cos. Lets Good Times Roll With Best Quarter in 13 Years," *Houston Chronicle*, 16 July 1966.
33. Rowan 1996 Annual Report: 2.
34. C. Robert Palmer, speech to Pioneer Oil Producers Society, April 21, 1997. Transcript: 9.
35. Paul Kelly, senior vice president, Rowan Cos., "Advanced Jackup Rig Breaking U.S. Drought," *The Oil and Gas Journal*, March 10, 1997: 62.
36. "Era Introduces the Future for Gulf of Mexico Flyers," *Grapevine* Fourth Quarter, 1997: 8.
37. Al Meyer, interviewed by Alex Lieber, July 10, 1998. Transcript: 8.
38. Rowan 1997 Annual Report: 7.
39. R.G. Croyle, interviewed by the author, March 30, 1998. Transcript: 16.
40. *Ibid.*: 17.
41. "Rowan Gets Letter of Intent," *The Wall Street Journal*, Sept. 5, 1997.
42. Rick von Flatern, "Reinventing Rowan," reprinted in a Rowan brochure from *Offshore Engineer* Jan. 1998.
43. Rowan 1997 Annual Report: 5.
44. *Ibid.*
45. Paul Kelly, interviewed by the author, Oct. 24, 1997. Transcript: 14.
46. Rick von Flatern, "Reinventing Rowan," reprinted in Rowan brochure from *Offshore Engineer* Jan. 1998.
47. Paul Kelly, interviewed by the author, Oct. 24, 1997. Transcript: 17.
48. Remarks by C. Robert Palmer, Rauscher Perice Energy Conference, September 15-18, 1997: 4-5.
49. C. Robert Palmer, speech to the Pioneer Oil Producers Society, April 21, 1997, transcript: 10.

INDEX